BUSINESS ESSENTIALS
(SUPPORTING HNC/HND AND FOUNDATION DEGREES)

Managing Financial Resources and Decisions

Course Book

In this September 2007 first edition

- full and comprehensive coverage of the key topics within subject

- activities, examples and quizzes

- practical illustrations and case studies

- index

- fully up to date as at August 2007

- coverage mapped to the Edexcel Guidelines for HND/HNC Business Core Unit 2

BPP
LEARNING MEDIA

BUSINESS ESSENTIALS

First edition September 2007

ISBN 9780 7517 4474 3

British Library Cataloguing-in Publication Data

A catalogue record for this book is available from the British Library

Printed in Great Britain by WM Print

45-47 Frederick Street

Walsall, West Midlands

WS2 9NE

Published by

BPP Learning Media Ltd

BPP House, Aldine Place

London W12 8AA

www.bpp.com/learningmedia

We are grateful to Edexcel for permission to reproduce the Guidelines for
the BTEC Higher Nationals in Business.

CONTENTS

INTRODUCTION

This is the first edition of BPP Learning Media's dynamic new **Business Essentials** range. It is the ideal learning solution for all students studying for business-related qualifications and degrees, and the range provides concise and comprehensive coverage of the key areas that are essential to the business student.

Qualifications in Business are traditionally very demanding. Students therefore need learning resources which get straight to the core of the topics involved, and which build upon students' pre-existing knowledge and experience. The BPP Learning Media Business Essentials range has been designed to meet exactly that need.

Features include:

- In depth coverage of essential topics within business-related subjects
- Plenty of activities, quizzes and topics for class discussion to help retain the interest of students and ensure progress
- Up to date practical illustrations and case studies that really bring the material to life
- A glossary of terms and full index

In addition, the contents of the chapters are comprehensively mapped to the **Edexcel Guidelines**, providing full coverage of all topics specified in the HND/HNC qualifications in Business.

Each chapter contains:

- An introduction and a list of specific study objectives
- Summary diagrams and signposts to guide you through the chapter
- A chapter roundup, quick quiz with answers and answers to activities.

Further resources

Lecturers whose colleges adopt the Business Essentials range (minimum of 10 copies for each relevant unit) are entitled to receive **free practice assignments and answers** for the units concerned. While remaining under the copyright of BPP Learning Media, these can be copied and distributed to students as desired.

BPP Learning Media CD Roms will also be available early in 2008 to complement some titles within the series. These provide interactive learning modules for the key topics in the subject.

BPP Learning Media
2007

Other titles in this series:

Generic titles

Economics *

Accounts *

Business Maths *

Core units for the Edexcel HND/HNC Business qualification

Unit 1	Marketing
Unit 2	Managing Financial Resources and Decisions
Unit 3	Organisations and Behaviour
Unit 4	Business Environment
Unit 5	Business Law *
Unit 6	Business Decision Making
Unit 7	Business Strategy
Unit 8	Research Project

Specialist units (endorsed title routes) for the Edexcel HND/HNC Business qualification

Units 9-12	Finance
Units 13-16	Management
Units 17-20	Marketing
Units 21-24	Human Resource Management
Units 25-28	Company and Commercial Law *

* CD Roms available spring 2008.

For more information, or to place an order, please call 0845 0751 100 (for orders within the UK) or +44(0)20 8740 2211 (from overseas), e-mail learningmedia@bpp.com, or visit our website at www.bpp.com/learningmedia.

If you would like to send in your comments on this Course Book, please turn to the review form at the back of this book.

STUDY GUIDE

This course book includes features designed specifically to make learning effective and efficient.

(a) Each chapter begins with a summary diagram which maps out the areas covered by the chapter. There are detailed summary diagrams at the start of each main section of the chapter. You can use the diagrams during revision as a basis for your notes.

(b) After the main summary diagram there is an introduction, which sets the chapter in context. This is followed by learning objectives, which show you what you will learn as you work through the chapter.

(c) Throughout the text, there are special aids to learning. These are indicated by symbols in the margin,

Signposts guide you through the course book, showing how each section connects with the next.

Definitions give the meanings of key terms. The *glossary* at the end of the course book summarises these.

Activities help you to test how much you have learnt. An indication of the time you should take on each is given. Answers are given at the end of each chapter.

Topics for discussion are for use in seminars. They give you a chance to share your views with your fellow students. They allow you to highlight holes in your knowledge and to see how others understand concepts. If you have time, try 'teaching' someone the concepts you have learnt in a session. This helps you to remember key points and answering their questions will consolidate your knowledge.

Examples relate what you have learnt to the outside world. Try to think up your own examples as you work through the course book.

Chapter roundups present the key information from the chapter in a concise format. Useful for revision.

Weblinks indicate useful websites for your own research.

(d)   The wide **margin** on each page is for your notes. You will get the best out of this book if you interact with it. Write down your thoughts and ideas. Record examples, question theories, add references to other pages in the course book and rephrase key points in your own words.

(e)   At the end of each chapter, there is a **chapter roundup**, a **quick quiz** with answers and an **assignment**. Use these to revise and consolidate your knowledge. The chapter roundup summarises the chapter. The quick quiz tests what you have learnt (the answers often refer you back to the chapter so you can look over subjects again). The assignment (with a time guide) allows you to put your knowledge into practice. Answer guidelines for the assignments are at the end of the course book.

(f)   At the end of the course book, there is a glossary of key terms and an index.

MANAGING FINANCIAL RESOURCES AND DECISIONS

BPP
LEARNING MEDIA

Chapter 1:
SOURCES OF FINANCE

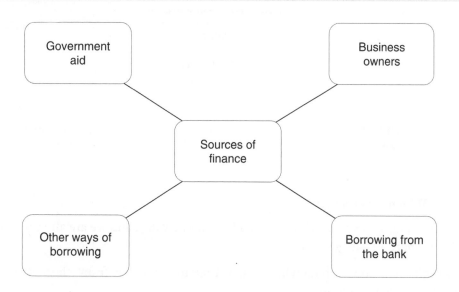

Introduction

Finance is at the very centre of business and management. Even if you have no direct responsibility for managing financial resources you ought to be aware that anything that anybody does in a business organisation either costs money, or generates money, or both.

In this chapter we are going to begin by looking at where that money comes from and the implications of obtaining money from different sources. In the next chapter we look more specifically at the sources of finance available to larger organisations (almost always companies).

This chapter introduces a number of topics, such as cash flow management, that are explored in greater depth later on in this Course Book.

Your objectives

In this chapter you will learn about the following.

- Identification and evaluation of alternative sources of finance
- Importance of ownership to the financing of a business
- When and for what reasons a bank loan might be available
- Other ways of borrowing money
- The variety of grants that are available

1 SOURCES OF FINANCE

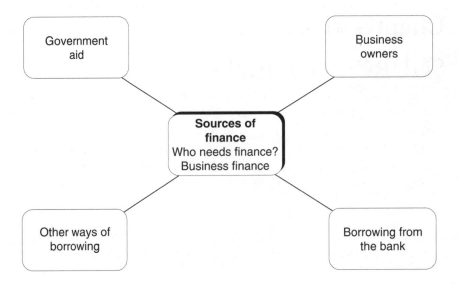

1.1 Who needs finance?

Finance means money. We all need it and use it every day, and we are all very interested to know where we can get more of it.

Let's begin by thinking about where you or I might get money from (short of stealing it) if we wanted some right now.

(a) We might use *our own* money – money in the bank or in our pocket or purse, that we have saved for later use.

(b) We might *borrow* from a friend, or use a credit card. If we wanted lots of money we might get a loan from a bank or building society.

(c) We might be *given* some money: the government would give us money if we were entitled to some form of benefit.

(d) We might *earn* some money by doing something or selling something to someone else.

FOR DISCUSSION

Depending on your background, experiences and beliefs you probably feel differently about these different ways of getting money. Assuming you are not a criminal, for example, you would not dream of stealing money. Do you feel uncomfortable about the welfare state? Do you think that people should be allowed to have unlimited savings? Do you mind being in debt? What would you not be willing to do to earn money?

The word *finance* is usually used in a bigger sense than just 'money'. It is any arrangement that you make in exchange for the ability to do all the different things you want to do.

(a) If you want to buy a Mars bar and a newspaper you finance your snacking and reading activities with the cash in your pocket.

(b)   If you want to listen to the new Robbie Williams CD now, but pay for it out of next month's salary, you finance this with your credit card.

(c)   If you want to drive a car and can't pay for it in cash you get a three year loan from the bank to finance yourself: you probably never see the actual money.

However, because your savings and day to day cash have to come from somewhere, and because people you borrow from expect to be paid back eventually, you have to do something that generates income. If you are very lucky – if you win the National Lottery say – you may be able to live off the interest generated by your savings. Most people, though, have to go to work to generate income. They have to sell their time and talents to an employer, or become self-employed.

Personal finance is an interesting and complex subject in its own right. However, in this book we are only interested in how businesses manage their finances.

1.2   Business finance

Businesses are set up with the object of making profits for their owners. A business, whether it be the local newsagent or a massive company like W H Smith's, has exactly the same need for, and sources of, finance as you and I.

(a)   *The business has some money of its own*

If you started up a newsagent's business, say, you would probably have to put in some money from your savings to buy your initial stocks of sweets and cigarettes and newspapers and to pay bills like rent and electricity.

A company like W H Smith has money of this sort in the form of what people paid when they bought *shares* in the company. The money is owned by the 'company' of shareholders.

(b)   *The business borrows money from the bank*

The newsagent might get his bank to agree to let him have an overdraft some of the time to tide him over periods when he has paid for stock but not yet sold it on to customers.

W H Smith might borrow millions of pounds from the bank over a term of many years to finance the building of new shops.

(c)   Some businesses are helped out with their financing by *Government grants*, especially new businesses and businesses in deprived areas.

(d)   Some businesses receive money from venture capitalists (organisation set up specifically to find profitable uses for spare funds) or from private individuals known as Business Angels (these have often been seen in the entertainment industry).

(e)   All businesses will generate money by making sales. Some of this money will then be used to pay interest to the bank on its lending and to pay off part of the amount loaned.

We hinted above that the idea of ownership of a business is important to the subject we are discussing. We had better look at this in a little more detail.

2   BUSINESS OWNERS

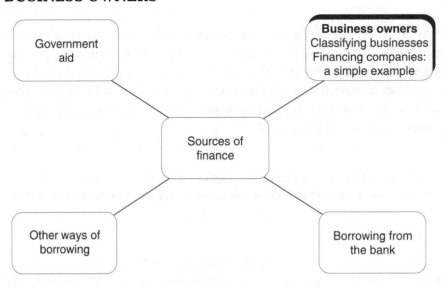

2.1   Classifying businesses

There are several different ways of classifying a business: for example, is it big or small; is it a service provider like a bank, a manufacturer like a car maker or a trader like a shop?

> **Activity 1**   **(15 minutes)**
>
> Divide into groups of three to four students. Each group should brain-storm to list as many businesses with a local presence that they can think of in, say, three minutes. Then the group should sub-divide the businesses into traders (wholesale and retail), service businesses and manufacturers; also, the group should rank them as large or small businesses, and discuss whether they are purely local businesses or part of large national or multinational businesses. This will enable you to start relating your studies to the world around you.

From the point of view of finance the most important distinction is the ownership of the business. This is partly a matter of how many people own the business, and partly a matter of the legal status of the business.

One owner: sole traders

A sole trader is a business that is owned by one person. This does not necessarily mean that only one person works for the business: a newsagent will typically be a sole trader but he will often have shop assistants working for him.

However, a sole trader is directly involved in the running of the business, he provides the money to start up the business (the *capital*), and all the profits that it makes belong to him.

For example, a self-employed plumber typically does all the plumbing work himself, he buys all the tools needed and a van to get about in, and the money he is paid goes directly into his pocket.

Two or more persons: partnerships

A partnership is an agreement between two or more persons to engage in business in common with a view to profit. It is desirable that partners have a written partnership agreement outlining important points such as the agreed shares of capital contributions and shares of profit, but there is nothing in law to say that any such written agreement is required.

Many small businesses are partnerships: three plumbers might get together in this way, for example, to share office space, or to offer a wider range of services to the same customers, or so that they can afford, and make full use of, expensive specialised equipment.

The 'professions' of law, medicine and accountancy are also often set up as partnerships (doctors and solicitors are not allowed to operate in any other way whereas firms of accountants are now able to operate as 'limited liability partnerships' (LLPs)).

Two or more owners: companies

A company is a form of business that has two or more owners (although it can have only one) but which is separate in law from the people who own and control it.

This is quite a hard concept to understand when you first encounter it. You need to be aware that the law recognises not just individual human beings as persons, but also 'corporate bodies', in other words, companies. (An individual human being is called a *natural person;* a company is called an *artificial person*.)

If a 'person' is recognised as such in law, the person then has certain legal rights and certain legal obligations.

(a)   The most important *right* that a person has in the context of finance is the right to own property, for example money or machines.

(b)   The most important *obligation* in this context is that a person has the responsibility for paying back financial debts.

A limited company is one whose owners' liability to pay back debts is limited to the amount that they put in. This is an advantage to the investor in a limited company, who knows that if the company in which he invested is hugely successful, he may get back many times the amount he invested. If the business 'goes broke', he may lose his investment, but his house, car and other personal possessions are safe.

Note that it is the shareholders' liability that is limited. The company is a separate person in law and its liability is *unlimited*.

The company is the most important form of business. Let's look at a simple example to make sure that the implications of trading as a company are clearly understood.

2.2 Financing Companies: a simple example

EXAMPLE: FINANCING A COMPANY: A SIMPLE EXAMPLE

A limited company is owned by shareholders. For example:

(a) Zosie, Adam and Shiva want to set up a holiday home business, and they have £100,000 between them with which to do so. They go to a solicitor, and ask the solicitor to incorporate a company, which they decide to call Ecalpimos Ltd.

(b) Ownership of a company, by and large, is determined by the number of shares a person owns. Let's assume that the legal documents by which Ecalpimos Ltd is brought into existence state that the: 'authorised share capital of the company is to be £100,000 shares of £1 each'. This means that ownership is divided into 100,000 units with a face value of £1. It is decided that Zosie, Adam and Shiva will purchase all the shares.

If Zosie puts in £40,000 and Adam and Shiva each contribute £30,000, and the shares are purchased at their nominal value (ie £1 each) then Zosie will own 40% of Ecalpimos and the other two will own 30% each.

(c) The £100,000 now belongs to Ecalpimos Ltd, as it has been exchanged for the shares. If the money is used to buy a rundown property, that property belongs to Ecalpimos Ltd, not to Zosie, Adam and Shiva.

(d) Imagine that Ecalpimos Ltd makes a profit in the first year of trading of £1,000. This is distributed to the shareholders according to the size of their shareholding: Zosie will get £400, and Adam and Shiva will get £300 each. Such a distribution is called a dividend.

(e) Also, if Zosie, Adam and Shiva disagree on some issue relating to the management of the company, then Zosie has 40% of the votes, and Adam and Shiva 30% each.

(f) Most importantly, imagine you have lent Ecalpimos Ltd a sum of money with which to buy a hotel. Unfortunately the hotel burns down and, because it was not insured, Ecalpimos Ltd has no money to pay you back. You cannot get Zosie, Adam and Shiva to pay up from their own personal fortunes: the debt was owed by the company, not the individuals. This fact has a significant effect on the way the company's transactions are recorded and presented. (Example end)

Definitions

Capital is used with a number of slightly different meanings.

(a) Capital is the money with which a business *starts up* – your life savings, for example, or a large redundancy payment might be used to set up a business.

(b) Capital is the also the name given to the *assets* that are used in a business. If you use your redundancy money to buy a pub and all its contents, then the building, the furniture, the beer stocks and so on are all your capital.

(c) Sometimes capital is the name given to *money invested*, for example £10,000 savings in a building society or £10,000 worth of ICI shares.

An **asset** is something owned by a business, for example a factory or a van.

A **liability** is a debt owed by a business, for example an overdraft at the bank.

Activity 2   (15 minutes)

The definitions in the box above are very important so make sure you understand them. Label the following items as 'capital', 'asset', 'liability', or 'none of these'.

(a) Cash in the bank

(b) A computer, bought on hire purchase

(c) An amount owed to a hire purchase company

(d) A rented building

(e) A factory full of machinery

(f) An employee

(g) Profits made by the business in previous years and not paid out to shareholders as dividends

(h) A tax bill

(i) Cash paid to settle the tax bill

On the next two pages we set out in tabular form the advantages and disadvantages of these basic kinds of financial and legal structure. (Any terms that you don't understand will be explained shortly.)

NOTES

Owner/manager finance – sole traders and partnerships

	Advantages for the business	*Disadvantages for the business*
Formation	Relatively simple and cheap to set up; no need to publish accounts (see 'shareholder finance').	With no track record, it could be hard to get credit from suppliers and bank.
Capital structure	Owner(s) provide capital and the business is totally independent.	Owner has total liability for debts. (Partners have total liability for *all* debts of the firm.) Owners may not have sufficient personal or business resources for growth.
		Borrowing required to finance expansion and also to cover times when there is a delay in collecting cash from customers.
		Finance is limited by maximum number of partners (20 except for some professional firms) but this is not usually a problem.
Management	Sole trader has total control over the management of the business, which enables him to offer a personal service to customers and potential customers.	Could result in overwork for owner and difficulties in management, particularly as the business grows.
	In a partnership, cover for sickness and holiday is available. Partners may be made responsible for different areas of the business, so specialisation is possible.	The presence of more than one 'manager' could give rise to danger of disagreement or slow decision-making between the partners. Continuity of the business could be a problem with the death or retirement of a key partner. One partner's work in business matters is binding on all other partners.
Profitability	Profits are distributed only to the owner(s); tax advantages over being an employee.	Potentially a loss of business/ profit during sole trader's absence from the business, eg due to sickness or holiday.

Shareholder finance – limited companies

	Advantages for the business	*Disadvantages for the business*
Formation	None	Complex and expensive to set up. Greater legal controls on management, eg submission of annual accounts to the Companies' House. Published accounts may give away sensitive trading information.
Capital structure	Large potential membership to provide capital and resources. Shareholders' liability is limited to the amount asked by the company for their shares. Ownership of the company is transferable by selling share-holding.	
Management	Day-to-day management can be made the responsibility of 'expert' managers.	
Profitability	Profits can either be distributed to shareholders as dividends or retained in the business to help future activities.	Shareholders may demand larger dividends than the business can afford.

The legal implications of different financial structures

Shareholder finance	*Owners/manager finance*
Separate legal entity (company).	Partners grouped in a relationship, ie no separate entity.
Shareholders' liability limited.	Liability for business debts usually unlimited.
Company (not its members) owns its assets.	Partners jointly own partnership property, sole traders own property personally.
Capital subscribed by shareholders may only be repaid to them under rules designed to protect interests of creditors.	Owners may (by mutual agreement) withdraw capital as they wish – but unpaid creditors of the business may claim against them personally.
A company must have one or more directors. A shareholder has no involvement in management (unless he is also a director or employee).	Owners are entitled to participate in management.
A company always has a written constitution (memorandum and articles of association).	A sole trader or partnership may exist without any written partnership agreement.
A company must usually deliver annual accounts, annual returns and other notices to Companies' House and maintain resisters – all open to public inspection.	A partnership must disclose the names or the partners. But no one except a partner has any right to inspect accounts (although accounts have to given to the tax authorities). Likewise sole traders.
A company may offer potential lenders of finance security by way of a 'charge' over its assets including current assets.	Partners and sole traders cannot provide security by a charge on goods.

NOTES

We shall consider the financing of companies in much more detail in the next chapter. In the rest of this chapter we shall discuss ways of borrowing money and ways of getting people to give you money.

For most businesses the bank is the first place to turn to if the owners do not have enough ready cash to set up the business and keep it running.

3 BORROWING FROM THE BANK

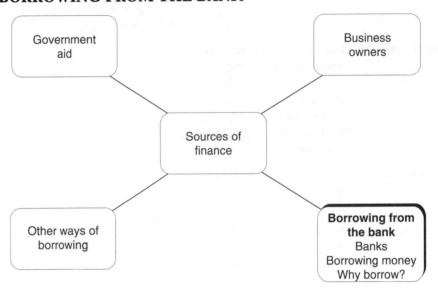

3.1 Banks

There are different types of banks which operate within the banking system, and you will probably have come across a number of terms which describe them.

(a) Clearing banks are the banks which operate the so-called 'clearing system' for settling payments (eg payments by cheque by bank customers).

(b) The term 'retail' banks is used to describe the traditional High Street banks, Barclays, NatWest, etc. The term 'wholesale' banks refers to banks which specialise in lending in large quantities to major customers. The clearing banks are involved in both retail and wholesale banking but are commonly regarded as the main 'retail' banks.

(c) Merchant banks are banks which offer services, often of a specialised nature, to corporate customers – companies.

All but the smallest businesses make extensive use of banks. The main functions and activities of banks can be summarised as follows.

(a) Providing a payments mechanism ie a way in which individuals, firms and government can make payments to each other. The 'clearing system' of the clearing banks is the major payments mechanism in the UK, and it enables individuals and firms to make payments by cheque. The banks are also a source from which individuals and firms can obtain notes and coins.

(b) Providing a place for individuals, firms and government to store their wealth, for example in current accounts or deposit accounts. Banks compete with other financial institutions to attract the funds of individuals and firms.

(c) Lending money in the form of loans or overdrafts.

(d) Acting as 'financial intermediaries': they accept deposits from people who have surplus wealth and lend it to those that need to borrow.

(e) Providing customers with a means of obtaining foreign currency, or selling foreign currency, whenever they require it.

For the moment we are concerned with item (c), getting the bank to lend money to a business. Let's think about the circumstances in which a bank might be prepared to do this.

3.2 Borrowing money

If you want to borrow money the people lending it to you will usually only be prepared to do so if they are sure of the following.

(a) They will be repaid within a reasonable time.

(b) They will make more for themselves by lending it to you (and making you pay interest) than they would from doing something else with their money.

FOR DISCUSSION

You have £10,000. You can put it in the building society and earn 3% interest. Alternatively you can lend it to a friend who says she is willing to pay 4% interest.

What further information would you want before you decide what to do?

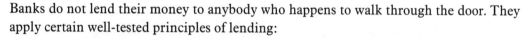

Banks do not lend their money to anybody who happens to walk through the door. They apply certain well-tested principles of lending:

(a) They look at the *character* of the person or business asking for the loan. Can they be trusted – for example have they borrowed and repaid money in the past?

(b) Is the borrower *able to repay?* If it is a business, is it a profitable one and are there enough spare profits to be able to afford the interest and the periodic repayments of portions of the loan?

(c) Will the bank *make money* out of the loan? If the bank itself has to pay out 3% interest to people who deposit money in their accounts then it will have to charge more than 3% interest to people who borrow money.

(d) The bank will want to know the *purpose* of the loan. They won't lend you money so that you can engage in drug-dealing, for example. If you intend to gamble the money you want to borrow on the 3.30pm at Cheltenham the bank will not take the risk. The main reasons for borrowing are discussed in a moment.

(e) The *amount* of the loan is partly dependent on whether the borrower can afford to repay capital and interest and what *security* there is available (see below). For many business loans, however, the bank prefers the customer to have a significant personal stake in whatever the loan is for – the bank will put up £10,000 to help buy a new machine, say, if the business puts up the remaining £10,000 needed.

(f) The *repayment terms* of the loan are very significant. These do not just include how long the loan will continue (say, for three or five years) and how much of each regular payment is of capital, and how much of interest, but also the circumstances in which the bank can call in the loan early. For instance, the terms may state that the entire loan should become repayable, with penalty interest, if more than two consecutive payments are late.

(g) The bank will need some form of *security* which it can turn to if the loan is not repaid. This is just like a mortgage: if you can't afford your mortgage repayments your house (the security) will be repossessed. Likewise, a bank will take some sort of charge over a business's assets. This means that the bank has a legal right to seize the assets if the loan is not repaid.

Together, these points make up a commonly-used acronym for the principles applied by the lending banker: CAMPARI

Character of borrower

   Ability to borrow and repay

      Margin of profit for the banker

         Purpose of the loan

            Amount of the loan

               Repayment terms

                  Insurance against non-payment (security)

Clearly you can't just go along to a bank and ask for wads of money with which to do what you like. Here are the most typical and legitimate reasons for using the bank as a source of finance.

3.3 Why borrow?

Broadly speaking, a business will wish to borrow from the bank for one or more of three purposes.

(a) To purchase a business as a whole
(b) To fund the purchase of fixed assets (capital finance) like buildings or cars
(c) To fund day-to-day activities ('working capital' or 'trading finance')

Buying a business

There are two main circumstances in which a business might be bought.

- As a totally new venture, possibly starting from scratch
- As an expansion of an existing business

New ventures are risky undertakings for businessmen: 80% of all new small businesses fail within the first five years. However, the new ventures of today may turn out to be tomorrow's Dyson, so a bank will always consider lending in order not to miss an excellent future customer, and so as not to have a reputation for being unsupportive of enterprise and initiative.

An existing business, say a small retailer, may see a good opportunity for expansion when the chance arises to purchase another business, such as a warehousing operation. This is a form of new venture, but is probably less of a risk for the bank because the borrower has more experience of running a business.

In addition to new ventures and takeovers there are other circumstances in which a business is purchased.

(a)   Professional people, such as doctors, dentists or accountants, seeking to set up in practice.

(b)   A management buyout, where the managers of a business purchase it from its existing owners.

(c)   Purchasing a franchise, for instance an individual might wish to set up a fast-food outlet within the framework of an international organisation which grants franchises.

FOR DISCUSSION

Why might managers be interested in buying the business they work for?

Think about issues like ownership, control and rewards. You might find it helpful to consider what advantages and disadvantages there would be for you if you were offered the chance to be one of the owners of your own employer.

2006 saw a record level of MBO transactions in the UK. What factors may have contributed towards this?

Buying fixed assets

Another very common reason for a business to borrow is in order to finance the purchase of new fixed assets. These are things like machines or premises that are used to generate income for a business over a long period of time. Banks try to ensure that the loan in some way matches the asset's life.

Hence a loan to purchase computer equipment will be *short term* (since computer systems become rapidly out of date, particularly in an expanding business) whilst one to purchase a factory will be *long term*. A mortgage over the latter will be good security, which is not the case with computer equipment.

Banks will also want to be sure that all the relevant costs of purchase have been included in the borrower's plan.

- Installation and testing costs
- Cost of any rebuilding
- Staff retraining costs

Such costs may reduce the profitability of the project and strain the business's cash flow to such an extent that the repayments cannot be met.

Day to day finance – bank overdraft

Day to day financing or 'working capital' is one of the most common forms of borrowing. Finance is needed for this purpose because stocks often take a long time to turn into cash: the business has to have them, whether customers buy them or not, but in the meantime the suppliers of the stocks must be paid.

Suppose A Ltd buys some stocks for resale from Z Ltd in month 1 on 30 days credit. It sells the stock to B Ltd at a profit at the beginning of month 2 and at the same time pays Z Ltd. But B Ltd takes 45 days to pay for the stocks. Hence until the middle of month 3 A Ltd has a cash deficit of the amount which it paid its supplier, Z Ltd. This deficit must be financed (the money must come from somewhere) and the most usual source is a bank overdraft.

Terms of a business overdraft are usually set out as follows.

(a) *Repayment:* repayable on demand with review dates set every twelve months or so to decide whether the amount of overdraft allowed needs to be increased.

(b) *Amount*: the account should fluctuate between debit and credit, the debit balance not to exceed a certain level and the average balance to be well within that limit.

(c) *Security:* usually an overdraft is secured by a charge over (a right to possession of) the business's assets.

(d) *Interest:* interest is calculated on the daily balance.

We shall be looking at trade credit and the management of working capital in much more detail in later chapters. However, we have not yet finished with borrowing: there are other ways of borrowing money besides a loan from the bank.

4 OTHER WAYS OF BORROWING

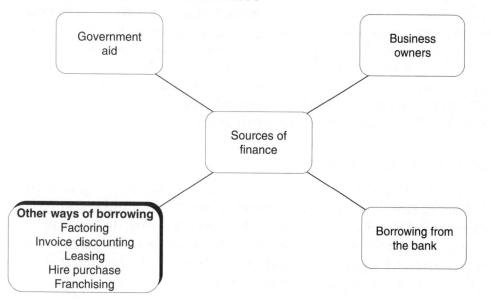

4.1 Factoring

Some businesses might have difficulties in financing the amounts owed by customers (debtors). There are two main reasons for this.

(a) If a business's sales are rising rapidly, its total debtors will rise quickly too. Selling more on credit will put a strain on the company's cash flow. The business, although making profits, might find itself in difficulties because it has too many debtors and not enough cash.

(b) If a business grants long credit to its customers, it might run into cash flow difficulties for much the same reason. Exporting businesses must often allow long periods of credit to foreign buyers, before eventually receiving payment, and their problem of financing debtors adequately can be a critical one.

Factors are organisations that offer their clients a financing service to overcome these problems. They are prepared to advance cash to the client against the security of the client's debtors. The business will assign its debtors to the factor and will typically ask for an advance of funds against the debts which the factor has purchased, usually up to 80% of the value of the debts.

In addition, the factor may provide a debtor management service, whereby it takes over the control and collection of debts from the client.

For example, if a business makes credit sales of £100,000 per month, the factor might be willing to advance up to 80% of the invoice value (here £80,000) in return for a commission charge, and interest will be charged on the amount of funds advanced.

The balance of the money will be paid to the business when the customers have paid the factor, or after an agreed period.

This service gives the business immediate cash in place of a debt (which is a promise of cash in the future). If the business needs money to finance operations, borrowing against trade debts is therefore an alternative to asking a bank for an overdraft.

The appeal of factor financing to growing firms is that factors might advance money when a bank is reluctant to consider granting a larger overdraft. Advances from a factor are therefore particularly useful for rapidly growing companies, that need more and more cash to expand their business quickly, by purchasing more stocks and allowing more credit sales than they would otherwise be able to do. However, factoring companies are generally reluctant to assist companies with less than a year's trading behind them, and which do not have much of a track record in business yet, because of the strong risk that a new company might get into financial difficulties.

4.2   Invoice discounting

Invoice discounting is related to factoring and many factors will provide an invoice discounting service. Invoice discounting is the purchase of a selection of invoices, at a discount. For example, if your business had just redecorated the Town Hall it might have sent the Council an invoice for £5,000. This would be an easy invoice to sell on for cash because the Council are very likely to pay. An invoice for £5,000 sent to 'A Cowboy & Co' would not be so easy to sell for immediate cash!

The invoice discounter does not take over the management of all the business's debtors', and the arrangement is purely for the advance of cash. A business should only want to have some invoices discounted when it has a temporary cash shortage, and so invoice discounting tends to consist of 'one-off deals'. Since the discounter does not control debt administration, and relies on the client to collect the debts for him, it is a more risky operation than factoring and so the discounter might only agree to offer an invoice discounting service to reliable, well-established companies.

Activity 3   **(15 minutes)**

(a)   What are the financial costs of bank loans, factoring and invoice discounting?

(b)   What is the financial cost of obtaining finance by issuing shares in a company?

4.3   Leasing

A lease is an agreement between two parties, the lessor and the lessee.

(a)   The *lessor* owns an asset, but grants the lessee use of it.

(b)   The *lessee* does not own the asset, but uses it, and in return makes payments to the lessor.

Leasing is therefore a form of rental. Leased assets are usually things like plant and machinery, and cars and commercial vehicles, but might also be computers, ships, aeroplanes, oil production equipment, office equipment and so on.

Operating leases are agreements between a lessor and a lessee where the period of the lease is fairly short, less than the useful life of the asset, so that at the end of one lease agreement, the lessor has two options.

(a)   Lease the same equipment to someone else, and obtain a good rental for it; or

(b)   Sell the equipment at a second-hand value.

With an operating lease the lessee is in effect renting the asset.

Finance leases are lease agreements between the user of the leased asset (the lessee) and a provider of finance (the lessor) for the main part of the asset's expected useful life, if not its entire useful life.

The lessor never has physical possession of the asset, even though he owns it. The lessee is responsible for the upkeep, servicing and maintenance of the asset. The lessor is not involved in this at all.

The lessee effectively owns the asset under a finance lease, although in law the lessor owns it.

What are the attractions of leasing to the supplier of the equipment, the lessee and the lessor?

(a)   The supplier of the equipment is paid in full at the beginning. The equipment is sold to the lessor, and apart from obligations under guarantees or warranties, the supplier is free from all further financial concern about the asset.

(b)   The lessor invests finance by purchasing assets from suppliers and makes a return out of the lease payments from the lessee. Provided that a lessor can find lessees willing to pay the amounts he wants to make his return, the lessor will make good profits on his deals.

(c)   It is natural to want to own an asset instead of 'rent' one, and so the attractions of leasing to the lessee might not seem so obvious. However, under a finance lease, the lessee has use of the asset as though he were the real owner, and the lessor does not interfere at all. Leasing has its advantages.

   (i)   The lessee may not have enough cash to pay for the asset, and may have difficulty obtaining a bank loan to buy it, and have to rent it in one way or another if he is to have use of the asset at all.

   (ii)   Leasing may be cheaper than a bank loan. The cost of payments under a loan might exceed the cost of a lease.

4.4   Hire purchase

Hire purchase (HP) is a form of borrowing whereby an individual or business purchases goods on credit and pays for them by instalments. The HP contract is arranged by the vendor of the goods but is usually between the customer and a finance company.

- The supplier sells the goods to the finance company

- It delivers the goods to the customer who will eventually purchase them

- The hire purchase arrangement exists between the finance company and the customer.

NOTES

The finance company will nearly always insist that the hirer should pay a deposit towards the purchase price, perhaps as low as 15%, or as high as 33%. In contrast, with a finance lease, the lessee does not usually have to make any down-payment.

Goods bought by businesses on hire purchase include company vehicles, plant and machinery, office equipment and farming machinery. Hire purchase arrangements for fleets of motor cars are quite common, and most car manufacturers have a link with a leading finance house for point-of-sale hire purchase credit (for example, Rover and Lombard North Central).

Hire purchase is similar to leasing, with the exception that ownership of the goods passes to the hire purchase customer on payment of the final instalment, whereas a lessee never becomes the legal owner of the goods.

The benefits of hire purchase, like leasing, include the following.

(a) A business can obtain assets now and pay for them over a period of time. This avoids putting a strain on the business cash flows.

(b) A business can budget its relevant costs and cash flows accurately with fixed interest rate HP finance.

(c) Hire purchase is fairly simple to arrange, and a useful alternative to borrowing from a bank.

Activity 4   **(15 minutes)**

Using the above terminology, what sort of arrangements are being made in the following domestic situations?

(a) Mark rents a TV.

(b) Lucy buys a Volkswagen Golf car and agrees to allow the Volkswagen dealer to arrange the finance.

(c) Mark wants his banker to help out until he receives his salary cheque in 3 weeks time.

(d) Lucy needs assistance to buy a new flat.

4.5 Franchising

Franchising is the means by which a large number of chains have grown very rapidly in the last decade. The franchisor has a successful business (selling hamburgers, pizzas or printing, for example) and instead of establishing branches under its own name it licenses franchisees to use its name, corporate identity and so on. The franchisees actually run the business, employing staff as necessary.

In return for what can be a substantial licence fee, the franchisees receive the following.

(a) They are trained before starting.

(b) Their premises are fitted out with the appropriate equipment and decor (the cost of doing this is likely to be loaned to the franchisee by the franchisor).

(c) They must usually buy most or all of their trading stock and other supplies from the franchisor.

(d) They benefit considerably from the marketing and advertising of the franchisor.

(e) They do not have to make pricing or marketing decisions themselves as these are made by the franchisor (at least in outline).

The franchisor is usually willing to put a lot of effort into helping the franchisees because the public perceives the chain as a chain and not as a collection of disparate outlets all using the same name. Thus, if the McDonalds outlet in Macclesfield (a franchise) is up to scratch, then customers will not be deterred from visiting the McDonalds outlet in Pontefract (owned and run by McDonalds plc itself).

The franchisor benefits from the arrangement even where it has no outlets of its own. Because the franchisees are the legal owners of the outlets, the franchisor is freed from the administrative burden of maintaining a branch network and employing large numbers of staff. Its income comes from the licence fees and from collecting an agreed percentage of profits made by the franchisees. This produces a steady stream of cash, less liable to fluctuate and less risky than relying on profits generated by its own branches. The franchisor's cash flow should improve and its need for borrowing decrease.

The franchisee benefits from the 'handholding' of the franchisor, especially when the franchisee has not been self-employed before. He or she is free to concentrate on running the business without having to think about marketing, choosing between suppliers and so on. For all these reasons, franchising has proved attractive to many people made redundant with large redundancy payments, or to people taking early retirement from a first career, with a lump sum from their pension fund to invest.

Activity 5   **(15 minutes)**

(a) Earlier we said that there are three main reasons why a business might borrow money. What are those reasons, and which applies to:

   (i) Factoring and invoice discounting?
   (ii) Leasing and hire purchase?
   (iii) Franchising?

(b) What are the costs, financial and otherwise, of franchising?

Finally in this chapter we turn to 'money for nothing'! You may be getting, say, local authority assistance in financing your studies, because it is seen as a good thing to have an educated population. Similarly, it is in the interests of society as a whole that businesses are given a chance to succeed, so financial support is available.

5 GOVERNMENT AID

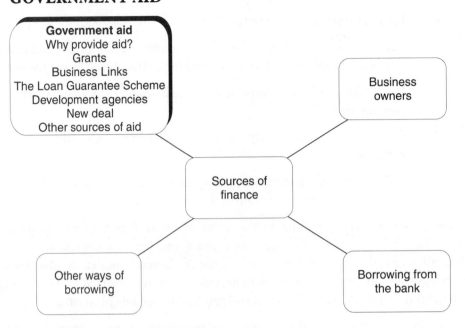

5.1 Why provide aid?

Governments are keen that businesses should start up and prosper because successful businesses provide employment and create wealth for the country. A healthy economy needs a steady flow of new enterprises to answer the needs of tomorrow's markets and offset the effects of the decline of other industries.

The UK Government provides finance to companies in cash grants and other forms of direct assistance, as part of its policy to help develop the national economy, especially in high technology industries and in areas of high unemployment.

5.2 Grants

These are a package of measures offered by the Department for Business, Enterprise and Regulatory Reform to businesses in the UK, including some regional selective grant assistance. There is a network of 'Business Links' (or equivalent outside England), which are local business advice centres.

The basics

A *grant* is a sum of money given to an individual or business for a specific project or purpose.

A grant usually covers only part of the total costs involved. However, as long as the individual or organisation keep to any conditions attached to the grant, it will not have to be repaid.

Grants to help with business development are available from a variety of sources, such as the Government, European Union, Regional Development Agencies, Business Links, local authorities and some charitable organisations.

These grants may be linked to business activity or a specific industry sector. Some grants are linked to specific geographical areas, eg those in need of economic regeneration.

Government grants and support

The government provides support to businesses both financially, in the form of grants and through access to networks of expert advice and information.

Government grants are almost always awarded for a specific purpose or project and are usually for **proposed projects** only – not for those that have already started.

Types of grants

The main groups who award grants are:

- The Government
- The European Union
- Regional Development Agencies in England, Scottish Enterprise, the Welsh Development Agency and Invest Northern Ireland
- Local authorities or local councils and local development agencies
- Business Links
- Chamber of Commerce
- County Enterprise Boards

Some funding is also distributed through colleges and the Learning and Skills Council (LSC).

Innovation, research and development

There are numerous grants available to encourage investment in innovation, research and development.

Training

The Learning and Skills Council and some 'British Links' (see para 5.3) provide grants for training and skills development.

Economic regeneration

Businesses based in areas classified as **assisted areas** may benefit from a grant if they stimulate regional development, urban regeneration or an improvement in employment prospects.

5.3 Business Links

Help with consultancy costs is provided by the network of 'Business Links', which are local business advice centres.

5.4 The Small Firms Loan Guarantee Scheme

The Small Firms Loan Guarantee Scheme is intended to help small businesses obtain a loan from a bank, when a bank may otherwise be unwilling to lend because the business cannot offer the security that the bank would want.

To be eligible, a UK company must have a turnover of up to £5.6 million and be up to five years old.

Under the scheme the bank can lend up to £250,000 to firms trading for more than two years, without security being given over *personal* assets or a personal guarantee being required of the borrower. However, all available *business* assets must be used as security if required. The government will guarantee the bulk (75%) of the loan, while the borrower must pay an annual premium (2%) on the guaranteed part of the loan.

EXAMPLE

As a result of the foot and mouth outbreak in 2001 the scope and terms of the SFLGS (previously restricted to larger wholesale and manufacturing type businesses) were temporarily extended to help a wider range of businesses overcome the ensuing difficulties, especially in the tourism sector. As a result of the Graham Review, changes to the SFLG were made in December 2005 to focus more on newer business.

5.5 Regional Development Agencies (RDAs)

The UK Government set up **development agencies** which have been given the task of encouraging the development of trade and industry in their areas. The main strategy of the agencies has been to encourage the start-up and development of small companies, although they will also give help to larger companies in certain circumstances.

The assistance that a development agency might give to a firm could include the following.

    (a)   Free factory accommodation, or factory accommodation at a low rent

    (b)   Financial assistance

        (i)   An interest relief grant for a bank loan. A company developing its business in an agency-covered area might obtain a bank loan, and the development agency will agree to compensate the bank for providing the loan at a low rate of interest.

        (ii)   Direct financial assistance in the form of share capital or loans

5.6 New Deal

In 1998 the **New Deal** was launched by the Labour Government, designed to give employers financial support towards the salary and training costs of young, disabled and/or long-term unemployed people, with the aim of reducing the level of unemployment.

5.7 Other sources of aid

Local authorities are often keen to attract new businesses into their area (or to help existing businesses expand) because of the benefits to the local community in creating more jobs and, therefore, spending power to the benefit of all local businesses. The new business may provide a market (or act as a supplier) for other local businesses, which is also beneficial. Grants, loans and advice are therefore likely to be available from the authority or its economic development unit.

The **Prince's Trust** provides grants of up to £5,000 for 18–30 year olds. Successful applicants are usually disadvantaged and have been unable to obtain funds from other lenders.

Activity 6   **(15 minutes)**

In what other ways can governments help businesses (or hinder them) besides providing finance directly?

Think about the impact of government polices on matters such as education, transport, the environment and so on, as well as economic policy.

Chapter roundup

- 'Finance' is money, or, in broader terms, it is a monetary arrangement made in exchange for the ability to do something. The basic sources of money are savings, borrowings, grants and earnings.

- The way in which a business is financed is closely linked with the ownership of the business. The three main forms of business are sole traders, partnerships and companies.

- Banks are the principal source of borrowed money for business purposes. Banks apply principles such as ability to repay and security before they agree to lend.

- Businesses borrow to purchase a business as a whole, to purchase fixed assets or, most commonly, to finance day-to-day trading.

- Other ways of borrowing include factoring and invoice discounting, leasing and HP, and franchising.

- A large variety of government grants are available for businesses that meet certain criteria.

Quick quiz

1   Why do individuals have to do something that generates income?

2   Why do businesses have to do something that generates more?

3   List four sources of business finance.

4   List the three major forms of business ownership.

5   In what sense is a limited company limited?

6   What are the owners of a limited company called?

7   What is the difference between 'wholesale' and 'retail' banks?

8   What principles will a bank apply when considering whether to lend money to a business?

9   What is an overdraft used for?

10   What is the difference between factoring and invoice discounting?

11   What are the advantages of leasing and hire purchase?

12   What advantages does franchising have to a person new to business ownership?

13   What are possible disadvantages of franchising?

Answers to quick quiz

1   To provide for ourselves (and possibly for our families).

2   To make profits for their owners.

3   Owners, bank loans, bank overdrafts, hire purchase, factoring, etc.

4   Sole trader, partnership, limited company.

5   The owners cannot lose more than their investment.

6   Shareholders.

7   'Wholesale' banks lend to major businesses, whilst 'retail' banks deal with the public.

8   Character of borrower, ability to repay, use of loan, interest charged, amount of borrowings and security. (See section 3.2.)

9   To finance fluctuating working capital requirements.

10   Factoring involves a third party collecting all debts. Invoice discounting involves only 'selling' a number of debts to a third party (See sections 4.1 and 4.2.)

11   Leasing allows the lessee to take effective ownership of an asset he might not be able to buy outright. Hire purchase also spreads an asset's cost but the final payment of the HP will mean that the customer owns the goods. (See sections 4.3 and 4.4.)

12   The franchisee can concentrate on the day-to-day running of the business. Other elements of the business such as, marketing and suppliers are taken care of already (See section 4.5.)

13   Lack of complete freedom, cost of franchise, possible disagreement with franchiser.

Answers to activities

1 The answer to this activity depends on your local area. You may be surprised at the number of service businesses, and at the number of small, local businesses.

2 (a) Asset

(b) Asset

(c) Liability

(d) None of these (the rent is an expense)

(e) Assets

(f) None of these (the employee's wages are an expense, but businesses do not own people)

(g) Capital

(h) Liability

(i) None of these (it is another expense)

3 (a) The cost of a bank loan is the interest paid to the bank. There may also be an *arrangement fee* when the loan is first taken out. (Bank charges are not a cost of borrowing: they are a cost of having a bank account.)

Factoring and invoice discounting costs are the factors' *commission charge* and *interest* on the funds borrowed.

(b) *Dividends* usually have to be paid to the shareholders, if only to stop them selling their shares.

4 (a) This is a sort of operating lease

(b) This is hire purchase

(c) This is a bank overdraft

(d) This is a bank loan (a mortgage loan)

5 (a) The three reasons and their application are:

- To finance working capital (factoring/invoice discounting)
- To purchase fixed assets (leasing/HP)
- To buy a business as a whole (franchising)

(b) There is a licence fee, possibly a premium charged on stocks (they may be available more cheaply from other suppliers), and a percentage of profits. The other main cost is the possible dissatisfaction or frustration caused by the lack of overall control of the business.

6 A wide-ranging question!

Items you could have mentioned as help:

(a) Low taxes

(b) Lack of red tape

(c) A buoyant economy

(d) Low interest rates

(e) An educated, skilled workforce

(f) Good infrastructure – roads, railways, etc

The reverse of all the above will be a hindrance.

Chapter 2:
FINANCING LARGE BUSINESSES

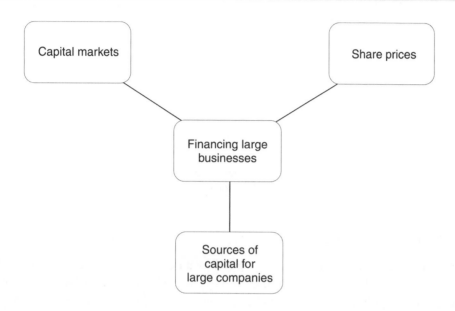

Introduction

When you read about businesses in the pages of a newspaper you will not find much about factoring arrangements or overdraft facilities. Most of what you read will be about events in institutions such as the Stock Exchange – things that go on in financial centres such as the City of London.

This is the world of large company finance in which, because much more finance is needed, there is a good deal more diversity and sophistication in both the range of options available and the number of parties who have an interest. If you work for a larger company it is both useful and important for you to understand that your company's policies and activities are not just the whim of the current managing director. They are, to quite a large extent, influenced by what is and is not acceptable to the City-based providers of finance.

Your objectives

In this chapter you will learn about the following.

- Sources of finance for larger businesses
- The chief providers of finance for larger businesses
- Alternative methods by which companies may raise finance

NOTES

1 CAPITAL MARKETS

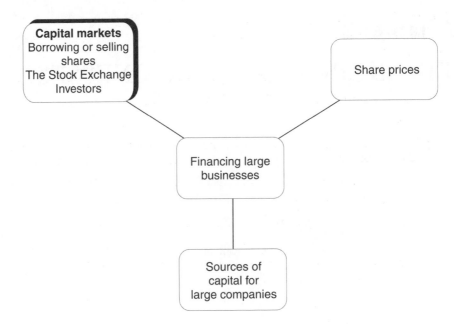

1.1 Borrowing or selling shares

Individuals often need to raise finance; eg to buy a house, a car, a television or furniture. They will in most cases borrow the money needed; their alternative sources will normally be a building society, a bank, a hire purchase or leasing company.

Small businesses often need to borrow, for similar reasons, and their alternatives are similar to those of individuals when they wish to buy business premises, lorries, new computer systems, etc.

Larger businesses also often have need for more funds for expansion purposes. However, they have an advantage over the individual and the small businessman. In addition to the various sources of borrowed money, they can often raise the finance they need by selling more shares in their company. So, instead of borrowing (which has to be paid back), they obtain permanent capital (on which the new shareholders will expect dividend income). Most investors (whether they be individuals with some surplus cash, or institutions, such as insurance companies, pension funds, etc) want to be assured that they can sell their investments at any time (hopefully at a profit, or possibly at a loss).

So most large public limited companies, which have the right to sell their shares to the public and to advertise their shares to the public, wish to be quoted on the London Stock Exchange. The Stock Exchange is in effect a second-hand shop, so that persons becoming shareholders of any plc quoted on the Stock Exchange can always get an up to date valuation of their shares and sell them through Stock Exchange member firms. The function of the Stock Exchange is to bring buyers and sellers together.

The Alternative Investment Market (AIM) is a similar 'second-hand shop' for smaller plcs which cannot meet the more stringent requirements needed to obtain a full Stock Exchange listing.

1.2 The Stock Exchange

The London Stock Exchange is an organised capital market based in London which plays an important role in the functioning of the UK economy. It is the main capital market in the UK.

(a) It makes it easier for large firms and the government to raise long term capital, by providing a 'market place' for borrowers and investors to come together.

(b) The Stock Exchange publicises the prices of quoted (or 'listed') securities, which are then reported in daily national newspapers such as the Financial Times. Investors can therefore keep an eye on the value of their stocks and shares, and make buying and selling decisions accordingly.

(c) The Stock Exchange tries to enforce certain rules of conduct for its listed firms and for operators in the market, so that investors have the assurance that companies whose shares are traded on the Exchange and traders who operate there are reputable. Confidence in the Stock Exchange will make investors more willing to put their money into stocks and shares.

(d) The index of share prices on the Stock Exchange acts as an indicator of the state of investor confidence in the country's economy. For example, if investors believe that interest rates are too low to curb inflation, they may sell shares and move their funds to other countries, causing a decline in share prices.

The price of shares on a stock market fluctuate up and down.

(a) The price of shares in a particular company might remain unchanged for quite a long time; alternatively, a company's share price might fluctuate continually throughout each day.

(b) The general level of share prices, as measured by share price indices (eg in the UK, by the All-Share Index and the FT-SE 100 or 'Footsie' Index), goes up or down each day.

Activity 1 **(15 minutes)**

Here is part of an article from the business pages of a quality newspaper.

'Scottish & Newcastle (S&N) is playing a dangerous game. The brewing group resolutely refused to admit that today's sombre interim results contained a profits warning – simply a kitchen sink load of reasons of why income might dive in its second half. S&N already took the heat out of today's statement by flagging up the effect of the weather on sales.

However, S&N uncovered its problems before July's dismal downpours and the true impact of this terrible month will only become clear in its second half. S&N is pointing the finger at every conceivable issue that might hurt its profits while at the same time it is seemingly confident it will not take a hit.

> The City seems to be buying this so far – an initial fall in shares has turned into a trickle. But if S&N does post a bad set of full-year financials, investors will take no prisoners. At this stage, with such a cloudy outlook, investors might reduce their shares in S&N until the skies clear.'
>
> *The Times Online*, August 7, 2007
>
> In the light of this, and if possible after glancing through the business pages of a newspaper such as *The Times* or the *Telegraph* or the *FT*, what factors do you think have an influence on share prices?

We have talked about 'investors' on the Stock Exchange. You may own a few shares yourself, but millions and millions of shares change hands on the Stock Exchange every day. Who is it that is doing all this buying and selling?

1.3 Investors

Providers of capital (investors) include private individuals, such as those who buy stocks and shares on the Stock Exchange, and those who invest in National Savings or building societies. However, there are some important groups of *institutional* investors which specialise in lending capital in order to make a return.

(a) *Pension funds.* Pension funds invest the pension contributions of individuals who subscribe to a pension fund, and of organisations with a company pension fund.

(b) *Insurance companies.* Insurance companies invest premiums paid on insurance policies by policy holders. If you think about it, insurance companies, like pension funds, must do something with the premiums they receive, and in practice, they invest the money to earn a return.

(c) *Investment trusts.* The business of investment trust companies is investing in the stocks and shares of other companies and the government. In other words, they trade in investments.

(d) *Unit trusts.* Unit trusts are similar to investment trusts, in the sense that they invest in shares of other companies. A unit trust comprises a 'portfolio' ie a holding of shares in a range of companies, perhaps with all the shares having a special characteristic, such as all shares in property companies or all shares in mining companies. The trust will then create a large number of small units of low nominal value, with each unit representing a stake in the total portfolio. These units are then sold to individual investors and investors will benefit from the income from an increase in value of their units ie their proportion of the portfolio.

(e) *Venture capital.* Venture capital providers are organisations that specialise in raising funds for new business ventures, such as 'management buy-outs' (ie purchases of firms by their management staff). These organisations are therefore providing capital for fairly risky ventures. A venture capital organisation that has operated for many years in the UK is Investors in Industry plc, usually known as '3i'. In recent years, many more venture capital organisations have been set up, for example by large financial institutions such as pension funds and banks.

The capital markets may be summarised in a simplified form in Figure 2.1 below.

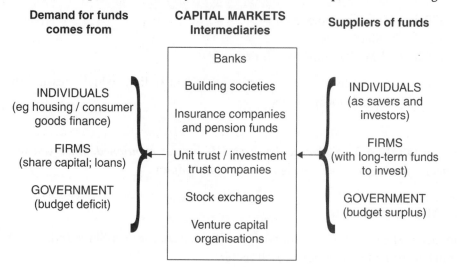

Figure 2.1 The capital markets

The news on the radio or the TV always includes an item telling you that 'the stock market fell today' or 'the stock market reached an all-time high'. While we are on the subject it is worth pausing for a moment to see what this means.

2 SHARE PRICES

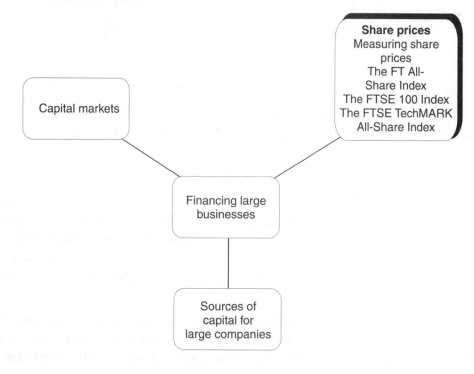

2.1 Measuring share prices

The *Financial Times* (FT) publishes various indices which measure the performance of the UK stock market, including the following.

- FTSE – All-Share Index
- FTSE 100 Share Index
- FTSE TechMARK All-Share Index

The *Financial Times* also publishes the FT-Actuaries World Indices, which measure the performance of international stockmarkets.

It will be useful to take a brief look at the three UK indices mentioned, since you will often see or hear references to them on the news or in the papers.

2.2 FTSE All share Index

The diagram below shows the composition of the FT-SE Actuaries All-Share Index, with the number of constituent companies in each sector.

There are a large number of indices which form a sort of tree (Figure 2.2):

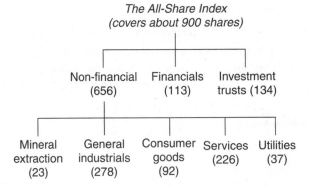

Figure 2.2 FTSE All-Share Index

The All-Share Index is representative of the market as a whole. Not only do the constituent companies cover all the major sectors, such as stores, construction, industrials etc, but together, they also account for around 98% of the total capital of UK listed companies.

2.3 The FTSE 100 Index

The FTSE 100 Index (known colloquially as the 'Footsie') is based on the average, weighted by the number of the shares in issue, of the prices of the shares of 100 leading companies. (The purpose of weighting is to give due prominence to the stock market value of the larger constituents and not to overstate the significance of the smaller companies.)

Between them, the companies which make up the FTSE 100 Index account for about 70% of the *value* of all quoted UK companies. As intended, the index covers a very substantial part of the market and is very closely correlated with the All-Share Index.

2.4 The FTSE techMARK All-Share Index

In 1999 the London Stock Exchange launched techMARK – an international market for innovative technology companies. As these companies have quite different risk/return characteristics from the more established mainstream wholesale/retail/manufacturing companies in the main FTSE Indices a special index is compiled consisting just of shares in business 'at the cutting edge of technical innovation'.

The FTSE 100 Index is calculated *once per minute* throughout the trading day.

Activity 2 (15 minutes)

The following market report is from the *Financial Times*. Read it and then answer the questions that follow.

> 'Share prices in London moved up again to all-time highs yesterday, measured by the stock market's main indices, the FTSE All-Share and the FTSE 100.
>
> There were, however, signs that the market's move to record levels could be running out of steam. Wall Street, one of the prime motivating forces behind the London market's recent rise, briefly penetrated the 5,000 level on the Dow Jones Industrial Average, shortly after the US market opened for trading. But it quickly dropped back to the mid-4980s, and around 2 hours after London closed for business the Dow was still jousting with the 5,000 mark.
>
> The failure of the US index to move decisively through 5,000 was one of a number of worrying signals affecting London. Others included the emergence of yet more profits warnings, notably from Rexam, the paper group, and a decline in international bond markets.
>
> Dealers said London had run into some determined selling pressure when it passed 3,630. "Above that level, we ran into some real selling,"' said one marketmaker.
>
> The FTSE 100 index finished the day a net 19.6 firmer at an all-time closing high of 3,628.8, after reaching a record intra-day peak of 3,639.5. The FTSE-A All-Share index ended at a best ever 1,776.87, up 7.47.'

(a) What do you think 'Wall Street' and the 'Dow Jones Industrial Average' mean?

(b) What is a 'profits warning'?

(c) What was the sentiment or mood of the UK stock market on this day?

This brief section is only meant as an introduction. We offer more advice on how to understand the share information given in newspapers in a later chapter.

Having introduced the providers of finance and the markets in which they operate we can now return to the businesses that want to use the finance. We are only concerned with companies now: these options are not available to sole traders and partnerships.

3   SOURCES OF CAPITAL FOR LARGE COMPANIES

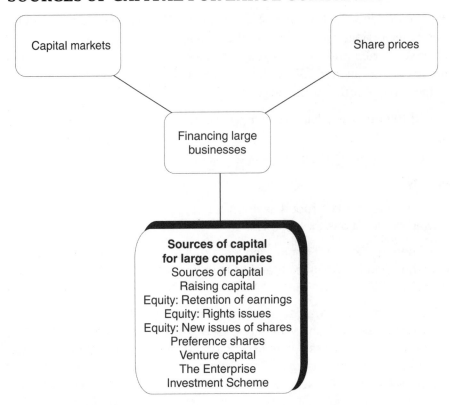

Capital markets

Share prices

Financing large businesses

**Sources of capital
for large companies**
Sources of capital
Raising capital
Equity: Retention of earnings
Equity: Rights issues
Equity: New issues of shares
Preference shares
Venture capital
The Enterprise
Investment Scheme

3.1   Sources of capital

A company must have capital to carry out its operations. Many companies start in a small way, often as family businesses that operate as a private company, then grow to the point where they become public companies and can invite the public to subscribe for shares. New capital is thus made available which enables the firm to expand its activities and achieve the advantages of large-scale production.

Definitions

> A **public company** or plc, is one that can invite the general public to subscribe for shares. A company has to be fairly large and reasonably well-established for there to be any point in doing this. Examples are Sainsbury, British Airways, Barclays Bank and so on.
>
> A **private company** is prohibited from offering its shares to the general public.
>
> Although nearly all of the biggest and best-known companies are public companies, private companies are far more numerous.

The principal sources of capital for a company include the following.

   (a)   *Issued share capital.* Share capital is usually in the form of 'ordinary shares' (equity). The ordinary shareholders are the owners of the company.

   (b)   *Retained profits and other reserves.* Retained profits are profits that have been kept within the company, rather than paid out to shareholders as dividends.

(c) *Borrowing*

    (i)   From banks (ie bank loans). These were mentioned as a source of credit in the previous chapter.

    (ii)   From investors. Investors might purchase 'debt securities' issued by the company. 'Securities' is a general term for any type of investment. Debt securities are 'IOUs', whereby the company promises to repay the debt at a certain date in the future, and until then, pays the investors interest on the debt. Debt capital includes debentures and, for larger companies, eurobonds and commercial paper.

Definitions

> **Equity** means simply the ordinary shares of a company.
>
> **Securities** is commonly used to mean any sort of investment that can be bought and sold in the financial markets. (Some would object to this definition, but this is how you will find the word used in financial writing.)
>
> **Debentures** are amounts loaned to a company. Strictly a 'debenture' is a document setting out the terms of a loan but you could buy, say, £10,000 in debentures, this being your portion of a loan of, say, £100m lent collectively by many people. Debentures are usually secured: ie lenders have the right to seize assets if the loan is not repaid.
>
> **Bonds** are very large fixed interest loans. The term is often used interchangeably with debentures. Commercial paper is just another term for this sort of loan.
>
> **Eurobonds** are bonds that are bought and sold on an international basis.

> **Activity 3**   **(5 minutes)**
>
> Spend about five minutes doing this activity, as often as you get the opportunity. Skim through the financial pages of a quality newspaper (ideally the 'Companies and Markets' section of the *Financial Times*) and see how many of these terms (or any new terms you find in this chapter) you can spot.

3.2 Raising capital

If a company wants to raise new capital from sources other than retained profits, it should establish whether it needs long term or short term capital. Short term capital can be obtained either by taking longer to pay suppliers, or by asking the company's bank for a short term loan or bigger overdraft facility.

Raising more long term capital would require the issue of more share capital or more loans. The ability to raise capital by issuing new shares will depend on the status of the company.

A large public limited company is usually in a better position to raise capital than smaller companies, private companies and non-incorporated businesses for the following reasons.

(a) The high standing of such companies makes investors and other creditors more willing to offer finance/credit.

(b) There is a well established 'machinery' for raising capital for plcs quoted on the Stock Exchange. A share issue will be organised for a firm by a merchant bank (known as an issuing house) or similar organisation.

(c) The limited liability of company shareholders usually makes large companies more willing to want to raise capital, in contrast to small company owner-directors, sole traders and partners, who accept greater personal financial risks when they borrow large amounts of capital.

The main source of new **lending** to companies, both long and short term, is the banks. New debenture stock is not often issued by companies to raise new funds because this stock must compete with government loan stock (gilts) to attract investors, and because they are more 'high risk', company debentures must generally offer a higher rate of interest than the interest rate on gilts.

Despite the existence of capital markets, it is not necessarily easy for firms to raise new capital, except by retaining profits. Small firms in particular find it difficult to attract investors, with the banks remaining as the major source of funds for such companies. The capital markets are dominated by institutional investors like pension funds, and these have tended to channel their funds into 'safe' investments such as 'blue chip' stocks and shares which are traded on the Stock Exchange or shares traded on the AIM, as well as government securities.

Factors in the choice of financing method

The first question when deciding on the most appropriate method of raising new finance is whether it should be in the form of **debt** (ie loans of some form, on which interest is paid) or **equity** capital (ie retained earnings, or new share issues, on which dividends are paid).

For companies, debt capital is a potentially attractive source of finance because interest charges reduce the profits chargeable to corporation tax, and thus the amount of tax payable. Thus an increase in **gearing** (the ratio of debt to equity capital) will lead to more of the companies' profits being available to pay dividends. However, higher gearing levels also lead to an increase in **financial risk** to the shareholders (as discussed in Chapter 6), who may thus require a higher rate of return to compensate for this risk. The overall impact of a gearing change on total cost of finance must be considered in order to determine the optimal gearing level to minimise overall costs of finance.

In addition, large amounts of debt can lead to increased risks of **bankruptcy** – where a company is in danger of not being able to meet its debt interest obligations if earnings fall below expected levels. A company nearing this level will want to seek extra finance from equity sources.

Finally, there may be **legal restrictions** on the company's power to borrow, through its Articles of Association, or the trust deeds of existing loan stock.

Several other factors will influence the choice of method of raising finance.

(a) The **profitability of the company** is obviously important. If the company is making small profits or even losses, it will be unable to raise much or any capital internally. It might also find it difficult to raise new long term funds externally. In such cases, the company might rely heavily on bank lending.

Definition

Profit in simple terms is the excess of income over expenditure. If you buy something for £10 and sell it for £20 you have £10 profit.

In business accounting, profit includes amounts owed by customers and takes into account amounts owed to suppliers. If you buy something with your credit card for £10 and sell it to someone else who gives you an IOU for £20 you have still made a profit of £10 on paper, even though no actual cash has changed hands.

Don't confuse 'profit' with cash!

(b) **The reason for wanting capital**. Capital for financing long term assets should be financed from long term sources, whereas current assets will be financed from a mixture of long term funds and current liabilities.

(c) **A profitable company can raise capital from retained profits**, and most new capital in the UK is currently obtained from this source. However, retaining profits means paying less in dividends and companies must achieve a sound balance between dividends and retained earnings.

(d) When a company wants to take over another, it might be able to pay for the takeover by means of a **share exchange** – issuing more of its own shares and giving these to the shareholders of the target company in exchange for their shares in that company. Companies seeking takeover opportunities commonly use share exchange arrangements in this way to finance their takeovers.

(e) **Interest rates on loan capital may be high**. If interest rates of gilts are high, then interest rates on company loan stock would have to be even higher to attract the institutional investors. In this case, rather than compete with the government, companies have tended to borrow from banks, often medium or short term.

(f) International companies sometimes **borrow in foreign currency**. Very large companies can borrow long term on the eurobond market.

(g) If **government grants** are available companies will, if feasible, seek to obtain finance from this source, depending on the conditions which must be met for the grant to be obtained.

We will now go on to look at some of the methods of raising finance in more detail, focusing on the implications for the organisation and the advantages and disadvantages of each.

NOTES

3.3 Equity: retention of earnings

That part of profits which is undistributed (or 'retained') provides a common means of raising funds from shareholders. The funds belong to shareholders and, if not retained, would be distributed as dividends.

There are advantages to using retained earnings as a form of finance.

- Absence of 'brokerage costs' (merchant banks' fees)
- Simplicity and flexibility
- All gains from investment will still ultimately belong to existing shareholders

There are however, disadvantages.

- Shareholders' expectation of dividends may present a problem
- Insufficient earnings may be available

Activity 4 (5 minutes)

One of the advantages of retained earnings listed above is that 'all gains from investment still ultimately belong to shareholders'. What does this mean?

(Hint. Compare retained earnings with borrowed money.)

3.4 Equity: Rights issues

A company which already has a Stock Exchange listing will commonly issue further shares through a rights issue. A rights issue involves the offer of new shares, at a discount below market value, to current shareholders in proportion to their current shareholding.

The shareholder may 'take up' the rights and buy the shares offered at the specified price. Alternatively, he may sell his rights in the markets.

Advantages of a rights issue include the following.

(a) A rights issue is relatively simple and cheap (compared to a new issue of shares).

(b) Shareholders are given some choice.

(c) Large amounts of capital may often be raised.

(d) All gains from any investment will accrue to existing shareholders.

Disadvantages include the following.

(a) A rights issue is not feasible if small amounts of finance are required.

(b) If many shareholders sell their rights, existing shareholders may lose some control over the company.

3.5 Equity: New issues of shares

A new issue may be by offer for sale or by a placing.

(a) *Offer for sale*

The company sells shares at a fixed price per share to an issuing house, which sells the shares to the general public at a fixed price through a 'prospectus' (a sort of advertising brochure, but with strict rules about the information that must be given). In an 'offer for sale by tender' the issuing house sets a minimum price and invites bids for the shares at a price of at least that minimum price.

(b) *Placing*

In this case, the issuing house again purchases the shares, and sells them directly to its own clients and not generally to the public. This saves the costs of advertising and producing a prospectus. A placing may be unpopular with existing shareholders if they do not have the right to subscribe, since it involves selling shares at a discount to new shareholders.

A new issue has certain advantages.

- Suitability for raising large amounts of cash

- Avoidance of the need to raise cash from existing shareholders

- Reduction of the risk of a future takeover taking place, due to the introduction of new shareholders

A new issues also has disadvantages.

- The considerable expenses involved
- Difficulty in fixing an issue price, particularly in a volatile market
- Unsuitability for small amounts
- Dilution of the control of existing shareholders

3.6 Preference shares

Preference shareholders are entitled to a fixed rate of dividend which is paid before a dividend is paid to ordinary shareholders. (In other words, if there is £100 to distribute and preference shareholders are entitled to £90, ordinary shareholders have to make do with the £10 left over.) Like ordinary dividends, preference dividends can only be paid if there are profits available for distribution. Preference shares do not carry voting rights, so these shareholders do not have a say in the business's activities.

Most ordinary equity shares are **irredeemable,** in that the capital cannot (except in special circumstances involving application to a court to reduce the capital of the company) be repaid to the shareholder. This protects the creditors of the company since it helps to ensure that the company will have sufficient capital to cover any losses. Preference shares are however sometimes issued in redeemable form, such that they will be repurchased by the company which issues them at or after a specified date. As with other preference shares, the company may withhold the dividend if profits are insufficient, but in other respects redeemable preference shares are very similar to debentures.

3.7   Venture capital

Venture capital may be available from a number of sources.

- Clearing bank funds (for example 3i – Investors In Industry)
- Institutionally-backed funds (for example pension funds)
- Government-owned funds (for example British Technology Group – BTG)
- Other funds (for example Innotech; company 'in-house' venture capital units)

Venture capital is capital which is provided for the long term by means of equity investment, sometimes with a loan element as well.

The venture capitalist normally maintains a continuing involvement in the company's business. He is essentially looking for long-term increase in the value of his investment (a capital gain) rather than short-term dividends. Venture capital is often used to finance innovative or 'high-tech' industries, and accordingly the investment carries great risks. If the venture is successful, the venture capitalist may realise his investment through a flotation of the company – the launching of the company on the stock market.

Definitions

> A **capital gain** is the increase in value of an investment. If you buy 100 shares in ICI for £700 and sell them for £800 you make a capital gain of £100.
>
> A **flotation** (or 'going public') involves the issue of shares by a new company or a private company for sale to the general public. (So-called 'privatisation' is the same thing really: state-owned businesses are put into the hands of 'private' individuals from the general public.)

3.8   The Enterprise Investment Scheme

The Enterprise Investment Scheme (EIS) is intended to encourage investment in the shares of unquoted companies. When an individual subscribes for eligible shares in a qualifying company, the individual saves income tax at 20% on the amount subscribed up to a limit of £150,000 per individual in one tax year. Capital gains tax reliefs are also available.

The scheme includes a measure to encourage 'business angels' who introduce finance to small companies by allowing them to become paid directors of the companies they invest in without loss of tax relief.

Activity 5 (15 minutes)

Read the following passage from the *Financial Times* about a company called Cash Converters International (CCI) and answer the questions that follow.

> 'Cash Converters International, the Australia-based retailer, is coming to the Stock Exchange with a value of £23.9m.
>
> Some 34m shares, 34 per cent of the enlarged equity, have been placed at 23.8p, raising £8.1m before expenses. Proceeds will be used to fund expansion which is being concentrated on Europe.
>
> The company has 124 franchised stores, specialising in second-hand goods, in Australia with a further 68 in the UK, France, New Zealand, South Africa and Canada. It is forecasting operating profits of A$1.41m (£670,000) for the six months to December 31.
>
> Dealings are expected to start on November 30.'

(a) Suggest two ways of classifying the business of CCI.
(b) What is 'equity' and what, in numerical terms, is the 'enlarged equity'?
(c) What does 'placed' mean?
(d) What sort of 'expenses' might there be?
(e) What are 'dealings'?
(f) Why is CCI raising capital?

Chapter roundup

- The Stock Exchange (or for new and small public companies, the Alternative Investment Market) is the main market place for larger businesses. It also enforces rules of conduct and provides a barometer of the country's economy.

- Individuals invest in the stock market, but the most important participants are the institutions such as pension funds, insurance companies and unit trusts.

- Share prices for the market as a whole are measured by a number of indices, such as the FT-SE All-Share Index and the FT-SE 100.

- Companies can obtain finance by issuing share capital, by borrowing, by retaining profits or from grants. Various factors, such as financial structure, influence the choice of method of raising finance.

- Share capital (or equity finance) may be raised by a rights issue, a new issue, by issuing a different type of share such as preference shares, through venture capital providers or through the Enterprise Investment Scheme.

Quick quiz

1   What is the Alternative Investment Market?

2   Give four reasons for the importance of the Stock Exchange.

3   Who are the main providers of capital to the capital markets?

4   Which UK share price index could give you a good idea of the state of the market at, say, 11.42am on a Thursday?

5   What are retained profits?

6   Define the following terms:

(a) Equity
(b) Bond
(c) Securities
(d) Public company

7   How might a company finance the takeover of another company?

8   What is a rights issue?

9   What is venture capital?

10 What is the intention of the EIS?

Answers to quick quiz

1   The AIM provides a market for the shares of smaller companies who want a public listing but who cannot meet the full Stock Exchange's listing requirements. (See section 1.1)

2   (a) It provides a market place for borrowers (who need money) and investors (who have spare funds) to deal with each other

(b) It provides information for investors on the value of equities so they can make buying and selling decisions

(c) It polices the standards of listed companies so investors can be assured they are buying quality stocks.

(d) It provides indices on how confident investors are in the economy as a whole. (See section 1.2)

3   Private investors; institutional investors: pension funds, insurance companies, investment trusts, unit trusts and venture capital companies. (See section 1.3)

4   The FTSE 100 (recalculated every minute of each trading day). (See section 2.4)

5   Retained profits that have not been paid out to shareholders as dividends

6   (a) Equity is the ordinary share capital of a company

(b) A bond is a large fixed interest loan

(c) Securities comprise all types of investment which can be bought and sold on the world's capital markets. (See section 3.1)

(d) A company with the right to advertise its shares to the public (See section 3.1)

7   It may issue more of its shares in exchange for the shares of the company taken over. (See section 3.2)

8   A rights issue is an offer to existing shareholders of new shares in the company at a price below the current market value. Usually the number of shares offered is related to how many shares are already owned – for instance, for every five shares owned the shareholder may be able to buy two shares at a discount. (See section 3.4)

9   Venture capital is long-term funding of a company by another company in return for equity in their company; usually the provider of venture capital wants continuing involvement over a long period of time so that the capital invested will grow. (See section 3.7)

10   The EIS is intended to encourage investment in unquoted companies by offering tax breaks on income and capital gains. (See section 3.8)

Answers to activities

1   Share prices respond to:

(a) Factors related to the circumstances of individual companies eg news of a company's annual profits, or a proposed takeover bid.

(b) Factors related to the circumstances of a particular industry eg increased competition, or new government legislation or regulations for an industry, such as new laws on pollution controls or customer protection measures.

(c) Factors related to the circumstances of the national economy eg changes in interest rates, the latest official figures for the balance of trade, or price inflation.

2   (a) Wall Street is the location of the New York Stock Exchange. The Dow Jones Industrial Average is a share price index of 30 shares, the equivalent of the FT Ordinary Share Index (Dow Jones is the publisher of the *Wall Street Journal*.)

(b) This is an announcement by a company that its profits will be lower than had previously been expected. A profits warning usually results in a drop in a company's share price, because it means that the company is less valuable than was previously thought.

(c) The market reached an all-time high, reflecting a mood of optimism about the future of the economy and business performance. There were some indicators, however, that prices had gone as high as they would for the moment (or that they were about to fall).

3   This is an on-going exercise. You will probably think that the financial pages are very boring when you first start looking at them. However, it is worth persevering even if you don't understand much at first. With experience, and as you continue reading this book, more and more will become understandable, and you will begin to follow stories from day to day.

4   If money is invested by a company it might make a return of, say, 10%. For example you might buy a machine for £10,000 and use it to make things that you sell for a profit of £1,000 per year. If the money is borrowed this £1,000 is reduced by the interest charge paid to the bank. If retained earnings are used all of the £1,000 is available to be paid out to shareholders.

5   (a) It is a retailer. It is an international organisation based in Australia. It is a franchisor. You may have thought of other classifications.

       (b) Equity is another name for ordinary share capital. The 'enlarged equity' must be 100m shares if 34% of it is 34m.

       (c) When a company 'places' a new issue of shares it engages an issuing house (probably a merchant bank) which purchases the shares and then sells them directly to its clients. (This is an alternative to offering the newly issued shares to the general public.)

       (d) The main expenses will be any fees paid to the merchant bank and to other professionals such as lawyers and accountants.

       (e) This means that the shares will start to be bought and sold on the Stock Exchange.

       (f) According to the article the purpose is to fund expansion of the business in Europe.

Chapter 3:
FINANCE AS A RESOURCE

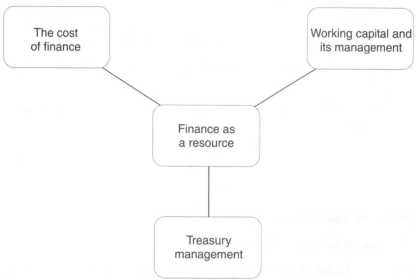

Introduction

You should now have a good idea of where finance comes from so we shall move on to see what a business does with it once it has obtained it.

The essence of management is effective use of *resources*. Resources include things like machines and staff. It is obvious that machines need to be operated properly and maintained if they are going to be used effectively. Likewise people need to be properly instructed and motivated if managers want to get the best out of them.

Money is also a resource, and hopefully personal experience has taught you that there is a need to be careful when using it and that it can be managed effectively.

The need to manage finance arises in business because finance has costs and these should be controlled. We have referred to these costs already in previous chapters and in Section 1 below we expand upon points already made – why a company needs a dividend policy, for example. Then we concentrate upon the day-to-day finance of a business – its working capital – and look in broad terms at how working capital is made up and why it needs to be managed. In the next chapter we go on to look in detail at the management of debtors, stocks and so on.

Your objectives

In this chapter you will learn about the following.

- The cost of various sources of finance
- Working capital and a business's operating cycle
- How a business's working capital requirement can be calculated
- The dangers of overtrading
- The functions of a treasury department

47

Managing Financial Resources and Decisions

1 THE COST OF FINANCE

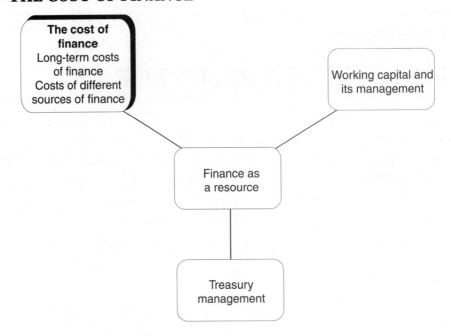

1.1 Long-term costs of finance

It is rare for finance to be provided for nothing.

Imagine that you spend £1 on a Lotto ticket and win £9 million. (You might imagine this all the time!) This should be enough to finance the rest of your life. The cost of obtaining the finance was £1. But what about the costs of managing such a large sum over the next 50 or more years?

(a) There will be fees to pay to financial consultants, stockbrokers and so on who advise you on how to invest wisely.

(b) There will be fees and commissions to pay to practically any institution you choose to invest the money with.

(c) The winnings are tax-free, but any income generated by investments in the future are not. Even if you have a huge binge and spend £7m in the first week you would still have annual investment income from the remaining £2m of well over £100,000. Your income tax bill would be approximately £40,000 per year! If, in 10 years time, you sell one of your mansions at a profit you would have to pay capital gains tax. Tax is hugely complicated: you would need to pay a tax adviser, too.

FOR DISCUSSION

There are other, non-financial, costs to pay too. The loss of some aspects of your current lifestyle would not be without regret.

Produce a list of things that might change in an individual's life if he or she suddenly had great wealth.

Now see how far this translates into a business context if, say, a small owner-managed company is suddenly transformed into a large plc.

In the two preceding chapters we have already mentioned costs such as interest or dividends that are associated with different methods of obtaining finance. We expand upon this in the next section.

Activity 1   **(15 minutes)**

Things only get committed to long-term memory if you run them through your mind over and over again. A good way of taking the pain out of learning from a book is to use cross-references like the one in the signpost above proactively.

Whenever you see such a cross-reference take action! Flick back or forward in the book until you find the passage referred to. Then quickly read or re-read it. This book has a detailed index to help you find topics.

1.2 Costs of different sources of finance

The costs (financial and otherwise) of our four basic sources of finance are as follows.

(a) *Share capital* or owners' savings

   (i) **Dividends in cash**. If you own say 100 shares in ICI, the company would pay you a dividend of so many pence per share twice a year. If ICI paid a dividend of 20p per share in March and in September the cost of your dividend to the business would be $100 \times £0.20 \times 2 = £40$. (If the 100 shares had cost you, say, £800 this is equivalent to an interest rate of $£40/£800 = 5\%$.)

      The amount of dividend paid is up to the company's management, within certain legal constraints. However, shareholders usually expect the amount they receive in dividends to **increase** over time and to be reasonably consistent from year to year. For some investors dividends are as significant a source of income as a salary is for an employee: for them if a company decides to halve its dividend suddenly it is like telling an employee 'we are going to halve your salary'. The employee would leave as soon as possible, and likewise investors would desert the company. So the company is by no means free to pay whatever dividend it likes.

      Dividends also have some quite complicated tax implications, both for investors and for companies. These are well beyond the scope of this book.

   (ii) **Scrip dividends**. Sometimes, instead of paying out dividends in the form of cash, a company pays them in the form of new shares. These are called scrip dividends.

      For example, instead of paying you a £20 dividend ICI might offer you an alternative of two new shares in ICI plus £4 in cash. The number of shares would depend on the market value of a share at the time the dividend was decided – in our example we have assumed this was £8.

      The advantage is that the company retains far more cash, which it can use to develop the business.

NOTES

(iii) The cost of providing shareholders or owners with **information** about the performance of the business. This is considerable in the case of a plc: it includes the cost of glossy financial reports, Annual General Meetings at glamorous locations, audit fees and the administrative costs of complying with legal and Stock Exchange requirements for disclosure of information to shareholders.

(iv) If funds are not needed immediately there may be a cost associated with investing them (bank charges, commission, advisers' fees) until they are wanted for use in the operations of the business.

(b) *Borrowed funds*

(i) **Interest** is the main cost. If you take out a loan of £100,000 and pay 10% interest, the cost is £10,000 per year.

The rate of interest may either be fixed or variable. A variable rate is usually the bank 'base rate' (effectively dictated by the government's economic policy) plus an extra amount (a premium) so that the bank makes a profit. For example there may be a base rate of 5% plus a premium of 3% giving the overall rate of 8%. If the base rate rises to 6% the overall rate will rise to 9%.

On the whole businesses prefer fixed rate loans because they then know for certain how much their future costs are going to be.

(ii) **Tax relief** on interest reduces the cost of debt capital. Thus if a company is paying 10% interest on a loan of £100,000 the basic interest cost is £10,000, but this will be set against taxable profits. If the corporation tax rate is 30%, this will mean a tax saving of 30% × £10,000 = £3,000 (assuming there are sufficient profits against which to offset the full £10,000). The net cost is thus £7,000.

(iii) There will often be an initial arrangement fee to cover the lender's administrative costs on setting up the loan. (Such costs are incurred in checking references, setting up data on a computer system and so on.)

(iv) Factors charge commission for advancing funds as well as interest for the period during which a debt remains unpaid.

(v) Do not forget that the loan itself has to be repaid, too. For example a loan of £4,000 over four years might have to be repaid at a rate of £250 per quarter.

(vi) Financial and non-financial costs arise from the relationship between the borrower and the lender. The lender will require the borrower to provide it with regular information about the performance of the business, and this will have a cost as well as creating the uncomfortable feeling of being watched.

The business generally is less in control of its fortunes. If it goes through a bad patch the lender might demand immediate repayment, effectively closing the business down.

Sole traders and partners are often required to put up their personal property as security for a business loan. This puts a good deal of psychological pressure on the borrower and may have damaging effects on their personal life and relationships.

(vii) A useful concept in many circumstances is opportunity cost. Instead of paying interest of £10,000 a year the business could do something else with that £10,000 that might help to generate income.

For example, if the company could spend the £10,000 a year on extra advertising this might generate an extra £15,000 of profits. Taking out the loan and paying interest means that the opportunity to earn this extra £15,000 is lost. The opportunity cost is £15,000.

As another example, if a loan is secured on the assets of the business, the business has more limited opportunities to do what it likes with its assets, eg sell them.

Definition

The **opportunity cost** of an action is the value of the alternative action which you go without because you do the first action.

Activity 2 **(15 minutes)**

(a) By taking out a loan of £50,000 a business can buy new machinery which will generate extra profit of £10,000 per year. The interest rate is 10%.

What is the opportunity cost if the business spends £5,000 a year on advertising instead of taking out the loan?

(b) What, if anything, is the opportunity cost of paying a dividend?

(c) *Government grants* may appear to be without cost. However there may well be opportunity costs associated with eligibility for a grant. Being based in a certain region, for example, may deprive a business of certain sales opportunities.

There will also be certain administrative costs to cover applying for the grant and (probably) filling in forms on a regular basis to reassure the grant-giving authority that the business is still eligible to receive it.

(d) *Retained earnings*
   (i) A business's sales are only generated by incurring costs such as wages, rent, materials, electricity and so on.
   (ii) Businesses have to pay tax on their earnings.
   (iii) Dividends are a cost of retained earnings as well as a cost of share capital. If dividends are not paid, shareholders' goodwill will be lost.
   (iv) Like capital not needed immediately, retained earnings may be invested in the short term and this will have certain costs.
   (v) The concept of **opportunity costs** is again relevant here. For example, if £50,000 of retained earnings is to be used for Project A, this will reduce the amount of capital available for other, alternative, projects. If the best of the alternative projects is expected to yield a return of, say, 15%, then the cost of using the finance for Project A is the 15% return lost on the best alternative.

NOTES

Activity 3 (15 minutes)

Share capital and retained profits appear to have similar costs. What is the difference between them?

We have mentioned that a certain amount of administration is required to obtain finance in the first place. A good deal more is needed to look after it from day to day when that finance is put to work.

2 WORKING CAPITAL AND ITS MANAGEMENT

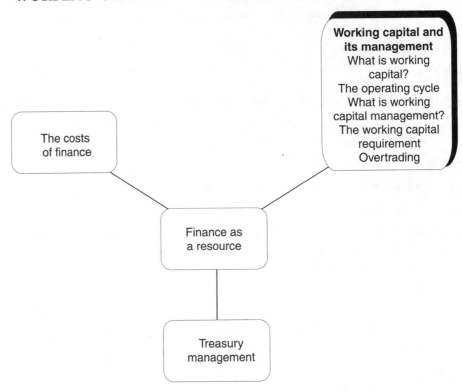

2.1 What is working capital?

The working capital of a business can be defined as its current assets less its current liabilities. Current assets comprise cash, stocks of raw materials, work in progress and finished goods and amounts receivable from debtors. Current liabilities comprise creditors who have to be repaid within 1 year, and may include amounts owed to suppliers of raw materials ('trade creditors'), taxation payable, dividend payments due, short term loans and so on.

Every business needs to be able to maintain day-to-day cash flow. It needs enough to pay wages and salaries as they fall due and enough to pay creditors if it is to keep its workforce and ensure its supplies. Maintaining adequate working capital is not just important in the short term. Sufficient 'liquidity' must be maintained in order to ensure the survival of the business in the long term as well. Even a profitable company may fail if it does not have adequate cash flow to meet its liabilities as they fall due.

52

EXAMPLE

In a recent set of accounts, Microstrategy (a software company in the internet business-to-business sector) reported a profit of $8.9m. However their cash flow statement revealed that their operating cash flows for the period were ($2.5m).

Definitions

> **Current assets** are cash, stocks and debtors.
>
> **Fixed assets** are things, like buildings and machines, that a business intends to keep and use for a long period.
>
> **Current liabilities** are amounts that must be paid out within 1 year.
>
> **Liquid assets** are assets that are easily converted into cash. For example Sainsbury's can easily convert packets of washing powder (stock) into cash by selling them. Cash itself is included when measuring the liquidity of a business.
>
> A **resource** is a means of doing something. A business's resources are sometimes referred to as the 4 Ms – manpower, machinery, materials and money.

Cash becomes available and liabilities fall due. Let's consider the pattern of events more formally. All businesses have what is known as an operating cycle.

2.2 The operating cycle

The connection between investment in working capital and cash flow may be illustrated by means of the 'operating cycle' or 'working capital cycle'.

The operating cycle may be expressed as a period of time – 40 days, say

    (a)   Raw material stocks are obtained from suppliers.

    (b)   Raw materials are held in stock until they are issued to production (work-in-progress). At this time, additional liabilities (for labour and other expenses) may be incurred.

    (c)   On completion of production, the finished goods are held in stock until sold, perhaps on credit.

    (d)   Trade creditors for raw materials are paid

    (e)   Cash is received when the debt is collected

    (f)   The operating cycle is the period between the payment of cash to creditors (cash out) and the receipt of cash from debtors (cash in).

If it takes longer to turn stocks and debtors into cash, or the payment period to creditors shortens:

    (a)   The operating cycle will lengthen

(b)   The investment in working capital will increase.

A business needs to make decisions about how much stock to hold, how soon to pay creditors, how long to wait until debtors are chased for payment and so on. Let's look at some factors that influence these decisions.

2.3   What is working capital management?

Ensuring that sufficient liquid resources are maintained is a matter of working capital management. This involves achieving a balance between the requirement to minimise the risk of not having enough cash to pay creditors and the requirement to maximise the earnings made by using assets. An excessively conservative approach to working capital management resulting in high levels of cash holdings will harm profits because the opportunity to make a return on the assets tied up as cash will have been missed. For example more stock could have been bought and sold.

The volume of current assets required will depend on the nature of the company's business. For example, a manufacturing company will require more stocks than a company in a service industry. As the volume of output by a company increases, the volume of current assets required will also increase.

Even assuming efficient stock holding, debt collection procedures and cash management, there is still a certain degree of choice in the total volume of current assets required to meet output requirements. Policies of low stock-holding levels, tight credit and minimum cash holdings may be contrasted with policies of high stocks (to allow for safety or buffer stocks) easier credit and sizeable cash holdings (for precautionary reasons).

Current liabilities are often a cheap method of finance (suppliers' invoices, or trade creditors, do not usually carry an interest cost) and companies may therefore consider that, in the interest of higher profits, it is worth increasing current liabilities, taking the maximum credit possible from suppliers. Too long a credit period may damage the company's relationship with the supplier though. A balance must be struck so that the company guarantees quality supplies.

FOR DISCUSSION

Make a list of the different types of business that you and your colleagues work in or know of – banks, supermarkets, dot.coms, building firms or whatever.

How do the different types vary in their need to hold stocks? What are stocks in each case?

The operating cycle and working capital management will be clearer if we look at a numerical example. Take some time over the next passage to make sure that you understand the logic of it and where the numbers are coming from.

2.4 The working capital requirement

Computing the working capital requirement is a matter of calculating the value of current assets less current liabilities, perhaps by taking averages over a one year period. First we need to introduce a few new terms.

Definitions

> **Turnover** is just another word for sales.
>
> **Raw materials** are items that are processed to make the finished product. For example steel is a raw material used to make cars.
>
> **Overheads** are expenses on things not used directly in the production of the finished item, for example factory rental or the cost of lighting a factory.
>
> Some overheads change depending on how much is produced – for example if the factory is running for longer it will need to be lit for longer. These are called **variable overheads**.
>
> Other overheads do not change no matter how much is produced. For example factory rent has to be paid whether the factory runs for 8 hours or 24 hours a day. These are called **fixed overheads**.

WORKED EXAMPLE: WORKING CAPITAL

The following data relate to Horn Ltd, a manufacturing company.

Turnover for the year	£1,500,000

Costs as percentages of sales	%
Materials	30
Labour	25
Variable overheads (eg lighting)	10
Fixed overheads (eg rent)	15
Selling and distribution costs	5

The operating cycle is as follows, on average.

(a) Debtors take 2.5 months before payment
(b) Raw materials are in stock for 3 months
(c) Work-in-progress represents 2 months worth of half produced goods
(d) Finished goods represents 1 month's production
(e) Credit is taken as follows:

Materials	2 months
Labour	1 week
Variable overheads	1 month
Fixed overheads	1 month
Selling and distribution	0.5 months

Work-in-progress and finished goods are valued at material, labour and variable expense cost. What is Horn Ltd's working capital requirement?

SOLUTION

The working capital requirement of Horn Ltd (assuming the labour force is paid for 50 working weeks a year) can be computed as shown below.

(a)   The annual costs incurred will be as follows.

		£
Materials	30% of £1,500,000	450,000
Labour	25% of £1,500,000	375,000
Variable overheads	10% of £1,500,000	150,000
Fixed overheads	15% of £1,500,000	225,000
Selling and distribution	5% of £1,500,000	75,000

(b)   The average value of current assets will be as follows.

		£	£
Raw materials	3/12 450,000		112,500
Work-in-progress			
Materials (50% complete)	1/12 450,000	37,500	
Labour (50% complete)	1/12 375,000	31,250	
Variable overheads (50% complete)	1/12 150,000	12,500	
			81,250
Finished goods			
Materials	1/12 450,000	37,500	
Labour	1/12 375,000	31,250	
Variable overheads	1/12 150,000	12,500	
			81,250
Debtors	2.5/12 1,500,000		312,500
			587,500

(c)   Average value of current liabilities will be as follows.

		£	£
Materials	2/12 450,000	75,000	
Labour – 50 weeks	1/50 375,000	7,500	
Variable overheads	1/12 150,000	12,500	
Fixed overheads	1/12 225,000	18,750	
Selling and distribution	0.5/12 75,000	3,125	
			(116,875)

(d)   Working capital required (£(587,500 – 116,875)) = 470,625

> **Activity 4**   **(15 minutes)**
>
> What would Horn Ltd's working capital requirement be if debtors took only one month before payment and finished goods stock were increased to two months' production? Do your own calculations then see if you agree with a colleague.

Many businesses fail because they do not have a proper understanding of their working capital requirements, or do not keep proper control over their requirements. This can happen even if, on the face of it, the business is doing very well. Unfortunately it is possible for a business to do too well: this is called over-trading.

2.5 Overtrading

Overtrading happens when a business tries to do too much too quickly with too little long term capital, so that it is trying to support too large a volume of trade with the capital resources at its disposal.

Even if an overtrading business operates at a profit, it could easily run into serious trouble because it is short of money. Such liquidity troubles stem from the fact that it does not have enough capital to provide the cash to pay its debts as they fall due.

Other causes of overtrading are as follows.

(a) When a business repays a loan, it often replaces the old loan with a new one. However a business might repay a loan without replacing it, with the consequence that it has less long term capital to finance its current level of operations.

(b) A business might be profitable, but in a period of inflation, its retained profits might be insufficient to pay for replacement fixed assets and stocks, which now cost more because of inflation. The business would then rely increasingly on credit, and eventually find itself unable to support its current volume of trading with a capital base that has fallen in real terms.

Symptoms of overtrading are as follows.

(a) There is a rapid increase in turnover.

(b) There is a rapid increase in the volume of current assets and possibly also fixed assets. The rate at which stock and debtors are turned into cash might slow down, in which case the rate of increase in stocks and debtors would be even greater than the rate of increase in sales.

(c) There is only a small increase in proprietors' capital (perhaps through retained profits). Most of the increase in assets is financed by the following methods of credit.

(i) Trade creditors. The payment period to creditors is likely to lengthen.

(ii) A bank overdraft, which often reaches or even exceeds the limit of the facilities agreed by the bank.

In the next chapter we are going to look in detail at the management of the various components of working capital. We conclude with a few brief words about managing large volumes of cash. The details of treasury management are very complicated – well beyond the scope of this book – but you should know that treasury management exists in large organisations.

NOTES

Managing Financial Resources and Decisions

3 TREASURY MANAGEMENT

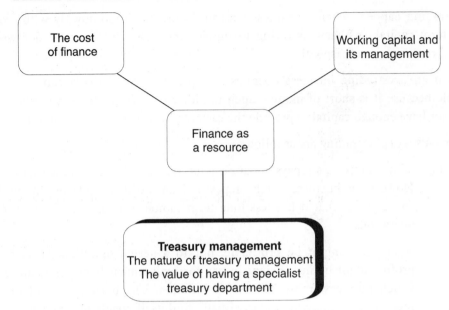

3.1 The nature of treasury management

Large companies rely heavily on the financial and currency markets. These markets are volatile, with interest rates and foreign exchange rates changing continually and by significant amounts. To manage cash and currency efficiently, many large companies have set up a separate treasury department.

A treasury department, even in a very large organisation, is likely to be quite small, with perhaps a staff of three to six qualified accountants, bankers or corporate treasurers working under the treasurer. In some cases, where the company or organisation handles very large amounts of cash or foreign currency dealings, and often has large cash surpluses, the treasury department might be a little bigger.

3.2 The value of having a specialist treasury department

The following are advantages of having a centralised specialist treasury department.

(a) Centralised management:
  (i) Avoids having a mix of cash surpluses and overdrafts in different localised bank accounts
  (ii) Facilitates bulk cash flows, so that lower bank charges can be negotiated

(b) Larger volumes of cash are available to invest, giving better short term investment opportunities.

(c) Any borrowing can be arranged in bulk, at lower interest rates than for smaller borrowings, and perhaps on the eurocurrency or eurobond markets.

(d) A specialist treasury department will employ experts with knowledge of dealing in forward contracts, futures, options, eurocurrency markets, swaps and so on. (These are all methods of minimising the risk of losses because of interest rate changes or changes in exchange rates.) Localised departments could not have such expertise.

BPP
LEARNING MEDIA

58

Activity 5   **(15 minutes)**

(a) ABC plc sells £10,000 worth of goods to a customer in France. The exchange rate is 1.55 euros to the pound, so ABC sends an invoice for 15,500 euros. One month later the customer pays the invoice. By this time the exchange rate is 1.58 euros to the pound.

How much does ABC plc receive, in pounds?

(b) ABC plc buys 50,000 euros worth of materials from a supplier in France and receives an invoice for 50,000 euros. The exchange rate is 1.55 euros to the pound.

ABC plc pays the invoice one month later. By this time the exchange rate is 1.5 euros to the pound.

(i) How much would ABC plc have paid out, in pounds, if it had paid the invoice upon receipt?

(ii) How much did ABC plc actually pay, in pounds?

FOR DISCUSSION

In the light of Activity 5, and taking your personal views into account, discuss the pros and cons of the the UK remaining excluded from the euro currency zone.

Chapter roundup

- Finance cannot be obtained without incurring costs of some description. Besides interest and dividends there are arrangement fees and commissions, the costs of information provision, opportunity costs, and non-financial costs such as loss of control.

- Part of the finance raised is invested in working capital: cash, stocks and debtors less short-term creditors. The relationship between the components is reflected in the business's operating cycle.

- Working capital management involves achieving a balance between the risk of having too little cash to pay debts and having too much cash that is not earning profits. Different types of business have different working capital requirements.

- If a business does not control its working capital needs it runs the risk of over-trading not having enough cash to pay debts as they fall due because it is trying to do too much too quickly or with an inadequate capital base.

- Large businesses with substantial cash flows often have a specialised treasury department to manage short- and long-term investment, foreign currency risks and so on.

NOTES

Quick quiz

1 What expectations do shareholders have about dividends?

2 What is a scrip dividend?

3 Why do businesses prefer fixed rate loans?

4 What is an opportunity cost?

5 Define working capital.

6 What does 'liquidity' mean?

7 What are the symptoms of overtrading?

8 What are the advantages of having a specialist treasury department?

9 What is the operating cycle?

10 What are fixed assets?

Answers to quick quiz

1 To be paid consistently; to increase over time

2 A dividend paid in the form of additional shares rather than cash

3 They know for certain their future interest costs

4 The value of an alternative action foregone

5 A business's working capital is represented by its current assets (cash, debtors, stock) less its current liabilities (amount to be paid within one year). (See section 2.1)

6 The degree of ease or difficulty a business has in paying its creditors on time.

7 Rapid increase in turnover, current assets and (possibly) fixed assets, with a decreasing rate at which stock and debtors are turned into cash. Rapid increase in credit as a source of finance, as opposed to proprietor's capital; trade creditors and overdraft may be used to finance fixed asset purchases, for instance. (See section 2.5)

8 A small number of accounts, either of cash surplus or overdrafts, means better investment and borrowing checks can be made. Expertise will also allow for a wider range of investment vehicles (futures, options etc) to be accessed. (See section 3.2)

9 The operating cycle is the movement of cash through the elements of working capital. (See section 2.2)

10 Fixed assets are items which the business intends to use, and generate profit from, over more than one year. Typically they include land, buildings, machinery, cars, computers and furniture. (See section 2.1)

Answers to activities

1   There is no solution, but don't forget that it is a good habit to learn proactively by looking backwards and forwards through anything you are reading and making links between different parts of the material.

2   (a) The opportunity cost is the £10,000 extra profit that would be earned if the machinery were bought.

   (b) The opportunity cost is the profit that could be earned if the dividend money were invested in business activities.

3   Share capital is money from a source external to the business. Retained profits is money generated within the business. Both would be repaid to the shareholders if the business were to close down, but only after all creditors had been paid.

4

	£	£
Original working capital requirement		470,625
Original debtors	312,500	
Revised debtors (1/12 × 1,500,000)	125,000	
Decrease		(187,500)
Original finished goods stock (1 month)	81,250	
Revised finished goods stock (2 months)	162,500	
Increase		81,250
Revised working capital requirement		364,375

5   (a) ▮15,500 ÷ 1.58   = £9,810

   (b) (i)   ▮50,000 ÷ 1.55   = £32,258
         (ii)   ▮50,000 ÷ 1.5   = £33,333

ABC plc has lost out on each foreign exchange transaction. It might equally have gained if the exchange rate movements had been different. Hence the need for treasury management in companies that engage in a great deal of foreign transactions.

Chapter 4:

MANAGING DEBTORS, CREDITORS, STOCKS AND CASH

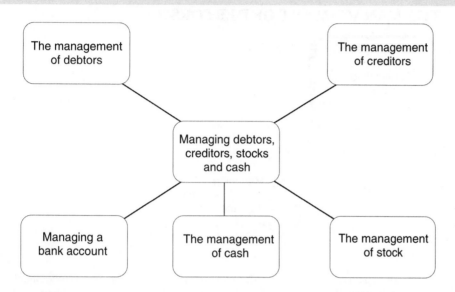

Introduction

In this chapter we are going to look in more detail at the components of working capital and think about the choices available to managers to ensure that working capital is used as effectively as possible.

For example, how much time should customers be allowed before they are expected to pay for their goods? If a supplier offers a discount for payment within the week is it worth taking that discount? You perhaps make decisions of this sort in your personal finances – should you pay off the whole of your credit card bill, say, or just the minimum amount? Should you pay the phone bill as soon as it arrives (and so go overdrawn at the bank) or should you wait for the red final demand (by which time your salary will have been paid into the bank)?

In a business, decisions of this nature can have a major impact on the amount of working capital required.

Your objectives

In this chapter you will learn about the following.

- The factors that influence a business's policies for granting credit and collecting debts
- The procedures for debt collection and credit control
- The use of trade credit as a source of finance
- The costs of holding stock and methods to minimise such costs

NOTES

- The situations in which cash flow problems may arise

- Methods of easing cash shortages

- The usefulness of cash budgets for monitoring cash flow and the preparation of a simple cash budget

- Services and techniques for managing cash in the bank

1 THE MANAGEMENT OF DEBTORS

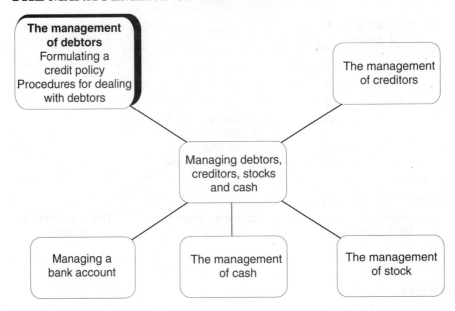

1.1 Formulating a credit policy

Several factors should be considered by management when a policy for managing debtors is formulated.

(a) The administrative costs of debt collection.

(b) The procedures for controlling credit granted to individual customers and for debt collection.

(c) The cost of the additional finance required for any increase in the volume of debtors (or the savings from a reduction in debtors). As we saw in the previous chapter this cost might be for bank overdraft interest, or the cost of long term funds (such as loan stock or equity).

(d) Any savings or additional expenses in operating the credit policy (for example the extra work involved in pursuing slow payers).

(e) The ways in which the credit policy could be implemented. For example
   (i) Credit could be eased by giving debtors a longer period in which to settle their accounts. The cost would be the resulting increase in average debtors.
   (ii) A discount could be offered for early payment. The cost would be the amount of the discounts taken.

(f) The effects of easing credit, which might include the following.

    (i) To encourage a higher proportion of 'bad' debts (debts that are never repaid).

    (ii) An increase in sales volume.

Provided that the extra profit from the increase in sales exceeds the increase in expenses, bad debts, discounts and the finance cost of an increase in working capital, a policy to relax credit terms would be worthwhile.

Definitions

A **bad debt** is a debt that is never repaid. This happens quite a lot in business, unfortunately. For example X Ltd might buy something on credit from your firm but soon afterwards goes out of business owing far more to all its suppliers than there is cash or assets available to repay the debts. The debt to you would never be recovered.

Trade debtors are people who owe you money because they have bought products or services from your business. (Non-trade debtors ('other debtors') are people who owe you money for other reasons: for example you may have earned 70 days interest on a bank deposit but not yet have received the money because it is only paid every 3 months.)

Trade creditors are people you owe money to because you have bought things from them that go into making your product or service. (Other creditors include employees, the tax man, the landlord for rent and so on.)Definition text

Activity 1	(10 minutes)

Think about debts that you owe such as your phone bill or electricity bill. How do the companies concerned try to encourage you to pay your debt?

The following are main areas which ought to be considered in connection with the control of debtors.

- Paperwork
- Debt collection policy
- Discount policy
- Credit control
- Credit insurance

We shall have a brief look at each of these areas in turn.

1.2 Procedures for dealing with debtors

Sales paperwork should be dealt with promptly and accurately.

(a) Invoices should be sent out upon or immediately after delivery.

(b) Checks should be carried out to ensure that invoices are accurate.

(c) The investigation of customers' queries and complaints should be carried out promptly.

(d) Monthly statements should be issued promptly so that all items on the statement might then be included in customers' monthly settlements of bills.

The debt collection policy

The overall debt collection policy of the firm should be such that the administrative costs and other costs incurred in debt collection do not exceed the benefits from incurring those costs.

Some extra spending on debt collection procedures might:

- Reduce bad debt losses.

- Reduce the average collection period, and therefore the cost of the investment in debtors.

Beyond a certain level of spending, however, additional expenditure on debt collection would not have enough effect on bad debts or on the average collection period to justify the extra administrative costs.

For example, suppose that a company is considering whether its current policy should be discarded in favour of Option 1 or Option 2?

	Current policy	Option 1	Option 2
Annual expenditure on debt collection Procedures	£240,000	£300,000	£400,000
Bad debt losses (% of sales)	3%	2%	1%
Average collection period	2 months	1.5 months	1 month

Current sales are £4,800,000 a year, and the cost of obtaining finance for working capital works out at around 15%.

	Current policy £	Option 1 £	Option 2 £
Average debtors (£4,800,000 ÷ 2/12, etc)	800,000	600,000	400,000
Reduction in working capital	–	200,000	400,000
(a) Interest saving (15% of reduction)	–	30,000	60,000
Bad debt losses (sales value)	144,000	96,000	48,000
(b) Reduction in losses	–	48,000	96,000
Benefits of each option (a) + (b)		78,000	156,000
Extra costs of debt collection		(60,000)	(160,000)
Benefit/(loss) from option		18,000	(4,000)

Option 1 is preferable to the current policy because the benefits exceed the costs. Option 2 is worse than the current policy.

Activity 2   **(10 minutes)**

(a) If debtors take an average of 10 days to pay and total sales for a year are £500,000, what is the average amount of debtors?

(b) If the average debtors total is £140,000 and sales for the year total £2,800,000 what is the average collection period (in days)?

Discount policies

A discount may be allowed for early payment of debts. Such an incentive:

- Affects the average collection period.

- Affects the volume of demand (and possibly, therefore, indirectly affects bad debt losses).

To see whether the offer of a discount for early payment is financially worthwhile we must compare the cost of the discount with the benefit of a reduced investment in debtors.

For example, based on past experience a company might predict that if a 2% early payment discount is offered, 50% of customers will take advantage of it. If annual sales are £1m the cost of the discount will be $2\% \times 50\% \times £1m = £10,000$. The saving from reduced working capital needs (since debtors are paying up more quickly) might be £12,000. It would therefore be worthwhile to offer the discount.

Credit control

Credit control involves the initial investigation of potential credit customers and the continuing control of outstanding accounts.

The main points to note are as follows.

(a) New customers should give two good references, including one from a bank, before being granted credit.

(b) Creditworthiness can be checked through a credit rating agency such as Dun and Bradstreet.

(c) A new customer's credit limit should be fixed at a low level and only increased if his payment record subsequently warrants it.

(d) For large value customers, a file should be maintained of any available financial information about the customer. This file should be reviewed regularly. Information is available from the following sources.

    (i) An analysis of the company's annual report and accounts.

    (ii) Other sources of financial information, such as newspaper cuttings, printouts from websites, specialised financial information services (Reuters, Bloomberg, Datastream) and Extel cards (sheets of accounting information about public companies in the UK, and also major overseas companies, produced by Extel).

(e) Government bodies such as the Department for Business, Enterprise and Regulatory Reform and the Export Credit Guarantee Department will be able to advise on overseas companies.

(f) Press comments may give information about what a company is currently doing (as opposed to the historical results in Extel cards or published accounts which only show what the company has done in the past).

(g) The company could send a member of staff to visit the company concerned, to get a first-hand impression of the company and its prospects. This would be advisable in the case of a prospective major customer.

(h) Aged lists of debts should be produced and reviewed at regular intervals. An 'aged list' shows how long each debt has been outstanding.

(i) The credit limit for an existing customer should be periodically reviewed, but it should only be raised if the customer's credit standing is good.

(j) It is essential to have procedures which ensure that further orders are not accepted from nor goods sent to a customer who is in difficulties. If a customer has exceeded his credit limit, or has not paid debts despite several reminders, or is otherwise known to be in difficulties, sales staff and warehouse staff must be notified immediately (and not, for example, at the end of the week, by which time more goods might have been supplied).

An organisation might devise a credit-rating system for new individual customers that is based on characteristics of the customer (such as whether the customer is a home owner, and the customer's age and occupation). Points would be awarded according to the characteristics of the customer, and the amount of credit that is offered would depend on his or her credit score.

Activity 3   **(15 minutes)**

Design a credit application form appropriate for the credit customers of a grocery wholesaler.

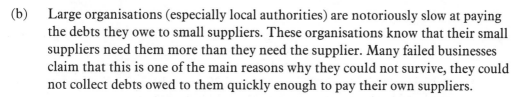

FOR DISCUSSION

(a)   A moral dilemma: if you owed a company £2,000 but you knew it was about to go out of business and that you would not be chased for the debt by the receivers for at least a year, would you pay now or wait? Assume that you have the £2,000 available now.

(b)   Large organisations (especially local authorities) are notoriously slow at paying the debts they owe to small suppliers. These organisations know that their small suppliers need them more than they need the supplier. Many failed businesses claim that this is one of the main reasons why they could not survive, they could not collect debts owed to them quickly enough to pay their own suppliers.

Suggest what could be done to help small businesses in this respect. Think about things like possible government measures, whether a factoring service would be available to a very small company (see Chapter 1) and what the company could do to help itself.

Credit insurance

Companies might be able to obtain insurance against certain debts going bad through a specialist 'credit insurance' firm. A company cannot insure against all its bad debt losses, but may be able to insure against losses above the normal level.

When a company arranges credit insurance, it must submit specific proposals for credit to the insurance company, stating the name of each customer to which it wants to give credit and the amount of credit it wants to give. The insurance company will accept, amend or refuse these proposals, depending on its assessment of each of these customers.

Credit insurance is normally available for only up to about 75% of a company's potential bad debt loss. The remaining 25% of any bad debt costs are borne by the company itself. This is to ensure that the company does not become slack with its credit control and debt collection procedures, for example by indulging in overtrading and not chasing slow payers hard enough.

Interest on overdue debts

In 1998 the UK Government introduced The Late Payment of Commercial Debts (Interest) Act which initially allowed small businesses (under 50 employees) and the public sector to claim interest on overdue debts from large companies. Since August 2002 this is extended to all commercial traders being able to claim interest from each other. The rate of interest is calculated as the base rate (Bank of England) for the end of the day payment terms ended, plus 8%. It is applied on a simple interest basis.

Don't forget factoring and invoice discounting as a means of getting early payment from debtors. Go back to Chapter 1 if you need a refresher. We now turn to creditors.

NOTES

2 THE MANAGEMENT OF CREDITORS

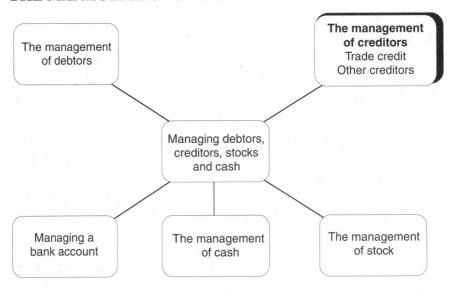

2.1 Trade credit

Taking credit from suppliers is a normal feature of business. Nearly every company has some trade creditors waiting for payment.

The management of trade creditors involves:

- Attempting to obtain satisfactory credit from suppliers
- Attempting to extend credit during periods of cash shortage
- Maintaining good relations with regular and important suppliers

Activity 4	**(5 minutes)**

What might your firm have to do to obtain credit from a supplier?

(You may like to look back at the section on credit control to give you some ideas.)

Trade credit is a source of short-term finance because it helps to keep working capital down. It is usually a cheap source of finance, since suppliers rarely charge interest (but see above). However, trade credit will have a cost, whenever a company is offered a discount for early payment, but opts instead to take longer credit.

For example, suppose that X Ltd has been offered credit terms from its major supplier of '2/10, net 45'. That is, a cash discount of 2% will be given if payment is made within 10 days of the invoice, and payments must be made within 45 days of the invoice.

The company has the choice of paying 98p per £1 on day 10 (to pay before day 10 would be unnecessary), or to invest the 98p for an additional 35 days and eventually pay the supplier £1 per £1. The decision as to whether the discount should be accepted depends on the opportunity cost of investing 98p for 35 days. What should the company do?

Suppose that X Ltd can invest cash to obtain an annual return of 25%, and that there is an invoice from the supplier for £1,000. The two alternatives are as follows.

	Refuse discount	*Accept discount*
	£	£
Payment to supplier	1,000.00	980
Return from investing £980 between day 10 and day 45:		
£980 × 35/365 × 25%	23.50	
Net cost	976.50	980

It is cheaper to refuse the discount because the investment rate of return on cash retained, in this example, exceeds the saving from the discount.

Although a company may delay payment beyond the final due date, thereby obtaining even longer credit from its suppliers, such a policy would be inadvisable (except where an unexpected short-term cash shortage has arisen). Unacceptable delays in payment will worsen the company's credit rating, and additional credit may become difficult to obtain. In addition, if you are both small businesses, you may become liable for interest.

So, managing creditors involves many of the same considerations as managing debtors. The important exceptions are mentioned next.

2.2 Other creditors

There is usually less scope for flexibility with other types of short term creditors. Things like rent and tax and dividends have to be paid out in full on certain specific dates.

(a) Rent is usually payable on the quarter days 25 March, 24 June, 29 September and 25 December.

(b) Corporation tax has to be paid nine months after the end of a company's accounting year.

(c) Employees expect to be paid regularly, usually just before the end of every calendar month.

(d) Income tax collected from employees has to be paid over to the **HM Revenue and Customs** by 19th of every month.

(e) VAT collected by a business has to be paid over every three months.

'Management' in such cases is a matter of ensuring that what is due gets paid on time and that the finance is available when needed. This is especially important with tax because the fines for late payment can be very heavy. Because payment dates are known in advance it is possible to plan ahead: this is what cash budgeting is all about, and we shall return to this topic later in this chapter.

3 THE MANAGEMENT OF STOCKS

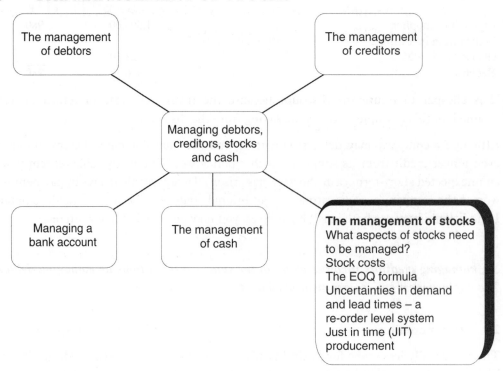

The management of debtors

The management of creditors

Managing debtors, creditors, stocks and cash

Managing a bank account

The management of cash

The management of stocks
What aspects of stocks need to be managed?
Stock costs
The EOQ formula
Uncertainties in demand and lead times – a re-order level system
Just in time (JIT) producement

3.1 What aspects of stocks need to be managed?

Almost every company carries stocks of some sort, even if they are only stocks of consumables such as stationery. For a manufacturing business, stocks (sometimes called inventories), in the form of raw materials, work in progress and finished goods, may amount to a substantial proportion of the total assets of the business.

Some businesses attempt to control stocks on a scientific basis by balancing the costs of stock shortages against those of stock holding.

The control of stocks from a financial point of view may be analysed into three parts.

(a) The **economic order quantity (EOQ)** model can be used to decide the optimum order size for stocks which will minimise the costs of ordering stocks plus stockholding costs.

(b) If **discounts for bulk purchases** are available, it may be cheaper to buy stocks in large order sizes so as to obtain the discounts.

(c) Uncertainty in the demand for stocks and/or the supply lead time may lead a company to decide to hold **buffer stocks** (thereby increasing its investment in working capital) in order to reduce or eliminate the risk of 'stock-outs' (running out of stock).

Definitions

Lead time is the time between starting something and finishing it. Thus **supply lead time** is the time between placing an order for an item and actually receiving it. **Production lead time** is the time between starting to make something and completing it.

It may not have occurred to you in the past that it actually costs money for, say, Tesco to have a shelf full of washing powder. Before we look at the EOQ model and so on it will be useful to have a better idea of what the costs of having stock are.

3.2 Stock costs

Stock costs can be conveniently classified into four groups.

(a) **Holding costs** comprise the cost of capital tied up, warehousing and handling costs, deterioration, obsolescence, insurance and pilferage.

(b) **Procuring costs** depend on how the stock is obtained but will consist of ordering costs for goods purchased externally, such as clerical costs, telephone charges and delivery costs.

(c) **Shortage costs** may include the following.
   (i) The loss of a sale and the profit which could have been earned from the sale.
   (ii) The extra cost of having to buy an emergency supply of stocks at a high price.
   (iii) The cost of lost production and sales, where the stock-out brings an entire process to a halt.

(d) **The cost of the stock itself,** the supplier's price or the direct cost per unit of production, will also need to be considered when the supplier offers a discount on orders for purchases in bulk.

Small businesses mainly use trial and error and past experience to decide how much stock to hold, but a more scientific approach is needed when there is a large investment in stock. The EOQ model is one such approach.

3.3 The EOQ formula

The economic order quantity (EOQ) is the optimal ordering quantity for an item of stock which will minimise costs.

The EOQ can be calculated using a mathematical formula, the details of which is beyond the scope of your studies. In its simplest form we make the following assumptions.

(a) Demand is constant
(b) The lead time is constant or zero
(c) Purchase costs per unit are constant (ie no bulk discounts)

EXAMPLE

Suppose the demand for a commodity is 40,000 units a year, at a steady rate. It costs £20 to place an order, and 40p to hold a unit for a year. We want to find the order size to minimise stock costs, the number of orders placed each year, and the length of the stock cycle. The EOQ will tell us to order 2,000 units each time, so there will be 40,000/2,000 = 20 orders placed each year. This means that the stock cycle is once every 52 ÷ 20 = 2.6 weeks. Total costs will be (20 × £20) for ordering, plus £800 a year stock holding costs (2,000/2 = 1,000 units on average held, at 40p a unit).

This approach can be modified to take account of discounts for bulk purchases. So long as you understand the basic principle, however, there is no need for us to go into further detail.

You must have had personal experience of trying to buy an item only to find that the shop has none left. How can this be avoided?

3.4 Uncertainties in demand and lead times: a re-order level system

When the volume of demand is uncertain, or the supply lead time is variable, there are problems in deciding what the re-order level should be. By holding a 'safety stock', a company can reduce the likelihood that stocks run out during the re-order period (due to high demand or a long lead time before the new supply is delivered). The average annual cost of such a safety stock would be:

Quantity of safety stock (in units)   ×   Stock holding cost per unit per annum

Because stock can be a major investment, and because these days many items tend to be at least partly tailor-made to customer requirements rather than standard models, some new ideas about managing stock have become popular. JIT is the best-known of these ideas.

3.5 Just-in-time (JIT) procurement

In the past decade, there have been developments in the inventory policy of some manufacturing companies which have sought to reduce their stocks of raw materials and components to as low a level as possible. This approach differs from other models, such as the EOQ model, which seek to minimise **costs** rather than inventory levels.

Just-in-time procurement and stockless production are terms which describe a policy of obtaining goods from suppliers at the latest possible time (ie when they are needed) and so avoiding the need to carry any materials or components stock.

Reduced stock levels mean that a lower level of investment in working capital will be required.

JIT will not be appropriate in some cases. For example, a restaurant might find it preferable to use the traditional economic order quantity approach for staple non-perishable food stocks but adopt JIT for perishable and 'exotic' items. In a hospital, a stock-out could quite literally be fatal and JIT would be quite unsuitable.

A system of just-in-time procurement depends for its success on a smooth and predictable production flow, and so a JIT policy must also be aimed at improving production systems, eliminating waste (rejects and reworked items), avoiding production bottlenecks and so on. Successful JIT also requires a very close mutually beneficial, working relationship with suppliers.

JIT is often associated with *Total Quality Management*, the basic principle of which is that the cost of preventing mistakes is less than the cost of correcting them once they occur (plus the cost of lost potential for future sales). The aim should therefore be to get things right first time consistently.

FOR DISCUSSION

JIT has complications for a business's suppliers. Not long ago in Japan the main suppliers to a particular industry decided to stop supplying on a JIT basis. Why do you think they might have done this?

4   THE MANAGEMENT OF CASH

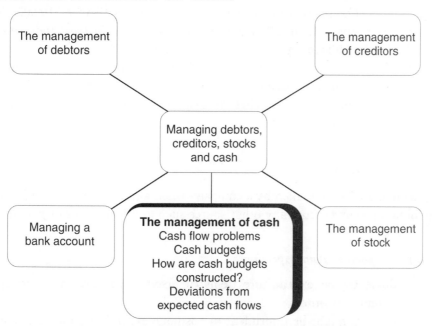

How much cash should a company keep on hand? The more cash which is on hand, the easier it will be for the company to meet its bills as they fall due and to take advantage of discounts. However, holding cash or near equivalents to cash has a cost – the loss of earnings which would otherwise have been obtained by using the funds in another way. The financial manager must try to balance liquidity with profitability.

4.1 Cash flow problems

In the previous chapter, we introduced the operating cycle, which connects investment in working capital with cash flows. Cash flow problems can arise in several ways.

(a) **Making losses**. If a business is continually making losses, it will eventually have cash flow problems.

(b) **Inflation**. In a period of inflation, a business needs ever-increasing amounts of cash just to replace used-up and worn-out assets. A business can be making a profit in accounting terms, but still not be receiving enough cash to buy the replacement assets it needs.

(c) **Growth**. When a business is growing, it needs to acquire more fixed assets, and to support higher amounts of stocks and debtors. These additional assets must be paid for somehow (or financed by creditors).

(d) **Seasonal business**. When a business has seasonal sales, it may have cash flow difficulties at certain times of the year, when cash inflows are low, but cash outflows are high, perhaps because the business is building up its stocks for the next period of high sales.

(e) **One-off items of expenditure**. There might occasionally be a single non-recurring item of expenditure that creates a cash flow problem.

    (i) The repayment of loan capital for, say, a 10-year £100,000 loan only repayable in full at the end of 10 years. Businesses often try to finance such loan repayments by borrowing again.

    (ii) The purchase of an exceptionally expensive item. For example, a small or medium-sized business might decide to buy a freehold property which then stretches its cash resources for several months or even years.

Methods of easing cash shortages

The steps that are usually taken by a company when a need for cash arises, and when it cannot obtain resources from any other source such as a loan or an increased overdraft, are as follows.

(a) *Postponing capital expenditure*

Some capital expenditure items (ie fixed assets) are more important and urgent than others.

    (i) It might be imprudent to postpone expenditure on fixed assets which are needed for the development and growth of the business.

    (ii) On the other hand, some capital expenditures are routine and might be postponable without serious consequences. The routine replacement of motor vehicles is an example. If a company's policy is to replace company cars every two years, but the company is facing a cash shortage, it might decide to replace cars every three years.

(b) *Accelerating cash inflows which would otherwise be expected in a later period*

The most obvious way of bringing forward cash inflows would be to press debtors for earlier payment. Often, this policy will result in a loss of goodwill and problems with customers. There will also be very little scope for speeding up payments when the credit period currently allowed to debtors is no more than the norm for the industry. It might be possible to encourage debtors to pay more quickly by offering discounts for earlier payment.

(c) *Reversing past investment decisions by selling assets previously acquired*

Some assets are less crucial to a business than others and so if cash flow problems are severe, the option of selling investments or property might have to be considered.

(d) *Negotiating a reduction in cash outflows, so as to postpone or even reduce payments*

There are several ways in which this could be done.

(i) Longer credit might be taken from suppliers. However, if the credit period allowed is already generous, creditors might be very reluctant to extend credit even further and any such extension of credit would have to be negotiated carefully. There would be a serious risk of having further supplies refused.

(ii) Loan repayments could be rescheduled by agreement with a bank.

(iii) A deferral of the payment of corporation tax could be agreed with HM Revenue and Customs. Corporation tax is payable nine months after a company's year end, but it might be possible to arrange a postponement by a few months. When this happens, HMRC will charge interest on the outstanding amount of tax.

(iv) Dividend payments could be reduced. Dividend payments are discretionary cash outflows, although a company's directors might be constrained by shareholders' expectations, so that they feel obliged to pay dividends even when there is a cash shortage.

None of these things can be done overnight, especially if it is necessary to sell things or hold negotiations. For these measures to be effective the business needs to know in advance when it is likely to be short of cash: it needs to prepare a cash budget.

4.2   Cash budgets

A cash budget is a statement in which estimated future cash receipts and payments are tabulated in such a way as to show the forecast cash balance of a business at defined intervals. For example, in December 20X6 an accounts department might wish to estimate the cash position of the business during the three following months, January to March 20X7. A cash budget might be drawn up in the following format.

EXAMPLE

	Jan £	Feb £	Mar £
Estimated cash receipts			
From credit customers	14,000	16,500	17,000
From cash sales	3,000	4,000	4,500
Proceeds on disposal of fixed assets		2,200	
Total cash receipts	17,000	22,700	21,500
Estimated cash payments			
To suppliers of goods	8,000	7,800	10,500
To employees (wages)	3,000	3,500	3,500
Purchase of fixed assets		16,000	
Rent and rates			1,000
Other overheads	1,200	1,200	1,200
Repayment of loan	2,500		
	14,700	28,500	16,200
Net surplus/(deficit) for month	2,300	(5,800)	5,300
Opening cash balance	1,200	3,500	(2,300)
Closing cash balance	3,500	(2,300)	3,000

In the example above (where the figures are purely for illustration) the accounts department has calculated that the cash balance at the beginning of the budget period, 1 January, will be £1,200. Estimates have been made of the cash which is likely to be received by the business (from cash and credit sales, and from a planned disposal of fixed assets in February). Similar estimates have been made of cash due to be paid out by the business (payments to suppliers and employees, payments for rent, rates and other overheads, payment for a planned purchase of fixed assets in February and a loan repayment due in January).

From these estimates it is a simple step to calculate the excess of cash receipts over cash payments in each month. In some months cash payments may exceed cash receipts and there will be a deficit for the month; this occurs during February in the above example because of the large investment in fixed assets in that month.

The last part of the cash budget above shows how the business's estimated cash balance can then be rolled along from month to month. Starting with the opening balance of £1,200 at 1 January a cash surplus of £2,300 is generated in January. This leads to a closing January balance of £3,500 which becomes the opening balance for February. The deficit of £5,800 in February throws the business's cash position into overdraft and the overdrawn balance of £2,300 becomes the opening balance for March. Finally, the healthy cash surplus of £5,300 in March leaves the business with a favourable cash position of £3,000 at the end of the budget period.

The usefulness of cash budgets is that they enable management to make any forward planning decisions that may be needed, such as advising their bank of estimated overdraft requirements or strengthening their credit control procedures to ensure that debtors pay more quickly. In our example, management might well be advised in December 20X6 to discuss with the bank the estimated need for an overdraft facility in February 20X7.

4.3   How are cash budgets constructed?

Constructing a cash budget in practice is a complex job because a great many forecasts need first to be formulated.

(a)   The sales or marketing department might produce estimates of the level of sales.

(b)   The credit control department might be able to supply information on how quickly debtors pay and what proportion of debts go bad.

(c)   The production or purchasing department might estimate the level of purchases required and the credit period to be taken from suppliers.

(d)   Other forecasts would need to be made about the dates and amounts of, for example, purchases and disposals of fixed assets.

An illustration of cash budgeting will give you a better idea of the forecasts that need to be made. Read carefully through the following example and then come back to the initial information and see if you can reproduce the cash budget without looking at the solution. You will probably find this quite hard. Allow at least half an hour

EXAMPLE: CASH BUDGET

Peter Blair has worked for some years as a sales representative, but has recently been made redundant. He intends to start up in business on his own account, using £15,000 which he currently has invested with a building society. Peter maintains a bank account showing a small credit balance, and he plans to approach his bank for the necessary additional finance. Peter asks you for advice and provides the following additional information.

(a)   Arrangements have been made to purchase fixed assets costing £8,000. These will be paid for at the end of September and are expected to have a five-year life, at the end of which they will possess a nil residual value.

(b)   Stocks costing £5,000 will be acquired on 28 September and subsequent monthly purchases will be at a level sufficient to replace forecast sales for the month.

(c)   Forecast monthly sales are £3,000 for October, £6,000 for November and December, and £10,500 from January 20X7 onwards.

(d)   Selling price is fixed at the cost of stock plus 50%.

(e)   Two months' credit will be allowed to customers but only one month's credit will be received from suppliers of stock.

(f)   Running expenses, including rent, are estimated at £1,600 per month.

(g)   Blair intends to make monthly cash drawings of £1,000.

Prepare a cash budget for the six months October 20X6 to 31 March 20X7.

SOLUTION

The opening cash balance at 1 October will consist of Peter's initial £15,000 less the £8,000 expended on fixed assets purchased in September, ie the opening balance is £7,000. Cash receipts from credit customers arise two months after the relevant sales.

Payments to suppliers are a little more tricky. We are told that cost of sales is 100/150 × sales. Thus for October cost of sales is 100/150 × £3,000 = £2,000. These goods will be purchased in October but not paid for until November. Similar calculations can be made for later months. The initial stock of £5,000 is purchased in September and consequently paid for in October.

The cash budget can now be constructed.

CASH BUDGET FOR THE SIX MONTHS ENDING 31 MARCH 20X7

	Oct £	Nov £	Dec £	Jan £	Feb £	Mar £
Payments						
Suppliers	5,000	2,000	4,000	4,000	7,000	7,000
Running expenses	1,600	1,600	1,600	1,600	1,600	1,600
Drawings	1,000	1,000	1,000	1,000	1,000	1,000
	7,600	4,600	6,600	6,600	9,600	9,600
Receipts						
Debtors			3,000	6,000	6,000	10,500
Surplus/(shortfall)	(7,600)	(4,600)	(3,600)	(600)	(3,600)	900
Opening balance	7,000	(600)	(5,200)	(8,800)	(9,400)	(13,000)
Closing balance	(600)	(5,200)	(8,800)	(9,400)	(13,000)	(12,100)

4.4 Deviations from expected cash flows

Cash budgets, whether prepared on an annual, monthly, weekly or even a daily basis, can only be estimates of cash flows. Even the best estimates will not be exactly correct, so deviations from the cash budget are inevitable.

This uncertainty about actual cash flows ought to be considered when the cash budget is prepared. It is desirable to prepare additional cash budgets based on different assumptions about sales levels, costs, collection periods, bad debts and so on.

A cash budget model constructed using a PC and a spreadsheet package will allow the sensitivity of cash flow forecasts to changes in estimates of sales, costs and so on to be analysed.

By planning for different eventualities, management should be able to prepare contingency measures in advance and also appreciate the key factors in the cash budget.

Activity 5	**(30 minutes)**

If you have access to a spreadsheet package and know how to use it, try setting up the cash budget in the example shown above on it.

Then make a second copy of the budget and try making changes to the estimates to see their effect on cash flow.

Businesses do not, of course, have piles of notes and coins in their corporate trouser pockets or purses. Most financial transactions only happen on paper. There are certain aspects of managing a business bank account of which you should be aware of.

5 MANAGING A BANK ACCOUNT

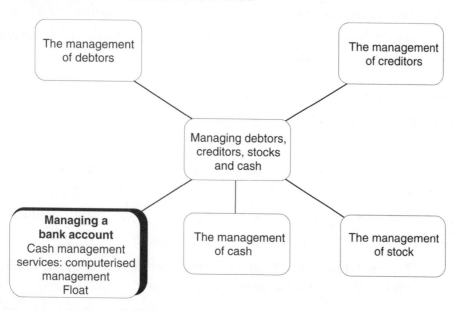

5.1 Cash management services: computerised management

Most banks now offer a cash management service for both business and personal customers. A company with many different bank accounts can obtain information about the cash balance in each account through a computer terminal in the company's treasury department linked to the bank's computer or via the internet. The company can then arrange to move cash from one account to another and so manage its cash position more efficiently and make optimal use of its funds deposited with banks or in various money market investments. A cash management service can be provided to a company with several bank accounts in the UK, or, through an international network of banks, to a multinational company with accounts in different currencies in various countries.

The cash management services provided by the banks comprise three basic services.

(a) *Account reporting*
   (i) Information is given about the balances on sterling or currency accounts whether held in the UK or overseas, including details of any uncleared items that have been paid in but not yet added to the account. (As you know it can take several days for a cheque to 'clear'.)
   (ii) Forecast balance reports, which take into account uncleared items and automated entries such as standing orders and direct debits, can be obtained.
   (iii) Reports giving details of individual transactions can be obtained.

(b) *Funds transfer*

The customer can initiate sterling and currency payments through his terminal. Banks will also give customers with substantial cash 'floats' (see below) the opportunity to get in touch with money market dealers directly and deposit funds in the money markets.

(c) *Decision support services*

A rates information service, giving information on foreign exchange rates and deposit interest rates, can be used.

5.2 Float

The term 'float' is sometimes used to describe the amount of money tied up between two points in time.

(a) When a payment is initiated (for example when a debtor sends a cheque in payment, probably by post)

(b) And when the funds become available for use in the recipient's bank account.

There are three reasons why there might be a lengthy float.

(a) **Transmission delay**. When payment is sent through the post, it will take a day or longer for the payment to reach the payee.

(b) Delay in banking the payments received (**lodgement delay**). The payee, on receipt of a cheque or cash, might delay putting the cheque or the cash into his bank. The length of this delay will depend on administrative procedures in the payee's organisation.

(c) The time needed for a bank to clear a cheque (**clearance delay**). A payment is not available for use in the payee's bank account until the cheque has been cleared. This will usually take two or three days for cheques payable in the UK. For cheques payable abroad, the delay is much longer.

There are several measures that could be taken to reduce the float.

(a) The payee should ensure that the lodgement delay is kept to a minimum. Cheques received should be presented to the bank on the day of receipt.

(b) The payee might, in some cases, arrange to collect cheques from the payer's premises. This would only be practicable, however, if the payer is local. The payment would have to be large to make the extra effort worthwhile.

(c) The payer might be asked to pay through his own branch of a bank. The payer can give his bank detailed payment instructions, and use the credit clearing system of the **Bank Giro**. The Bank Giro is a means of making credit transfers for customers of other banks and other branches. The payee may include a Bank Giro credit slip on the bottom of his invoice, to help with this method of payment.

(d) The same effect may be achieved via **Internet banking**.

(e) **BACS** (Bankers' Automated Clearing Services Ltd) is a banking system which provides for the computerised transfer of funds between banks. In addition, BACS or Direct Credit is available to business customers of banks for making payments. The customer must supply a magnetic tape or disk to BACS, which contains details of payments, and payment will be made in two days. Direct Credit is now commonly used by companies for salary payments.

(f) For regular payments **standing orders** or **direct debits** might be used.

(g) **CHAPS** (Clearing House Automated Payments System) is a computerised system for banks to make same-day clearances (that is, immediate payment) between each other. Each member bank of CHAPS can allow its own corporate customers to make immediate transfers of funds through CHAPS. However, there is a large minimum size for payments using CHAPS.

Inefficient cash management

A lengthy float suggests inefficient cash management. But there are other types of delay in receiving payment from debtors, which might also suggest inefficient cash management.

(a) There is the delay created by the length of credit given to customers. There is often a 'normal' credit period for an industry, and companies might be unable to grant less time for payment than this.

(b) There are avoidable delays caused by poor administration (in addition to lodgement delay). These include the following.
  (i) Failure to notify the invoicing department that goods have been despatched, so that invoices are not sent promptly.
  (ii) Cheques from debtors being made out incorrectly, to the wrong company perhaps, because invoices do not contain clear instructions.

FOR DISCUSSION

There are lots of things that people do every day at work that have consequences for working capital – for example 'borrowing' a pen or an envelope for personal use, being impatient with a customer, or failing to pass on a message to a colleague.

Take these and as many other examples as you can think of and trace through their financial consequences to the various components of working capital.

NOTES

Chapter roundup

- Formulating a policy for managing debtors involves decisions about the administrative resources to be devoted to record-keeping and checking, the credit period allowed to customers, and the procedures for ensuring as far as possible that only customers likely to pay are granted credit in the first place.

- The earlier debtors pay the better. Early payment can be encouraged by good administration and by discount policies. The risk that some debtors will never pay can be partly guarded against by insurance.

- Management of creditors is largely a mirror image of debtors management. Trade creditors are a useful and cheap source of finance, but a successful business needs to ensure that it is seen as a good credit risk by its suppliers. Some creditors must be paid on specific dates. This must be remembered and cash must be available.

- Some businesses have a substantial proportion of their total assets tied up in stocks. Financial aspects of stock management consist of keeping the costs of procuring and holding stock to a minimum. The aim of Just-in-Time is to hold as little stock as possible and production systems need to be very efficient to achieve this.

- Cash flow problems arise because of factors such as growth and seasonal fluctuations. Careful management of the other components of working capital helps to avoid such problems. Monitoring cash requirements through careful cash budgeting and accurate forecasting is essential.

- Almost all of a business's cash is really a bank balance and careful monitoring and management of transactions at the bank will help to reduce bank charges and interest and to take advantage of opportunities to earn interest on deposits.

Quick quiz

1. List five factors that should be considered when formulating a policy for management of debtors.

2. What is a bad debt?

3. What is a collection period?

4. List five credit control procedures.

5. How should trade creditors be managed?

6. Is trade credit free to the buyer?

7. What are the four types of stock cost?

8. What is the difference between the EOQ and the JIT approach to stock management?

9. Why do cash flow problems occur?

10. Write out a skeleton cash budget.

11   How is a cash budget constructed?

12   What is a 'float' and why might it be lengthy?

Answers to quick quiz

1   Administrative costs of debt collection; procedures for controlling the granting of credit; cost of financing an increase in debtors/decrease in creditors; facets of credit policy, such as credit period allowed and discounts for early payment; effects of easing credit, such as increased bad debts or increased sales volume. (See section 1)

2   A debt that is never repaid.

3   The length of time between invoicing of goods or services and the payment of the bill.

4   References from new customers, checks with credit rating agencies; low credit limit initially; keeping up-to-date information; aged list of debtors; prompt and efficient action if a customer breaches its credit terms. (See section 1.2)

5   Obtain satisfactory credit from suppliers; attempt to extend credit in times of cash shortage; maintain good relations with regular and important suppliers. (See section 2.1)

6   Yes – early payment discount is forgone if payment is delayed, but interest on an outstanding debt is rarely charged by the seller. (See section 2.1)

7   Holding, procuring and shortage costs, plus the cost of the stock itself. (See section 3.2)

8   The EOQ approach aims to minimise stock costs; JIT seeks to minimise the level of stock. (See sections 3.3 and 3.5)

9   Because of: losses, inflation, growth, seasonality and large payments for fixed assets or to repay loans. (See section 4.1)

10

	June	July	August
Cash receipts			
Cash sales	100	150	300
Receipts from debtors	200	400	200
Selling fixed assets	300	–	100
	600	550	600
Cash payments			
To suppliers	100	150	200
To employees	50	50	60
To providers of finance	20	20	20
To tax authorities	20	20	25
Buying fixed assets	200		300
Overheads	50	50	60
	440	290	665

	June	July	August
Surplus/deficit for month	160	260	(65)
Opening cash	(360)	(200)	60
Closing cash	(200)	60	(5)

(See also section 4.2)

11   By aggregating forecasts from: sales and marketing, credit control and production. (See section 4.3)

12   'Float' is the term used to describe the period of time between when payment is received and when it is actually at the business's disposal. It may be lengthy because of transmission delay, lodgement delay or clearance delay. (See section 5.2)

Answers to activities

1   Firstly there is the bill itself: the invoice spells out how much you owe, with the total due shown as the most prominent figure. It gives you some information about how the bill was calculated and what period it covers so that you can check it. Typically you also get an envelope (sometimes even a pre-paid envelope) to make it easy for you physically to send off your payment. The slip you send back has most of the essential details pre-printed so there is minimum writing for you to do and minimum chance of mistakes such as the wrong account number.

Large companies often offer you the chance to pay by direct debit: this actually makes it much easier for the company to collect your debt, but there may be an incentive for you, too, such as a small discount.

In addition, you will probably be able to pay the bill over the Internet, involving a minimal amount of work on your part.

Other things you might have mentioned include glossy brochures making you 'feel good' about the company's services, and reminder letters (gentle at first but more threatening later) if you forget to pay.

2   (a) $10/365 \times £500,000 = £13,698.63$

      (b)   Let the average period = x

$$x = \frac{365 \times £140,000}{£2,800,000}$$

$$= 18.25 \text{ days}$$

3   It will probably include the following:

      (a)   Trading name
      (b)   Name of owners if sole trader or partnership
      (c)   Addresses of business and home addresses of owners
      (d)   Telephone and fax numbers
      (e)   Banker's name and address
      (f)   Two trade references
      (g)   How long in business
      (h)   Credit limit required
      (i)   Request for most recent accounts.

4   You need to look back to the section headed 'credit control' for a full answer. A firm would have to provide good references, maintain a good payment record, allow the supplier to pay a visit, and generally be known to be a successful business and a good credit risk.

5   Hopefully, your computer work was successful! You probably found that it was much easier to amend a cash flow when using a computer.

Chapter 5:
FINANCIAL STATEMENTS

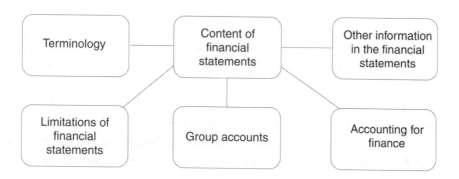

Introduction

So far we have traced the history of a business from the initial raising of money to finance it, through various aspects of the management of the business and its money until this point, where we come to the end result. The results of a business's activities are presented in financial terms in the form of what are commonly called the 'accounts'.

In this context 'accounts' means three statements: a balance sheet, a profit and loss account, and a cash flow statement.

This chapter describes these statements and illustrates the format in which they are usually presented. In the next chapter we shall see how the statements can be interpreted to give an idea of how well a business is performing.

Your objectives

In this chapter you will learn about the following.

- The terminology used in keeping accounts

- How a balance sheet and profit and loss account fit together, and what they look like

- Why cash flow statements are prepared and what sort of information they contain

- The range of information contained in the notes to published accounts

- Some of the peculiarities of group accounts

- The limitations of financial statements

- The meaning of an auditor's report

BPP
LEARNING MEDIA

1   TERMINOLOGY

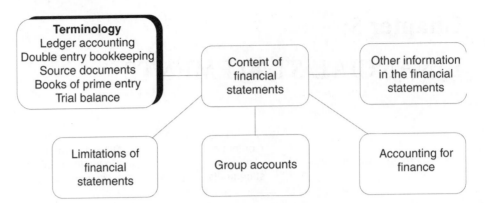

This chapter uses traditional UK accounting terminology. However, international terminology is increasingly being used. Therefore, although this Course Book uses the traditional UK terminology, where there are alternative international terms, these are referred to in the chapter.

1.1   Ledger accounting

What is ledger accounting?

It is common sense that a business should keep a record of the transactions that it makes, the assets it acquires and liabilities it incurs so that when the time comes to prepare a profit and loss account and a balance sheet, the relevant information can be taken from those records.

Ledger accounting is the process by which business keeps a record of its transactions:

(a)   in chronological order, and dated so that transactions can be related to a particular period of time; and

(b)   built up in cumulative totals. For example, a business may build up the total of its sales:

(i)   day by day (eg total sales on Monday, total sales on Tuesday);

(ii)   week by week;

(iii)   month by month;

(iv)   year by year.

Every business generates a large amount of financial information. The nominal ledger is a means of summarising such information.

The nominal ledger

Every business needs a means of summarising information required to meet the needs of internal and external users of accounting information.

Definition

> The **nominal** or **general ledger** is a file, hard or soft copy, which contains all the separate accounts of a business. In other words, a general ledger is an accounting record which summarises the financial affairs of a business.

The general or nominal ledger contains details of assets, liabilities and capital, income and expenditure and so profit and loss. It consists of a large number of different accounts, each account having its own purpose or 'name' and an identity or code. There may be various subdivisions, whether for convenience, ease of handling, confidentiality, security, or to meet the needs of computer software design.

Examples of accounts in the nominal or general ledger include:

- (a) Plant and machinery at cost (fixed asset);
- (b) Motor vehicles at cost (fixed asset);
- (c) Proprietor's capital (liability);
- (d) Stocks – raw materials (current asset);
- (e) Stocks – finished goods (current asset);
- (f) Total debtors (current asset);
- (g) Total creditors (current liability);
- (h) Wages and salaries (expense item);
- (i) Rent and rates (expense item);
- (j) Advertising expenses (expense item);
- (k) Bank charges (expense item);
- (l) Motor expenses (expense item);
- (m) Telephone expenses (expense item);
- (n) Sales (income);
- (o) Total cash or bank overdraft (current asset or liability).

Terminology

UK term	International term
Stock	Inventory
Debtors	Receivables
Creditors	Payables

We next look at the layout of a ledger account.

The format of a ledger account

If a ledger account were to be kept in an actual book rather than as a computer record, its format might be as follows.

ADVERTISING EXPENSES

Date	Narrative	Folio	£	Date	Narrative	Folio	£
2000							
15 April	JFK Agency for quarter to 31 March	PL 348	2,500				

Only one entry in the account is shown here, because the example is introduced simply to illustrate the general format of a ledger account.

There are two sides to the account, and an account heading on top. Thus, it is convenient to think in terms of 'T' accounts:

(a) on top of the account is its name eg capital, advertising expense etc;

(b) there is a left hand side, or *debit side*; and

(c) there is a right hand side, or *credit side*.

NAME OR TITLE OF ACCOUNT

Left hand side	£	*Right hand side*	£
DEBIT SIDE		CREDIT SIDE	

The words debit and credit have no other meaning in accounting except the left and the right side of an account respectively. Neither debit nor credit implies good or bad news – they simply mean the left or the right side of an account. Similarly, debiting an account only means recording a transaction on the left side of an account (any account) and crediting an account only means entering a transaction on the right hand side of an account.

FOR DISCUSSION

In your experience so far, do you think that the terms debit and credit are either good or bad? Or are they simply factual?

We will now look at the way transactions are recorded, using the system of double-entry accounting, in ledger accounts.

1.2   Double entry bookkeeping

Definition

Double entry bookkeeping is the method by which a business records financial transactions. An account is maintained for every supplier, customer, asset, liability, and income and expense. Every transaction is recorded twice so that for every *debit* there is an equal, corresponding *credit*.

Dual effect

Double entry bookkeeping is the method used to transfer our weekly/monthly totals from our books of prime entry into the nominal ledger.

Central to this process is the idea that every transaction has two effects, the **dual effect**. This feature is not something peculiar to businesses. If you were to purchase a car for £1,000 cash for instance, you would be affected in two ways.

(a) You own a car worth £1,000.
(b) You have £1,000 less cash.

If instead you got a bank loan to make the purchase:

(a) You own a car worth £1,000.
(b) You owe the bank £1,000.

A month later if you pay a garage £50 to have the exhaust replaced:

(a) You have £50 less cash.
(b) You have incurred a repairs expense of £50.

Ledger accounts, with their debit and credit side, are kept in a way which allows the two-sided nature of business transactions to be recorded. This system of accounting is known as the '**double entry**' system of bookkeeping, so called because **every transaction is recorded twice** in the accounts.

The rules of double entry bookkeeping

The basic rule which must always be observed is that **every financial transaction gives rise to two accounting entries, one a debit and the other a credit**. The total value of debit entries in the nominal ledger is therefore always equal at any time to the total value of credit entries. Which account receives the credit entry and which receives the debit depends on the nature of the transaction.

Definitions

- An **increase** in an **expense** (eg a purchase of stationery) or an **increase in an asset** (eg a purchase of office furniture) is a **debit**.

- An **increase** in **income** (eg a sale) or an **increase in a liability** (eg buying goods on credit) is a **credit**.

- A **decrease** in an **asset** (eg making a cash payment) is a **credit**.

- A **decrease** in a **liability** (eg paying a creditor) is a **debit**.

Have a go at the activity below before you learn about this topic in detail.

NOTES

Activity 1 (5 minutes)

Complete the following table relating to the transactions of a bookshop. (The first two are done for you.)

(a) Purchase of books on credit

    (i) creditors increase   CREDIT   creditors (increase in liability)

    (ii) purchases expense increases   DEBIT   purchases (item of expense)

(b) Purchase of cash register

    (i) own a cash register   DEBIT   cash register (increase in asset)

    (ii) cash at bank decreases   CREDIT   cash at bank (decrease in asset)

(c) Payment received from a debtor

    (i) debtors decrease
    (ii) cash at bank increases

(d) Purchase of van

    (i) own a van
    (ii) cash at bank decreases

How did you get on? Students coming to the subject for the first time often have difficulty in knowing where to begin. A good starting point is the cash account, ie the nominal ledger account in which receipts and payments of cash are recorded. The rule to remember about the cash account is as follows.

(a) A cash **payment** is a **credit** entry in the cash account. Here the **asset is decreasing**. Cash may be paid out, for example, to pay an expense (such as rates) or to purchase an asset (such as a machine). The matching debit entry is therefore made in the appropriate expense account or asset account.

(b) A cash **receipt** is a **debit** entry in the cash account. Here the **asset is increasing**. Cash might be received, for example, by a retailer who makes a cash sale. The credit entry would then be made in the sales account.

1.3 Source documents

You should have realised that most organisations exist to provide products and services in the ultimate hope of making profit for their owners, which they do by receiving payment in money for goods and services provided. Whenever such activities take place, they need to be recorded. They are recorded on what is called a document.

Whenever a business transaction takes place, involving sales or purchases, receiving or paying money, or owing or being owed money, it is usual for the transaction to be recorded on a document. These documents are the source of all the information recorded by a business. The documents used to record business transactions include:

(a) The sales order
(b) The purchase order
(c) The invoice
(d) The credit note
(e) The debit note
(f) The goods received note

We will now look at each of these documents in turn.

Sales order

A document showing the goods or services the customer wishes to buy.

Purchase order

A document sent by a business to a supplier ordering specified goods or services.

Invoice

An invoice relates to a sales order or a purchase order. When a business sells goods or services on credit to a customer, it sends out an invoice. The details on the invoice should match up with the details on the sales order. The invoice is a request for the customer to pay what he owes. Similarly, when a business buys goods or services on credit it receives an invoice from the supplier. The details on the invoice should match up with the details on the purchase order.

The invoice is primarily a demand for payment, but it is used for other purposes as well. Because it has several uses, an invoice is often produced on multi-part stationery, or photocopied, or carbon-copied. The top copy will go to the customer and other copies will be used by various people within the business.

What does an invoice show?

Most invoices are numbered, so that the business can keep track of all the invoices it sends out. Information usually shown on an invoice includes the following.

(a) Name and address of the seller and the purchaser

(b) Date of the sale

(c) Description of what is being sold

(d) Quantity and unit price of what has been sold (eg 20 pairs of shoes at £25 a pair)

(e) Details of trade discount, if any (eg 10% reduction in cost if buying over 100 pairs of shoes). We looked at discounts in an earlier chapter

(f) Total amount of the invoice including (in the UK) any details of VAT

(g) Sometimes, the date by which payment is due, and other terms of sale

Credit note

A document issued by the seller to show a reduction in the amount owed by the buyer. The reduction could be due to a variety of reasons such as:

(a) goods were not according to specifications;

(b) goods were damaged during packing or transit;

(c) goods were faulty.

A credit note is sometimes printed in red to distinguish it from an invoice. Otherwise, it will be made out in much the same way as an invoice, but with less detail and 'Credit Note Number' instead of 'Invoice Number'.

Debit note

A document issued by the buyer to show a reduction in the amount owed to the seller/supplier. More commonly, a debit note is issued by the buyer to the seller as a means of formally requesting a credit note. It may also be issued by the seller to increase the amount already owed by the buyer.

Goods Received Note (GRN)

This is a document which is filled in to record a receipt of goods, most commonly in a warehouse. It may be used in addition to suppliers' advice notes. Often the accounts department will require to see the relevant GRN before paying a supplier's invoice. Even where GRNs are not routinely used, the details of a consignment from a supplier which arrives without an advice note must always be recorded.

The source documents provide the evidence needed for recording business transactions in the accounting system. The transactions are first recorded in what are called books of prime entry.

1.4 Books of prime entry

We have seen that in the operation of a business, source documents are created. The details on these source documents need to be summarised, as otherwise the business might forget to ask for some money, or forget to pay some, or even accidentally pay something twice. In other words, it needs to keep records of source documents – of transactions – so that it can keep tabs on what is going on. When a business is small, it can keep all these details in a single binder or book. However, as the firm grows, it becomes impossible to keep all records in just one binder/book. Maintaining separate binders/books for similar transactions, eg a separate book only for credit sales, another one only for credit purchases and so on makes the process of recording and retrieving information far more manageable and efficient (as more than one person can work on recording information at the same time).

Definition

> **Books of prime entry** or **day books** refer to a set of 'books' in which transactions are initially recorded in the accounting system; it is in these 'books' that information is recorded from the source documents at the start of the accounting process. Each of the books record only a particular type of transaction eg credit sales, credit purchases etc.

The main books of prime entry which we need to look at for the purpose of fulfilling the requirements of the Guidelines are:

(a)   the sales day book;

(b)   the purchase day book;

It is worth bearing in mind that, for convenience, this chapter describes books of prime entry as if they are actual books. Nowadays, books of prime entry are often not books at all, but rather files hidden in the memory of a computer. However, the principles remain the same whether they are manual or computerised.

The sales day book

The sales day book is used to keep a list of all invoices sent out to customers each day. An extract from a sales day book might look like this.

SALES DAY BOOK

Date 20X1	Invoice	Customer	Sales ledger folio	Total amount invoiced £
Jan 10	247	Jones & Co	SL 14	105.00
	248	Smith Ltd	SL 8	86.40
	249	Alex & Co	SL 6	31.80
	250	Enor College	SL 9	1,264.60
				1,487.80

The column called 'sales ledger folio' is a reference to the sales ledger, part of the nominal ledger.

Most businesses 'analyse' their sales. For example, suppose that the business sells boots and shoes, and that the sale to Smith was entirely boots, the sale to Alex was entirely shoes, and the other two sales were a mixture of both.

Then the sales day book might look like this.

SALES DAY BOOK

Date 20X1	Invoice	Customer	Sales ledger folio	Total amount invoiced £	Boot sales £	Shoe sales £
Jan 10	247	Jones & Co	SL 14	105.00	60.00	45.00
	248	Smith Ltd	SL 8	86.40	86.40	
	249	Alex & Co	SL 6	31.80		31.80
	250	Enor College	SL 9	1,264.60	800.30	464.30
				1,487.80	946.70	541.10

This sort of analysis gives the managers of the business useful information which helps them to decide how best to run the business.

The purchase day book

A business also keeps a record in the purchase day book of all the invoices it receives. An extract from a purchase day book might look like this.

PURCHASE DAY BOOK

Date 20X1	Supplier	Purchase ledger folio	Total amount invoiced £	Purchases £	Electricity etc £
Mar 15	Cook & Co	PL 31	315.00	315.00	
	W Butler	PL 46	29.40	29.40	
	EEB	PL 42	116.80		116.80
	Show Fair Ltd	PL 12	100.00	100.00	
			561.20	444.40	116.80

You should note the following points.

(a) The 'purchase ledger folio' is a reference to the purchase ledger and its location in the nominal ledger, just as the sales ledger folio was to the sales ledger.

(b) There is no 'invoice number' column, because the purchase day book records other people's invoices, which have all sorts of different numbers.

(c) Like the sales day book, the purchase day book analyses the invoices which have been sent in. In this example, three of the invoices related to goods which the business intends to re-sell (called simply 'purchases') and the fourth invoice was an electricity bill.

1.5 Trial balance

Definition

A **trial balance** is a schedule which lists all the accounts of the ledger along with their balances in the appropriate debit or credit column. It is used to ensure that the equality of debits and credits has been maintained in preparing the ledger accounts.

The earlier section on double-entry has shown you the following.

(a) Each transaction is entered at least twice in the ledger: once as a debit and once as a credit.

(b) The £ amounts of debit and credit entered for each transaction are equal.

Since equal £ amounts of debits and credits are recorded for each and every transaction, it follows that if all the debits in the ledger are added up, they must equal the total of all the credits in the ledger.

Total debit £ amount = Total credit £ amount

 96

It is desirable that this equality is proven after all the transactions have been posted to the ledger but before the final accounts and the related financial statements are prepared. This proof of equality of debits and credits is obtained through the preparation of a trial balance.

The steps involved in preparing a trial balance are as follows.

(a) Find the balance on the ledger accounts

(b) Record the ledger account balances in the appropriate column of the trial balance

(c) Total each column

(d) Compare the totals of the two columns of the trial balance

Before you draw up a trial balance, you will have a collection of ledger accounts.

CASH

	£		£
Capital– Ron Knuckle	7,000	Rent	3,500
Bank loan	1,000	Shop fittings	2,000
Sales	10,000	Trade creditors	5,000
Debtors	2,500	Bank loan interest	100
		Incidental expenses	1,900
		Drawings	1,500
			14,000
		Balancing figure	6,500
	20,500		20,500

CAPITAL (RON KNUCKLE)

	£		£
		Cash	7,000

BANK LOAN

	£		£
		Cash	1,000

PURCHASES

	£		£
Trade creditors	5,000		

TRADE CREDITORS

	£		£
Cash	5,000	Purchases	5,000

RENT

	£		£
Cash	3,500		

SHOP FITTINGS

	£		£
Cash	2,000		

SALES

	£		£
		Cash	10,000
		Debtors	2,500
			12,500

DEBTORS

	£		£
Sales	2,500	Cash	2,500

BANK LOAN INTEREST

	£		£
Cash	100		

OTHER EXPENSES

	£		£
Cash	1,900		

DRAWINGS ACCOUNT

	£		£
Cash	1,500		

Given a series of accounts in which transactions have been recorded, the process of preparing a trial balance is as follows.

Step 1: *Finding the balance on the ledger accounts*

At the end of an accounting period all ledger accounts are 'balanced'. This means finding the balance in each account by going through the following procedure.

(a) Total all the debits in the account, ie find the total of the left side of the account.

(b) Total all the credits on the account, ie total the right side of the account.

(c) Subtract the lower side total from the higher side total.

(d) If the higher side is the debit side, ie if total debits exceed total credits, the account has a debit balance.

(e) If, on the other hand, the higher side is the credit side, ie if total credits exceed total debits, the account has a credit balance.

(f) If the debit and credit sides of an account are equal, the account has a zero balance.

In our example of Ron Knuckle, there is very little balancing to do.

(a) The trade creditors account and the debtors account balance off to zero.

(b) The cash account has a debit balance of £6,500.

(c) The total on the sales account is £12,500, which is a credit balance.

The remaining accounts have only one entry each, so there is no totalling to do.

Step 2: *Recording the balances*

Once all the accounts have been 'balanced', a list of all the accounts along with their balances is prepared. The crucial thing is that the debit balances are entered in the debit column and the credit balances are recorded in the credit column of the trial balance. This is illustrated below for Ron Knuckle's accounts.

	Debit £	Credit £
Cash	6,500	
Capital		7,000
Bank loan		1,000
Purchases	5,000	
Trade creditors	–	–
Rent	3,500	
Shop fittings	2,000	
Sales		12,500
Debtors	–	–
Bank loan interest	100	
Other expenses	1,900	
Drawings	1,500	

Step 3: *Totalling each column*

After all the accounts and their balances have been entered in the proper columns (debit balances in the left-hand column and credit balances in the right-hand column), the two columns are then totalled.

	Debit £	Credit £
Cash	6,500	
Capital		7,000
Bank loan		1,000
Purchases	5,000	
Trade creditors	–	–
Rent	3,500	
Shop fittings	2,000	
Sales		12,500
Debtors	–	–
Bank loan interest	100	
Other expenses	1,900	
Drawings	1,500	
	20,500	20,500

Step 4: *Comparing the totals*

The final step in preparing the trial balance is to make sure that the totals of the debit and the credit columns are equal.

In our example, the two columns do total to £20,500. But what if the trial balance shows unequal debit and credit balances?

If the two columns of the trial balance are not equal, this means that there are error(s) in recording the transactions in the accounts or that mistake(s) have been made in entering the balances in the trial balance. These errors need to be corrected before going any further.

However, it is possible for the trial balance to balance, ie for debit and credit column totals to be equal, and still to have errors present. The errors that a trial balance will not disclose are the following.

(a) The complete omission of a transaction, because neither a debit nor a credit is made

(b) The posting of a debit or credit to the correct side of the ledger, but to a wrong account, eg debiting furniture account as opposed to cash

(c) Compensating errors, eg an error of £100 is exactly cancelled by another £100 error elsewhere

(d) Errors of principle, eg cash received from debtors being debited to the debtors account and credited to cash instead of the other way round

EXAMPLE: TRIAL BALANCE

As at 30.3.20X1, your business has the following balances on its ledger accounts.

Accounts	*Balance*
	£
Bank loan	12,000
Cash	11,700
Capital	13,000
Rates	1,880
Trade creditors	11,200
Purchases	12,400
Sales	14,600
Sundry creditors	1,620
Debtors	12,000
Bank loan interest	1,400
Other expenses	11,020
Vehicles	2,020

We will now draw up a trial balance showing the balances as at the end of 31.3.X1.

Account	Debit	Credit
	£	£
Bank loan		12,000
Cash	11,700	
Capital		13,000
Rates	1,880	
Trade creditors		11,200
Purchases	12,400	
Sales		14,600
Sundry creditors		1,620
Debtors	12,000	
Bank loan interest	1,400	
Other expenses	11,020	
Vehicles	2,020	
	52,420	52,420

Activity 2 (20 minutes)

S Trader carries on a small business. The following balances have been extracted from his books on 30 September 20X0.

	£
Capital	24,239
Office furniture	1,440
Drawings	4,888
Stock	14,972
Purchases	167,760
Sales	184,269
Rent	1,350
Lighting and heating	475
Insurance	304
Salaries	6,352
Debtors	19,100
Creditors	8,162
Petty cash in hand	29

Task: Prepare a trial balance as at 30 September 20X0.

Once a trial balance has been balanced, the next step is to start preparing the financial statements.

2 CONTENT OF FINANCIAL STATEMENTS

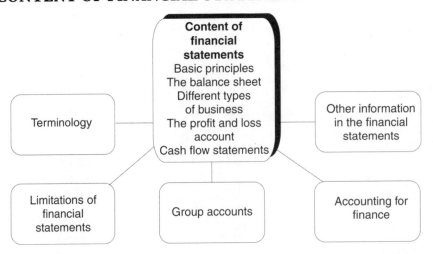

2.1 Basic principles

Businesses produce statements of their financial results for a number of reasons.

(a) In the case of companies, to comply with the law (Companies Act 1985).

(b) To inform the people who are interested in the company about its situation (the shareholders, employees, bank, HM Revenue and Customs, trade contacts, financial markets etc).

(c) To help management in managing the company.

A business's 'accounts' – more properly called 'financial statements' – can be confusing documents when you first encounter them. For the completely uninitiated we begin by setting out some basics.

The principles of a balance sheet and a profit and loss account are very simple. Suppose you decide on Wednesday to invest £100 of your savings in a business venture. This is represented in a balance sheet as follows.

BALANCE SHEET WEDNESDAY

	£
Net assets	
Cash at the bank	<u>100</u>
Capital	
Owner's capital	<u>100</u>

It 'balances' because net assets are equal to capital: they are both £100. Balance sheets *always* balance.

On Thursday you buy an item for £50 and some paint for £5. Later you sell the painted item for £70. You are very pleased with yourself and so you pay yourself £5 to have a drink. You also buy another £50 item and another £5 of paint.

This time we can draw up both a balance sheet and a profit and loss account. Note how the balance sheet has changed and how the profit, not squandered on drink, turns into *retained* profit.

PROFIT AND LOSS ACCOUNT THURSDAY

	£	£
Sales		70
Cost of sales	55	
Drawings or wages	5	
		(60)
Profit		10

Figures in brackets are negative.

BALANCE SHEET THURSDAY

	£
Net assets	
Stock (£50 item + £5 paint)	55
Cash at the bank (£100 – £55 + £70 – £5 – £55)	55
	110
Capital	
Owner's capital	100
Retained profit	10
	110

A full balance sheet and profit and loss account prepared by a company is no more complicated than this in principle, it just covers a longer period (typically one year) and shows more detail.

Activity 3　　　　　　　　　　　　　　**(15 minutes)**

(a)　If all the transactions in the example above had been done on credit (except your drink!) the net assets would include debtors (people who owe you money) and creditors (people to whom you own money). Can you draw up the balance sheet?

(b)　(i)　What is the value of the business if it stops trading on Thursday?

　　　　　Refer back to the balance sheet above (cash-based transactions)

　　(ii)　What is the value of the business if it carries on trading in exactly the same way (not on credit) for another four days but does not buy any stock on the last day?

(c)　Why are there two lots of £110 in the above balance sheet?

We shall now consider the basic structure and contents of detailed financial statements. These can be looked at in four stages: the balance sheet, the profit and loss account, the cash flow statement and the notes to the accounts.

2.2　The balance sheet

A balance sheet is a statement of the assets, liabilities and capital of a business at a given moment in time. The balance sheet can also be called the Statement of Financial Position.

It is like a 'snapshot' photograph, since it captures on paper a still image, frozen at a single moment in time, of something which is dynamic and continually changing.

Sometimes it is called the 'position statement', because it shows the financial position of a business at a given moment. A balance sheet is prepared to show the assets, liabilities and capital as at the end of the accounting period to which the financial accounts relate.

Balance sheets are nearly always presented in the format shown below, but because each business is different there can be some variations in classifications and presentation. However, one of the main aims of interpretation of financial statements is consistency between one company and the next and between one accounting period and the next.

Definition

> An **intangible fixed asset** is a fixed asset that does not have a physical existence. It cannot be 'touched'. A good example is a trade mark. 'Coca-Cola' is a trade mark. It is an asset because it helps the Coca-Cola company to make profits – people buy things with the trade mark Cola-Cola in preference to other types of cola.
>
> Fixed assets can also be termed non-current assets.

A LIMITED
BALANCE SHEET AS AT 31 MARCH 20X6

	Cost £	Depreciation £	Net Book Value £
Fixed assets			
Land and buildings	10,000	4,000	6,000
Plant and machinery	10,000	6,000	4,000
Vehicles	4,000	2,000	1,000
	24,000	13,000	11,000
Current assets			
Stock	2,900		
Debtors	8,600		
Cash in hand	2,500		
		14,000	
Creditors: amounts falling due in less than one year			
Bank overdraft	(1,500)		
Trade creditors	(2,000)		
Other creditors	(3,000)		
		(7,000)	
Net current assets			7,000
			18,000
Creditors: amounts falling due in more than one year			
Bank loan			(3,000)
			15,000
Capital and reserves			
Share capital			5,000
Profit and loss account			10,000
			15,000

> **Activity 4**   **(15 minutes)**
>
> (a) Although the totals are correct, there are two deliberate mistakes in the balance sheet figures shown above. See if you can find them.
>
> (b) What is 'net book value'?
>
> (c) Why do you think the 'profit and loss account' is shown as a single figure in the balance sheet?

2.3 Different types of business

In Chapter 1 we looked at the different types of business – companies, partnerships and sole traders. Does this affect the presentation of their balance sheets?

The top half of the balance sheet represents the **net assets** of the business and will be very similar for all types of business. Companies have to use particular wordings and layouts according to the Companies Act, whereas partnerships and sole traders can present it as they wish.

The bottom half of the balance sheet represents the **owner'(s') stake in the business.**

In a **company,** the owners are shareholders, whose initial stake is shown as share capital and subsequent profits earned shown as a balance on the profit and loss account, as in A Limited's balance sheet above.

In a **partnership,** the partners' individual stakes in the business are represented by capital accounts (used for their long-term investment) and, sometimes, current accounts (used to record profit shares, drawings, salaries, interest on capital accounts etc). So the bottom half of the balance sheet above, if it were a partnership, might look as follows:

Partners' capital		£
Capital accounts	Fred	2,000
	Sue	3,000
	Billy	4,000
Capital accounts	Fred	3,500
	Sue	1,850
–	Billy	650
		15,000

For a **sole trader,** the profits (or losses) each year are often transferred into the capital account, so that the bottom of the balance sheet would simply have one line:

Capital		15,000

Alternatively, it may show profit earned, or loss incurred, in the current year as follows:

Opening capital	1 April 2005	12,850
Profit for the year ended	31 March 2006	2,150
Closing capital	31 March 2006	15,000

2.4 The profit and loss account

A profit and loss account is a record of income generated and expenditure incurred over a given period. The profit and loss account can also be called the Statement of Financial Performance or, under international terminology, the income statement.

The period chosen will depend on the purpose for which the statement is produced. The profit and loss account which forms part of the 'published' annual accounts of a limited company will usually be made up for the period of a year, commencing from the date of the previous year's accounts. On the other hand, management might want to keep a closer eye on a company's profitability by making up a quarterly or monthly profit and loss account. These are known as management accounts.

Definition

Published accounts are not published in the sense that you can go and buy a copy in a bookshop or a newsagents. 'Published' means that they are available to the general public. You have to pay a small fee to a government body called Companies House to see them. All companies have to publish their accounts in this way.

Large public companies are usually happy to send out copies of their financial statements to anybody that asks.

Many businesses try to distinguish between a gross profit earned on trading activities, and a net profit after deducting all non-trading costs and adding any non-trading income. They do this by preparing a statement called the trading, profit and loss account.

(a) In the first part of the statement (the trading account) revenue from selling goods is compared with direct costs of acquiring or producing the goods sold, to arrive at a **gross profit** figure.

(b) In the second part of the statement (the profit and loss account), deductions and additions are made from gross profit to arrive at a **net profit** figure. The deductions are in respect of costs not directly linked with trading: indirect costs (or overheads). Similarly, the additions are in respect of income not directly linked with trading, and are usually called non-trading income.

Here is an example of a 'detailed' trading and profit and loss account.

B LIMITED TRADING AND PROFIT AND LOSS ACCOUNT
FOR THE YEAR ENDED 30 SEPTEMBER 20X6

	£	£
Sales		33,340
Cost of sales		
Opening stock	890	
Purchases	18,995	
	19,885	
Closing stock	(775)	
		(19,110)
Gross profit		14,230
Less expenses		
Bank charges	120	
Rent	2,400	
Postage and stationery	65	
Profit on sale of plant	(315)	
Wages	1,930	
Motor expenses	1,155	
Electricity	585	
Business rates	2,700	
Depreciation	2,069	
		(10,709)
Profit before taxation		3,521
Corporation tax		(810)
Profit after taxation		2,711
Dividend		(700)
Retained profit for the year		2,011

This level of detail would be useful for the company's own use and may be required by the HM Revenue and Customs. However, there is less information in a profit and loss account in the format normally used for publication. This is because the Companies Act only requires a limited amount of information to be disclosed.

C LIMITED PROFIT AND LOSS ACCOUNT
FOR THE YEAR ENDED 31 MARCH 20X6

	£	£
Turnover		21,000
Cost of sales		(9,000)
Gross profit		12,000
Administration expenses	4,000	
Distribution costs	2,000	(6,000)
Operating profit		6,000
Exceptional gain		1,000
Profit on ordinary activities before interest		7,000
Interest payable		(800)
Profit on ordinary activities before taxation		6,200
Tax on profit on ordinary activities		(1,475)
Profit for the financial year		4,725
Dividends		(1,225)
Retained profit for the financial year		3,500

The 'exceptional' gain might be receipt of insurance proceeds, or profit on disposal of part of the business or any other item which wouldn't be expected in the normal run of trading. (An exceptional loss can also arise.) Just like other profits, there is likely to be a tax charge on these gains, and this is included in the tax charge on ordinary activities.

'Ordinary activities' are precisely that – the things that the company usually does.

Terminology	
UK term	*International term*
Turnover	Revenue
Corporation tax	Income tax

Different types of business

How will the profit and loss account differ from the one above if the business were a partnership or sole trader?

Again, non-incorporated businesses have more flexibility about how they word and present their statement. They will often give greater information about expenses etc on the face of the P&L, and it will look more like that for B Limited, above.

Also, some items will not appear:

- **Corporation tax** is not payable by partnerships or sole traders. The partners or owner pay personal income tax on their share of the profits, but this is not shown on the business financial statements.

- **Dividends** are not paid. Instead, the partners will get a share of the profit; this split may be shown at the bottom of the profit and loss, and will be reflected in their capital/current account balances shown in the balance sheet. Sole traders simply get all of the profits earned and there is no equivalent to dividends in their profit and loss.

The balance sheet and the profit and loss account are the main financial statements. However, you may remember that we pointed out the distinction between profits and cash in an earlier chapter – profit takes account of money owed to you and money you owe to others, and it reflects 'notional' expenses like depreciation, so it is not the same as cash in the bank. An apparently profitable company can be in great difficulties in reality because it is short of cash. Where many investors are involved it is important to have a fuller picture of the state of the company.

2.5 Cash flow statements

A cash flow statement explains differences between profit and cash and also shows where a business gets its capital from and what uses it puts the capital to. Only large companies are required to produce a cash flow statement, though smaller companies can do so if they wish.

We will not describe the preparation of a cash flow statement in detail. However, you should certainly be aware of what the statement looks like because you are likely to encounter them in practice. Here is the standard format, together with the accompanying notes that companies have to produce.

Study the cash flow statement and then do the activity that follows.

XYZ LIMITED
CASH FLOW STATEMENT FOR THE YEAR ENDED 31 MARCH 20X6

Reconciliation of operating profit to net cash inflow from operating activities

	£'000
Operating profit	6,022
Depreciation charges	899
Increase in stocks	(194)
Increase in debtors	(72)
Increase in creditors	234
Net cash inflow from operating activities	6,889

Cash flow statement

	£'000
Net cash inflow from operating activities	6,889
Returns on investments and servicing of finance (note 1)	2,999
Taxation	(2,922)
Capital expenditure (note 1)	(1,525)
	5,441
Equity dividends paid	(2,417)
	3,024
Management of liquid resources (note 1)	(450)
Financing (note 1)	57
Increase in cash	2,631

Reconciliation of net cash flow to movement in net debt (note 2)

	£'000	£'000
Increase in cash in the period	2,631	
Cash to repurchase debenture	149	
Cash used to increase liquid resources	450	
Change in net debt*		3,230
Net debt at 1 April 20X5		(2,903)
Net funds at 31 March 20X6		327

NOTES TO THE CASH FLOW STATEMENT

1 *Gross cash flow*

	£'000	£'000
Returns on investments and servicing of finance		
Interest received	3,011	
Interest paid	(12)	
		2,999
Capital expenditure		
Payments to acquire intangible fixed assets	(71)	
Payments to acquire tangible fixed assets	(1,496)	
Receipts from sales of tangible fixed assets	42	
		(1,525)
Management of liquid resources		
Purchase of treasury bills	(650)	
Sale of treasury bills	200	
		(450)
Financing		
Issue of ordinary share capital	211	
Repurchase of debenture loan	(149)	
Expenses paid in connection with share issues	(5)	
		57

2   *Analysis of changes in net debt*

	As at 1 April 20X5 £'000	*Cash flows* £'000	*Other changes* £'000	*At 31 March 20X6* £'000
Cash in hand, at bank	42	847		889
Overdrafts	(1,784)	1,784		
		2,631		
Debt due within 1 year	(149)	149	(230)	(230)
Debt due after 1 year	(1,262)		230	(1,032)
Current asset investments	250	450		700
Total	(2,903)	3,230	–	327

	£
Operating activities	
Cash received from customers	79,006
Cash payments to suppliers	(43,690)
Cash paid to and on behalf of employees	(22,574)
Other cash payments	(4,938)
Net cash inflow from continuing operating activities	7,804
Net cash outflow in respect of discontinued activities and reorganisation costs	(915)
Net cash inflow from operating activities	6,889

Activity 5   **(45 minutes)**

The cash flow statement and its notes contain many reminders of topics you have encountered earlier in this book. See if you can answer the following questions.

(a) How has the company raised capital during the year?

(b) Does the company have a larger amount of borrowed money than of shareholders' capital?

(c) The reconciliation of operating profit to net cash flow from operating activities shows changes in the components of working capital. What might be the reasons for an increase in debtors and for an increase in creditors?

(d) What is a debenture loan?

(e) Is depreciation included anywhere in the cash flow statement or notes? Where, if so, or why not, if not?

(f) What cash has to be paid 'on behalf of' employees?

When you get hold of a company's financial statements you will probably find it difficult to locate the three main statements at first. An annual 'Report and Accounts' contains a wealth of other information about the company, which we shall look at now.

3 OTHER INFORMATION IN THE FINANCIAL STATEMENTS

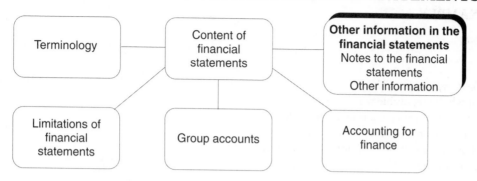

3.1 Notes to the financial statements

As the example of a cash flow statement shows, the notes to financial statements give supplementary information which can be useful.

- In analysing figures in the accounts
- In providing information not otherwise available from the accounts

An example of the extra detail to be found in the notes is the stocks note. In the notes in A plc's accounts, the stocks note might look like this.

EXAMPLE

	20X6	20X5
Stocks and work in progress	£	£
Raw materials and consumables	500	1,200
Work in progress	800	1,100
Finished goods and goods for resale	1,600	1,700
	2,900	4,000

Note that in published accounts the requirement is to show not only the current year's figures but also the previous year's. The previous year's figures are known as the *comparatives* because they allow users of the financial statements to see how much better or worse the company has done this year compared with last year.

Other figures in the accounts analysed in more detail are as follows.

(a) Fixed assets (tangible, intangible, investments)
(b) Debtors
(c) Creditors (current and long term)
(d) Interest payable
(e) Tax on profits
(f) Dividends payable

For example, long term creditors are analysed by the date the loan has to be repaid as well as by type of creditor. Here is an example.

NOTES

EXAMPLE

Loans

	20X6 £	20X5 £
Wholly repayable within five years	100,000	100,000
Not wholly repayable within five years		
Bank loan at 15% per annum, repayable in instalments of £10,000 from 1 January 20X7	60,000	60,000
US dollar loan at 14% per annum, wholly repayable on 31 December 20Y5	120,000	–
	280,000	160,000
Amounts repayable after five years other than by instalments	120,000	
Amounts repayable by instalments		
Within five years	150,000	140,000
After five years	10,000	20,000
	280,000	160,000
Included in current liabilities	30,000	–
	250,000	160,000

The US dollar loan is secured by a fixed charge on the freehold property, and the bank loans are secured by a floating charge on the assets of the company.

Information given elsewhere in the financial statements (not in the notes to the accounts) includes:

- Directors' pay and rewards
- Average number of employees
- Details of transactions with directors

This is useful information (although probably out of date by the time you get hold of the accounts) because it gives a fuller picture of the company's activities than that given by the main accounts.

Definition

A **director** of a company is a person who takes part in making decisions and managing a company's affairs. Private companies must have at least one director and public companies must have at least two. Directors have to be re-elected by the shareholders at regular intervals. Appointment as a director carries many duties. The law is complex, but in broad terms directors must be honest and not seek personal advantage and must also show reasonable competence in managing the company.

FOR DISCUSSION

The following is an extract from the *London Evening Standard*.

> **'Fat-cat pay surge widens gap**
>
> 'Boardroom pay has exploded by almost 30%, more than seven times the rate for ordinary workers. A survey today showed top company directors' pay packages soaring to record levels with the increase the biggest for many years.
>
> 'The 28% surge takes the average pay for a chief executive at one of Britain's biggest companies to £2.4m, almost 100 times average earnings. The going rate for a finance director is £1.1m.'
>
> *Evening Standard*, 2 October 2006

John Edmunds, former TUC President, was quoted as saying that all fat cats were 'greedy bastards'.

What is your opinion?

Besides the notes (which are required by law), large company annual reports usually have pictures of the directors, or of staff members at work, or of the company's buildings and machines, perhaps some charts, graphs and diagrams, and commentaries by leading figures in the company saying how well it is doing. Is any of this useful, or is it just hype?

3.2 Other information

Sometimes you can get useful information from other statements in the accounts. All financial statements must include a **directors' report** which is supposed to include, amongst other things, a fair review of the business for the year and an indication of future developments. As you would expect, however, the directors are rarely overwhelmingly frank about problems in the business nor are they likely, except where things are obviously going badly wrong, to be gloomy in their forecasts.

Another drawback is that (except for the directors' report) other information sent out with the accounts is not independently verified by auditors (see below) and therefore there is less likelihood of objectivity in the **chairman's report** or in a glossy brochure looking at the company's activities in detail than in the accounts.

In earlier chapters, we have looked at the various types of finance and their costs. How are these reflected in the financial statements of a business?

4 ACCOUNTING FOR FINANCE

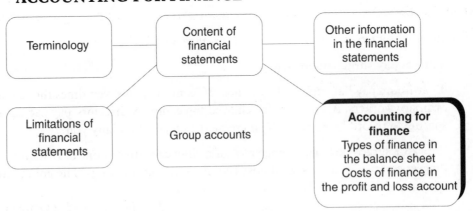

4.1 Types of finance in the balance sheet

Look back at the balance sheet in Section 2.2 of this chapter. Try to identify the sources of finance this company uses.

Although the standard balance sheet format divides into 'net assets' (the top half) and 'shareholders' funds' (the bottom half) we can present it in a different way to highlight its assets and the sources of finance used to finance them. This form of presentation is summarised for A Limited below:

	£
Total assets	
Fixed assets	11,000
Current assets	14,000
	25,000
Financed by	
Short-term creditors	7,000
Medium-term debt	3,000
Long-term equity	15,000
	25,000

This analysis shows clearly the mix of finance, with 60% being long-term (in the form of equity capital), 12% medium-term and 28% short-term. Total assets are 44% long-term (fixed) and 56% short/medium-term. Thus there appears to be a reasonably conservative matching of finance to investment, with more long-term capital than required to finance the current level of fixed assets.

4.2 Costs of finance in the profit and loss account

Activity 6 **(10 minutes)**

Look back at the profit and loss account for C Limited in Section 2.4. Try to identify the costs associated with the following forms of finance:

(a) Debt capital
(b) Equity capital
(c) Working capital

Most well-known companies are actually groups made up of a number of smaller companies. There are certain peculiarities about group accounts that you should know about.

5 GROUP ACCOUNTS

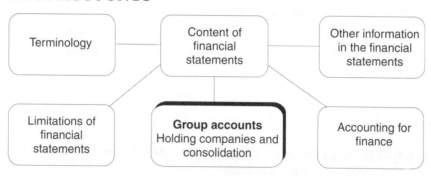

5.1 Holding companies and consolidation

When one company (a **holding company**) owns or controls a majority of the shares in another company or has a significant interest in another business (has '**Subsidiaries**' or '**Associates**'), it is required by law to prepare 'consolidated' accounts (or group accounts) which effectively show the assets, liabilities, income and expenses of the group as if it were one company instead of two or more legally separate entities.

For example, Unilever plc is a holding company that owns shares in numerous subsidiaries.

Unilever's accounts only show Unilever plc's results – you cannot see how well, say, Birds Eye Walls did, unless you apply to Companies House for the individual company accounts.

The basic method of **consolidation** is simply to add the accounts together but there are refinements, such as allowing for **minority interests**. These are the holders of the other shares in a subsidiary which is not 100% owned by the holding company; as shareholders they are entitled to a share of net assets if the subsidiary closes down. In consolidated accounts, they are treated as providers of long-term funds to the group, just like long-term creditors.

The purpose of consolidated accounts is to recognise that when a company controls other businesses, it could simply absorb their operations into its own, perhaps by setting up different divisions or branches. If it chooses to keep them as separate entities, then its own accounts would be misleading if it simply recorded its own trading results, assets and liabilities. There would be a single entry in the balance sheet for its subsidiaries, shown as investments, possibly at cost, and a single entry in the profit and loss account for dividends received from subsidiaries. This would not reflect the **economic realities** of the situation.

Group accounts always include the holding company's own balance sheet but need not include its own profit and loss account, although its profit then has to be disclosed separately. Details of subsidiaries will be given in a note and there will probably be some analysis, also by way of note, showing the group's turnover, profit and net assets broken down by geographical market and by class of business. This will help you to sort out which businesses engage in which activities and how profitable and significant each is.

NOTES

Large (generally group) companies have to use a layered format for the profit and loss account to highlight a number of important components of financial performance.

(a) Results of continuing operations (including the results of acquisitions), that is of those operations which continue during the financial year.

(b) Results of discontinued operations, that is those which have been sold or closed down during the financial year.

(c) Profits or losses on the sale or termination of an operation, costs of a fundamental reorganisation or restructuring and profit or losses on the disposal of fixed assets.

EXAMPLE

The 20X1 Interim Consolidated Profit and Loss Acount for Go-Ahead, a Newcastle based transport group, appeared as follows.

CONSOLIDATED PROFIT AND LOSS ACCOUNT

	Notes	Six months to 29 Dec X1 Unaudited £'000
Turnover: Group and share of joint ventures'		433,615
Less: share of joint ventures' turnover		(9,494)
Continuing operations		
ongoing		323,768
acquisition		100,353
Group turnover	3	424,121
Operating costs (exlcuding goodwill amortisation)		(400,323)
Goodwill amortisation		(452)
		(400,775)
Operating profit		
Continuing operations		
ongoing		24,727
acquisition		(1,381)
Group operating profit		23,346
Share of operating profit in joint ventures		712
Exceptional bid defence costs		
Profit on disposal of subsidiary trade and assets		–
Profit on ordinary activities before interest		24,058
Net interest payable		
group		(3,291)
share of joint ventures'		(54)
Profit on ordinary activities before taxation		20,713
Taxation	2	(6,565)
Profit on ordinary activities after taxation		14,148
Minority interests – equity		(1,891)
Profit attributable to members of the parent company		12,257
Dividends		(2,526)
Retained profit for the period		9,731
Prior year adjustment		(15,485)
Total recognised (losses)/gains since last report		(5,754)

	Notes	Six months to 29 Dec X1 Unaudited
Dividends per share		5.0p
Earnings per share		
basic	4	24.2p
adjusted	4	25.1p
diluted	4	24.2p

Definitions

Here are some terms you may find in published group accounts.

A **holding company** is a company which controls another, its subsidiary, by holding the majority of its shares. The term parent company is sometimes used instead.

A **subsidiary** is a company under the control of another company, its holding company or 'parent'.

An **associated company** is one in which a holding company has a very large interest, although it does not control it.

A **minority interest** is the shares held in a subsidiary by people other than the holding company. For example a holding company may own 95% of the shares and another person or company may own the other 5%.

Share premium is the amount paid for a new share in excess of the share's 'nominal value'. For example when the water industry was privatised shares had a nominal value of £1 but buyers had to pay a total of £2.40 to acquire them (spread over about a year and a half). The extra £1.40 is the share premium.

Goodwill is the amount paid to buy a business in excess of the value of its assets. For instance if you bought a newsagent's shop and its stock for £100,000 this might consist of £80,000 for the building and its contents and £20,000 because the newsagents was in a good location – by a station, say. The extra £20,000 is called goodwill.

We have already suggested that there are some drawbacks to using the information found in financial statements. Let's think about this in a bit more detail, and see how far we can trust the accounts we see.

6 LIMITATIONS OF FINANCIAL STATEMENTS

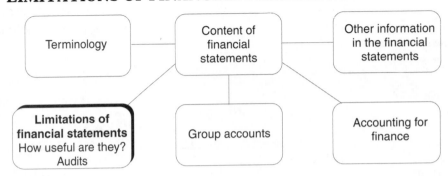

6.1 How useful are they?

Two very important drawbacks of financial statements are mentioned above.

(a) They are often out of date by the time you receive them.

(b) They are not audited in full, but only as far as required by statute.

To these we can add several other limitations.

(a) Accounts can only show the performance and standing of a business in financial terms – they cannot place a value on the staff or customer base, nor assess the business's competition.

(b) Accounts are a record of the past, not a predictor of the future.

(c) Although the Companies Acts and accounting standards are very detailed, they sometimes leave room for choice of accounting treatment and they do not cover every type of financial transaction encountered in business.

(d) The audit is not a guarantee that the accounts are 'correct'.

(e) Only companies whose turnover exceeds a certain threshold (recently increased from £1 million per annum to £5.6 million per annum) have to have an audit. Companies with a level of turnover under that amount may have an audit, but it is not compulsory.

6.2 Audits

An opinion poll looked at the public's expectations of audits. It revealed **a gap between the real purpose of audits and the public's perception of their purpose**. Most people believe that auditors set out to detect fraud and that an audit report guarantees the financial soundness of the company or even that the balance sheet shows the current value of the company. None of these is true.

Auditors are required by law to confirm that the financial statements give **a 'true and fair' view** of the company's position as at the balance sheet date. 'True and fair' is not defined in law, but it is generally assumed that as long as the accounts are materially correct and overall do not present a misleading picture, then the auditor can give a 'clean' audit report. To find out whether there are significant errors in the accounts, auditors review the overall reasonableness of figures in the accounts, and test representative samples of assets, liabilities and transactions. Rarely is every item checked as this would be impractical and very expensive. Errors which are found are not necessarily corrected, if they do not materially (ie significantly) alter the basic picture of the company's health and results shown by the original financial statements.

In an effort to reduce the gap between what the public expects and what the auditor actually does (the '**expectations gap**'), the Auditing Practices Board produced a standard on the audit report, SAS 600 Auditors Reports on Financial Statements. The following paragraphs are based on that standard.

Here is an example of an audit report that would be found in the accounts if the auditors are happy with them.

EXAMPLE: AUDIT REPORT

Independent auditors' report to the shareholders of XYZ Limited

We have audited the financial statements of (name of entity) for the year ended ... which comprise (state the primary financial statements such as the profit and loss account, the balance sheet, the cash flow statement, the statements of total recognised gains and losses) and the related notes. These financial statements have been prepared under the historical cost convention (as modified by the revaluation of certain fixed assets) and the accounting policies set out therein.

Respective responsibilities of directors and auditors

The director's responsibilities for preparing the annual report and the financial statements in accordance with applicable law and United Kingdom Accounting Standards (United Kingdom Generally Accepted Accounting Practice) are set out in the statement of director's responsibilities.

Our responsibility is to audit the financial statements in accordance with relevant legal and regulatory requirements and International Standards on Auditing (UK and Ireland).

We report to you our opinion as to whether the financial statements give a true and fair view and are properly prepared in accordance with the Companies Act 1985. We report to you whether in our opinion the information given in the directors' report is consistent with the financial statements.

In addition we report to you if, in our opinion, the company has not kept proper accounting records, if we have not received all the information and explanations we required for our audit, or if information specified by law regarding directors' remuneration and transactions with the company is not disclosed.

We read other information contained in the annual report and consider whether it is consistent with the audited financial statements. This other information comprises only (the Directors' Report, the Chairman's Statement, the Operating and Financial Review). We consider the implications for our report if we become aware of any apparent misstatements or material inconsistencies with the financial statements. Our responsibilities do not extend to any other information.

Basis of audit opinion

We conducted our audit in accordance with International Standards on Auditing (UK and Ireland) issued by the Auditing Practices Board. An audit includes examination, on a test basis, of evidence relevant to the amounts and disclosures in the financial statements. It also includes an assessment of the significant estimates and judgements made by the directors in the preparation of the financial statements, and of whether the accounting policies are appropriate to the company's circumstances, consistently applied and adequately disclosed.

We planned and performed our audit so as to obtain all the information and explanations which we considered necessary in order to provide us with sufficient evidence to give reasonable assurance that the financial statements are free from material misstatement, whether caused by fraud or other irregularity or error. In forming our opinion we also evaluated the overall adequacy of the presentation of information in the financial statements.

Opinion

In our opinion

- the financial statements give a true and fair view of the state of the company's affairs as at ... and of its profit (loss) for the year then ended;

- the financial statements have been properly prepared in accordance with the Companies Act 1985; and

- the information given in the directors' report is consistent with the financial statements.

Registered auditors

Date   *Address*

The auditors must distinguish between their responsibilities and those of the directors. To this end, a **statement of directors' responsibilities** should be included. This states that directors must do the following.

(a) Prepare financial statements for each financial year which give a true and fair view of the state of affairs of the company and of the profit or loss of the company for that period.

(b) Select suitable accounting policies and then apply them consistently.

(c) Make judgements and estimates that are reasonable and prudent.

(d) State whether applicable accounting standards have been followed, subject to any material departures disclosed and explained in the financial statements (large companies only).

(e) Prepare the financial statements on the basis that the company will continue in business when this is appropriate.

(f) Keep proper accounting records which disclose with reasonable accuracy at any time the financial position of the company and enable them to ensure that the financial statements comply with company law.

(g) Safeguard the assets of the company and hence take reasonable steps for the prevention and detection of fraud and other irregularities.

Activity 7   **(15 minutes)**

(a) Who is the auditors' report shown on the previous page prepared for?

(b) The report refers to 'significant estimates and judgements'. What sort of things do you think these might relate to? (Clue. Look at the balance sheet shown earlier.)

(c) What are the auditors reasonably sure about?

(d) Why is the auditors' opinion more credible than that of the directors responsible for actually preparing the financial statements?

In spite of these reservations it is possible to carry out a very thorough check of a company's health if we know how to interpret the information provided in financial statements. In the next chapter we shall see how this is done.

Chapter roundup

- Financial statements comprise:

    – Balance sheet
    – Profit and loss account
    – Cash flow statement

- An annual report and accounts will also contain notes to the financial statements, directors' and auditors' reports and usually a chairman's report.

- The balance sheet shows the business's financial position as at the balance sheet date whereas the profit and loss account shows its trading results, overheads, interest, tax and dividends for the year. The cash flow statement reconciles the trading profit to operational cash flows and shows other movements in cash for capital transactions and so on.

- Larger companies generally produce group accounts.

- The principal limitations of financial statements are that:

    – They are usually out of date by the time you receive them.

    – They can only tell you about the past of the company and its financial affairs.

    – There is sometimes confusion because of a company's chosen accounting policy.

Quick quiz

1   Why do companies produce financial statements?

2   Distinguish between a balance sheet and a profit and loss account.

3   What is the difference between gross and net profit?

4   What are the main headings in a cash flow statement?

5   Give four examples of information disclosed in the notes to the financial statements or elsewhere in the accounts.

6   What is a holding company?

7   What is the purpose of consolidated accounts?

8   What is an auditor required to do?

Answers to quick quiz

1 Because they have to (under the Companies Act 1985). Financial statements also keep the 'stakeholders' in the company (shareholders, employees, creditors, HM Revenue and Customs) informed as to its financial health, and they help managers to manage the company's resources. (See section 1.1)

2 A balance sheet presents a 'snapshot' of a company's net assets at a particular point in time, while a profit and loss account is a record of all the income and expenditure incurred over a period of time. (See sections 1.2 and 1.4)

3 Gross profit is simply the company's sales less the direct costs incurred in generating those sales. Net profit deducts other items of expenditure (administrative expenses, distribution costs) and adds other items of income (interest received, profit on sale of fixed assets). (See section 1.4)

4 Net cash inflow from operating activities, returns on investments and servicing of finance, taxation, capital expenditure, equity dividends paid, management of liquid resources, financing. (See section 1.6)

5 Analysis of figures for: fixed assets, debtors, creditors, interest payable, tax, dividends payable, directors' pay, average number of employees, transactions with directors. (See section 2.1)

6 A holding company owns or controls a majority of the shares in another company, or controls another business. (See section 4.1)

7 Consolidated accounts show the assets, liabilities, income and expenses of the group as if it was one entity. (See section 4.1)

8 To confirm that a set of accounts gives a 'true and fair view' of the company's position as at the balance sheet date. (See section 5.2)

Answers to activities

1 Payment received from a debtor

(i)	debtors decrease	CREDIT debtors (decrease in asset)
(ii)	cash at bank increases	DEBIT cash at bank (increase in asset)

Purchase of van

(i)	own a van	DEBIT van (increase in asset)
(ii)	cash at bank decreases	CREDIT cash at bank (decrease in asset)

2   S TRADER
        TRIAL BALANCE
        30 SEPTEMBER, 20X0

	Dr £	Cr £
Capital		24,239
Office furniture	1,440	
Drawings	4,888	
Stock	14,972	
Purchases	167,760	
Sales		184,269
Rent	1,350	
Lighting and heating	475	
Insurance	304	
Salaries	6,352	
Debtors	19,100	
Creditors		8,162
Petty cash	29	
	216,670	216,670

3   (a)

Net assets	£	£
Stock	55	
Debtors	70	
Cash (£100 – £5)	95	
		220
Creditors (£55 + £55)		(110)
		110
Capital		
Owner's capital		100
Retained profit		10
		110

The debtors have taken the place of cash in; the creditors have taken the place of cash out.

(b)   (i)   The value is the amount that will be received when the assets are disposed of. If the stock can be sold for the same amount as it was bought for this will be:

	£
Cash	55
Stock	55
	110

It is unlikely that the stock can be sold for as much as was paid for it (any buyer could simply go to the original supplier instead). The business's value is thus between £55 and £110.

(ii)   The business will make £10 profit per day. The value is therefore as follows.

	£
Original capital	100
Retained profit	50
	150

There is no stock so this will all be in cash.

Note that this is a simplified example. There are many other matters to take into account when selling a real business.

(c) There are *not* two lots of £110. A balance sheet shows two different ways of looking at the same £110, one in terms of the assets making up the £110 and the other in terms of who owns the £110.

4   (a) The depreciation figure for vehicles should be £3,000, not £2,000. One of the figures for creditors falling due in less than one year should be increased by £500 (it could be any one of the three amounts shown).

    (b) 'Book value' is the amount at which an asset or liability is valued 'on paper' ie in the business's accounting system. Net book value is the purchase price of the asset minus amounts charged to date for depreciation.

    (c) This is the value of all the profits that the company has made and not paid out in dividends in the past (it really means 'retained profits). When the business starts it will be nil. Every year the profit made by the company (as shown in its profit and loss account) will be added to the retained profits figure shown in the balance sheet.

If you do not understand this, go back to section 2.1 and work through it again.

5   (a) It has issued some ordinary share capital.

    (b) No. The 'interest paid' figure is tiny compared with the 'dividends paid' figure.

    (c) (i) Increase in debtors: debtors are paying more slowly or there are more of them or they are buying more.

        (ii) Increase in creditors: larger amounts are being bought, a longer time is waited before paying them or there are more of them.

    (d) A debenture loan is a long-term loan. A debenture is the name of the document setting out the terms of the loan.

    (e) Depreciation is not a cash flow. However, you should have spotted it in the reconciliation of operating profit to net cash flow from operating activities. This reconciliation adjusts the accounting profit (operating profit) for non-cash items to show the cash equivalent. Depreciation is therefore 'added back'.

    (f) A company collects employees' income tax and national insurance through the PAYE system and pays it over to the HM Revenue and Customs. Pension contributions may be included here, too.

6   (a) Debt capital – interest payable.

    (b) Equity capital – dividends.

    (c) Working capital – not separately identifiable. Bank overdraft interest and other short/medium-term loans will be included in the interest payable figure. Costs associated with supplier credit (eg loss of discounts) will be hidden within the cost of sales etc.

7   (a) The company's shareholders (not its managers).

    (b) Estimates would include such things as the current values of fixed assets and stocks; judgements would include matters such as whether some long-outstanding debts would ever be repaid.

    (c) That the financial statements are free from material misstatement. In other words, that there are no mistakes that would alter a user's view of the performance of the company.

    (d) Because the auditors are independent of the management of the company. The directors have a vested interest in making it look as though the company is doing well, because this would suggest that they are doing their jobs well.

Chapter 6:
EVALUATING FINANCIAL PERFORMANCE

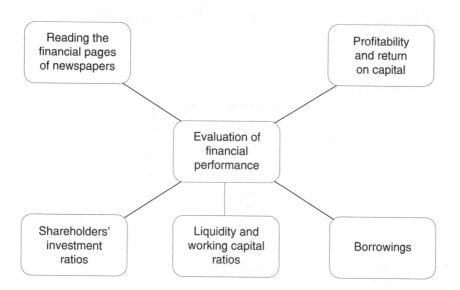

Introduction

In this chapter we revisit a great many of the topics that have been covered so far in this book, so you should find it a very useful memory jogger. If you cannot remember the meaning of some of the terms used this will show you that you need to go back and revise.

Having looked at the basic contents of a business's financial statements we are now going to consider how that information can be used. This is important whichever side of the fence you are on: if you are providing capital for companies as an investor you ought to take the trouble to check that those companies are performing well. If you are a manager of financial resources within a company you need to take into account how the results you achieve will be interpreted by others.

Your objectives

In this chapter you will learn about the following.

- The principles of interpretation of financial information, especially the importance of comparisons

- Why non-financial information is needed to supplement financial information

- How to calculate and interpret profitability ratios, especially ROCE and its components

- How to analyse a company's borrowings in terms of gearing and interest cover
- How to calculate liquidity and working capital ratios and comment on their significance
- How to calculate simple shareholders' ratios and be aware of their significance
- Share price information published in newspapers

1 EVALUATION OF FINANCIAL PERFORMANCE

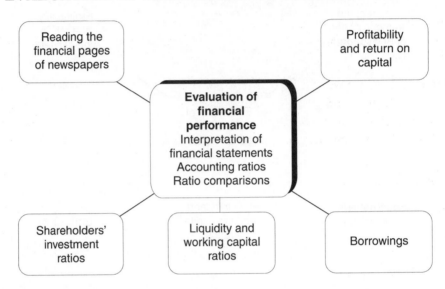

1.1 Interpretation of financial statements

As we have seen, the profit and loss account, the balance sheet and the cash flow statement are all sources of useful information about the condition of a business. But we need to know more about how to analyse and interpret them if they are to be truly useful. In this chapter we will examine the various additional figures which can be calculated from accounts and discuss what they can (and cannot) tell us about the business.

There are a few rules to bear in mind when using any method of interpretation.

(a) Always be aware of the context in which the business operates – manufacturing, service and finance companies will show very different results.

(b) Compare like with like. Try to eradicate unusual items like major write-offs or changes in policy which distort the comparison and disguise underlying trends.

(c) Findings should always be double-checked. Do not base your interpretation on the result of one fact only (such as a major decline in sales).

(d) To interpret effectively, the statements of more than one accounting period should be analysed to give an idea of the trend.

You can gain an initial overall impression of a business just by looking at the figures: is it a multi-million pound business, does it have lots of fixed assets, does it owe large amounts of money, and so on.

However a more sophisticated approach than this has been developed. This is ratio analysis, which involves comparing one figure against another to produce a ratio, and assessing whether the ratio indicates a weakness or strength in the company's affairs.

1.2 Accounting ratios

Broadly speaking, accounting ratios can be grouped into four categories: profitability and return; borrowings; liquidity and working capital; and shareholders' investment ratios.

Within each heading we will identify a number of standard measures or ratios that are normally calculated and generally accepted as meaningful indicators. However each individual business must be considered separately: a ratio that is meaningful for a manufacturing company may be completely meaningless for a financial institution.

1.3 Ratio comparisons

The key to obtaining meaningful information from ratio analysis is comparison. This may be:

(a) **External** – comparison with similar businesses and averages for the business sector within which the company operates; or

(b) **Internal** – comparison with previous periods and forecasts or budgeted results.

Ratio analysis on its own is not sufficient for interpreting company accounts. There are other items of information which should be looked at.

(a) Comments in the chairman's report and directors' report.

(b) The age and nature of the company's assets.

(c) Current and future developments in the company's markets, at home and overseas, recent acquisitions or disposals of a subsidiary by the company.

FOR DISCUSSION

Read through the following extract from an article in the *Financial Times*. How much of the information is of the sort that can be derived from financial statements and how much concerns the company's markets and competition?

'BPB advances as plasterboard market grows

'PB Industries, Europe's biggest plasterboard manufacturer, increased pre-tax profits almost 4 % to £78.9m in the six months to the end of September.

The increase would have been 13% but for a £7.5m exceptional loss on the sale of the group's Wireline mineral exploration business.

'BPB, which supplies about half of the European market, said demand for plasterboard had risen in spite of sluggish housing and construction markets. Operating profits increased from £76.6m to £86.6m.

'Plasterboard profits in France and Germany were largely flat and down narrowly in the UK.

'An increase in European plasterboard volumes of 5.5 % more than offset the slight fall in the UK.

'Sales volumes worldwide rose 3.5 %. Prices held steady in the main European markets but operating margins were trimmed by about half a percentage point reflecting increased raw material prices, principally paper.

'Mr Jean-Pierre Cuny, BPB's chief executive, said continuing expansion of the European market justified the group's decision to invest £50m in a plant in Berlin capable of producing 50m sq m of plasterboard a year.

'There has been concern about overcapacity in the German market which might cause a resurgence of the European price war that several years ago damaged BPB and its main competitors, Lafarge of France and Knuaf of Germany.

'Mr Cuny said yesterday that cuts in capacity and imports meant the net gain to supply would be only 10m sq m.

'Total building material profits rose by 9.5 % to £76.4m (£69.8m). Paper and packaging profits rose by half to £10.2m (£6.8m).

'Group turnover increased 15 % to £720.2m (£625m).'

Note. Get your tutor to explain any terms you don't understand. Most of the unfamiliar ones will be explained in this chapter.

We shall remind you of the need to compare with other companies and take account of market conditions wherever appropriate in this chapter.

EXAMPLE

To illustrate the calculation of many of the ratios we will use the following balance sheet and P & L account figures, with further information from the notes to the accounts.

FURLONG PLC
PROFIT AND LOSS ACCOUNT FOR THE YEAR ENDED 31 DECEMBER 20X5

	Notes	20X5	20X4
		£	£
Turnover	1	3,095,576	1,909,051
Operating profit	1	359,501	244,229
Interest	2	(17,371)	(19,127)
Profit on ordinary activities before taxation		342,130	225,102
Taxation on ordinary activities		(74,200)	(31,272)
Profit on ordinary activities after taxation		267,930	193,830
Dividend		(41,000)	(16,800)
Retained profit for the year		226,930	177,030
Earnings per share		12.8p	9.3p

FURLONG PLC
BALANCE SHEET AS AT 31 DECEMBER 20X5

	Notes	20X5 £	20X4 £
Fixed assets			
Tangible fixed assets		802,180	656,071
Current assets			
Stocks and work in progress		64,422	86,550
Debtors	3	1,002,701	853,441
Cash at bank and in hand		1,327	68,363
		1,068,450	1,008,354
Creditors: amounts falling due within one year	4	(881,731)	(912,456)
Net current assets		186,719	95,898
Total assets less current liabilities		988,899	751,969
Creditors: amounts falling due after more than one year			
10% first mortgage debenture stock 20Y1/20Y6		(100,000)	(100,000)
Provision for liabilities and charges			
Deferred taxation		(20,000)	(10,000)
		868,899	641,969
Capital and reserves			
Called up share capital	5	210,000	210,000
Share premium account		48,178	48,178
Profit and loss account		610,721	383,791
		868,899	641,969

NOTES TO THE ACCOUNTS

			20X5 £	20X4 £
1	*Turnover and profit*			
	(i)	Turnover	3,095,576	1,909,051
		Cost of sales	(2,402,609)	(1,441,950)
		Gross profit	692,967	467,101
		Administration expenses	(333,466)	(222,872)
		Operating profit	359,501	244,229
	(ii)	Operating profit is stated after charging:		
		Depreciation	151,107	120,147
		Auditors' remuneration	6,500	5,000
		Leasing charges	47,636	46,336
		Directors' emoluments	94,945	66,675
2	*Interest*			
		Payable on bank overdrafts and other loans	8,115	11,909
		Payable on debenture stock	10,000	10,000
			18,115	21,909
		Receivable on short term deposits	(744)	(2,782)
		Net payable	17,371	19,127

		20X5	20X4
3	*Debtors*	£	£
	Amounts falling due within one year		
	Trade debtors	884,559	760,252
	Prepayments and accrued income	89,822	45,729
	Advance corporation tax recoverable	7,200	–
		981,581	805,981
	Amounts falling due after more than one year		
	Advance corporation tax recoverable	9,000	7,200
	Trade debtors	12,120	40,260
		21,120	47,460
	Total debtors	1,002,701	853,441
4	*Creditors: amounts falling due within one year*		
	Trade creditors	627,018	545,340
	Accruals and deferred income	81,279	280,464
	Corporation tax	108,000	37,200
	Other taxes and social security costs	44,434	32,652
	Dividend	21,000	16,800
		881,731	912,456
5	*Called up share capital*		
	Authorised ordinary shares of 10p each	1,000,000	1,000,000
	Issued and fully paid ordinary shares of 10p each	210,000	210,000

2 PROFITABILITY AND RETURN ON CAPITAL

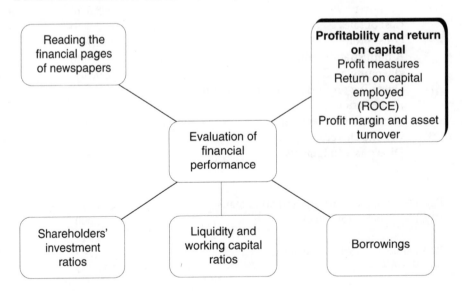

2.1 Profit measures

In our example, the company made a profit in both 20X5 and 20X4, and there was an increase in profit on ordinary activities between one year and the next

- of 52% before taxation
- of 38% after taxation

Activity 1   **(5 minutes)**

How are these figures calculated?

Profit on ordinary activities before taxation is generally thought to be a better figure to use than profit after taxation, because there might be unusual variations in the tax charge from year to year which would not affect the profitability of the company's operations over the long term.

Another profit figure that should be looked at is profit before interest and tax (PBIT). This is the amount of profit which the company earned before having to pay interest to the providers of loan capital (the amount it could have earned if it had its own capital and did not have to pay interest). By providers of loan capital, we usually mean longer-term loan capital, such as debentures and medium-term bank loans, which will be shown in the balance sheet as 'creditors: amounts falling due after more than one year'.

	20X5	20X4
	£	£
Profit on ordinary activities before tax	342,130	225,102
Interest payable (Note 2)	18,115	21,909
PBIT	360,245	247,011

PBIT shows a 46% growth between 20X4 and 20X5.

Activity 2   **(15 minutes)**

(a) The figure shown for 'Interest' in the profit and loss account for 20X5 is £17,371. Why have we used a different figure in the calculation above?

(b) Is 46% growth a good performance?

Ten pounds is a good profit if you only invest £20. It is not so good if you invest £20,000. We shall look at how this can be taken into account.

2.2   Return on capital employed (ROCE)

It is impossible to assess profits or profit growth properly without relating them to the amount of finance (capital) that was employed in making the profits. The most important profitability ratio is therefore return on capital employed (ROCE), which states the profit as a percentage of the amount of capital employed.

$$\text{ROCE} = \frac{\text{Profit on ordinary activities before interest and taxation}}{\text{Capital employed}}$$

Capital employed =   Shareholders' funds plus creditors: amounts falling due after more than one year

In our example, capital employed is calculated as follows.

$$20X5: £(868,899 + 100,000 + 20,000) = £988,899$$
$$20X4: £(641,969 + 100,000 + 10,000) = £751,969$$

These total figures are the total assets less current liabilities figures for 20X5 and 20X4 in the balance sheet.

	20X5	20X4
ROCE	$\dfrac{360,245}{988,899}$	$\dfrac{247,011}{751,969}$
	36.4%	32.8%

What does a company's ROCE tell us? What should we be looking for? There are 3 comparisons that can be made.

(a) The change in ROCE from one year to the next can be examined. In this example, there has been an improvement in ROCE from its 20X4 level.

(b) The ROCE being earned by other companies, if this information is available, can be compared with the ROCE of this company.

(c) A comparison of the ROCE with current market borrowing rates may be made.

   (i) What would be the cost of extra borrowing to the company if it needed more loans, and is it earning a ROCE that suggests it could make profits to make such borrowing worthwhile?

   (ii) Is the company making a ROCE which suggests that it is getting value for money from its current borrowing?

In this example, if we suppose that current market interest rates, say, for medium term borrowing from banks, is around 10%, then the company's actual ROCE of 36% in 20X5 might seem high.

However, there is always a chance that the company's fixed assets, especially property, are undervalued in its balance sheet, and so the capital employed figure might be unrealistically low, making ROCE unrealistically high. If the company had earned a ROCE of, say only 6%, then its return would have been below current borrowing rates and so disappointingly low.

Activity 3 **(5 minutes)**

Why does ROCE become unrealistically high if capital employed is unrealistically low?

We often sub-analyse ROCE, to find out more about why the ROCE is high or low, or better or worse than last year.

2.3 Profit margin and asset turnover

There are two factors that contribute towards a return on capital employed, both related to sales (or 'turnover').

(a) **Profit margin**. A company might make a high or low profit margin on its sales. For example, a company that makes a profit of 25p per £1 of sales is making a bigger return on its sales than another company making a profit of only 10p per £1 of sales.

(b) **Asset turnover**. Asset turnover is a measure of how well the assets of a business are being used to generate sales. For example, if two companies each have capital employed of £100,000 and Company A makes sales of £400,000 per annum whereas Company B makes sales of only £200,000 per annum, Company A is making a higher turnover from the same amount of assets (twice as much asset turnover as Company B) and this will help A to make a higher return on capital employed than B. Asset turnover is expressed as 'x times' so that assets generate x times their value in annual turnover. Here, Company A's asset turnover is four times and B's is two times.

Profit margin and asset turnover together explain the ROCE. The relationship between the three ratios can be shown mathematically.

Profit margin × Asset turnover = ROCE

$$\frac{\text{PBIT}}{\text{Sales}} \times \frac{\text{Sales}}{\text{Capital employed}} = \frac{\text{PBIT}}{\text{Capital employed}}$$

In our example:

		Profit margin		*Asset turnover*		*ROCE*
(a)	20X5	$\frac{360,245}{3,095,576}$	×	$\frac{3,095,576}{988,899}$	=	$\frac{360,245}{988,899}$
		11.64%	×	3.13 times	=	36.4%
(b)	20X4	$\frac{247,011}{1,909,051}$	×	$\frac{1,909,051}{751,969}$	=	$\frac{247,011}{751,969}$
		12.94%	×	2.54 times	=	32.8%

In this example, the company's improvement in ROCE between 20X4 and 20X5 is attributable to a higher asset turnover. Indeed the profit margin has fallen a little, but the higher asset turnover has more than compensated for this.

It is also worth commenting on the change in sales turnover from one year to the next. You may already have noticed that Furlong plc achieved sales growth of over 60% from £1.9 million to £3.1 million between 20X4 and 20X5. This looks like very strong growth, and this is certainly one of the most significant items in the P&L account and balance sheet.

FOR DISCUSSION

(a) Why do we say it 'looks like' very strong growth, not that it is very strong growth?

(b) Employees' skills and personalities are not 'assets' in a financial sense, but they contribute to sales. Is 'asset turnover' a good name for what is really being measured?

Is asset turnover more meaningful in some types of business than others?

NOTES

Activity 4 (30 minutes)

Calculate ROCE, profit margin and asset turnover for the following two companies. Compare and comment on the ratios you calculate.

Company A		Company B	
Sales	£1,000,000	Sales	£4,000,000
Capital employed	£1,000,000	Capital employed	£1,000,000
PBIT	£200,000	PBIT	£200,000

Gross profit margin and net profit margin

Depending on the format of the P & L account, you may be able to calculate the gross profit margin as well as the net profit margin. Looking at the two together can be quite informative.

EXAMPLE

Suppose that a company has the following summarised profit and loss accounts for two consecutive years.

	Year 1 £	Year 2 £
Turnover	70,000	100,000
Cost of sales	42,000	55,000
Gross profit	28,000	45,000
Other costs	21,000	35,000
Net profit	7,000	10,000

Although the net profit margin is the same for both years at 10%, the gross profit margin is not.

In Year 1 it is: $\dfrac{28,000}{70,000}$ = 40%

and in Year 2 it is: $\dfrac{45,000}{100,000}$ = 45%

The improved gross profit margin has not led to an improvement in the net profit margin. This is because other costs as a percentage of sales have risen from 30% in Year 1 to 35% in Year 2.

If capital could be obtained for nothing profits would be higher because businesses would not have to pay the costs of finance, notably interest. We shall now go on to see how the impact of borrowing capital can be measured using the accounting figures.

3 BORROWINGS

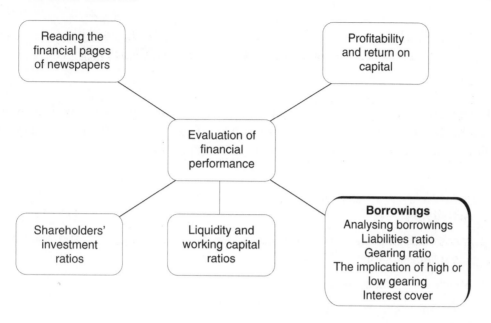

3.1 Analysing borrowings

Borrowing ratios are concerned with how much the company owes in relation to is size, whether its liabilities are getting larger or smaller, and whether its burden of liabilities seems heavy or light.

(a) When a company has high liabilities banks and other potential lenders may be unwilling to advance further funds.

(b) When a company is earning only a modest profit before interest and tax, and has large-scale borrowings, there will be very little profit left for share-holders after interest changes have been paid. And if interest rates were to rise, the company might find that the interest charges on overdrafts and loans might exceed its net profit before interest and taxes (PBIT). This might lead to the collapse and liquidation of the company.

3.2 Liabilities ratio

The liabilities ratio is the ratio of a company's total liabilities to its total assets.

(a) Assets consist of fixed assets at their balance sheet value, plus current assets.

(b) Liabilities consist of all creditors, whether amounts falling due within one year or after more than one year.

There is no absolute guide to the maximum safe liability ratio, but as a very general guide, you might regard 50% as a safe limit. In practice, many companies operate successfully with a higher ratio than this, but 50% is nonetheless a helpful benchmark. In addition, if the ratio is over 50% and getting worse, the company's position will be worth looking at more carefully.

In the case of Furlong plc the liabilities ratio is as follows.

	20X5	20X4
Total debts	$(881,731 + 100,000)$	$(912,456 + 100,000)$
Total assets	$(802,180 + 1,068,450)$	$(656,071 + 1,008,354)$
	= 52%	= 61%

In this case, the liabilities ratio is quite high, mainly because of the large amount of current liabilities. However, the ratio has fallen from 61% to 52% between 20X4 and 20X5, and so the company appears to be improving its position.

Activity 5   (10 minutes)

A company approaches a bank asking for a loan of £100,000. The company has a liabilities ratio of 100%.

Should the bank make the loan?

Give reasons for your answer.

3.3   Gearing ratio

Capital gearing is concerned with a company's long term capital structure. We can think of a company as consisting of fixed assets and net current assets (ie working capital, which is current assets minus current liabilities). These assets must be financed by long term capital of the company, which comprises:

    (a)   Share capital and reserves (shareholders' funds) which can be divided into:
         (i)   Ordinary shares plus reserves
         (ii)   Preference shares; plus

    (b)   Long-term loan capital: 'creditors: amounts falling due after more than one year'.

Like loan capital, preference share capital has a **prior claim** over profits before interest and tax, ahead of ordinary shareholders. Preference dividends must be paid out of profits before ordinary shareholders are entitled to an ordinary dividend, and so we refer to preference share capital and loan capital as 'prior charge capital'.

If you cannot remember what preference shares are, go back to Chapter 2.

The **capital gearing ratio** is a measure of the proportion of a company's capital that is prior charge capital. It is measured as:

$$\frac{\text{Prior charge capital}}{\text{Total capital}}$$

    (a)   Prior charge capital is capital carrying a right to a fixed return. It will include preference shares and debentures.

    (b)   Total capital is ordinary share capital and reserves plus prior charge capital plus any long term liabilities or provisions. (It is the same as 'total assets less current liabilities', a figure which you will find given to you in the balance sheet.)

As with the liabilities ratio, there is no absolute limit to what a gearing ratio ought to be. A company with a gearing ratio of more than 50% is said to be high-geared (whereas low gearing means a gearing ratio of less than 50%). Many companies are high geared, but if a high geared company is becoming increasingly high geared, it is likely to have difficulty in the future when it wants to borrow even more, unless it can also boost its shareholders' capital, either with retained profits or by a new share issue.

A similar ratio to the gearing ratio is the **debt/equity ratio**, which is the ratio of:

$$\frac{\text{Prior charge capital}}{\text{Ordinary share capital and reserves}}$$

This gives us the same sort of information as the gearing ratio, and a ratio of 100% or more would indicate high gearing.

In the example of Furlong plc, we find that the company, although having a high liabilities ratio because of its current liabilities, has a low gearing ratio. It has no preference share capital and its only long term debt is the 10% debenture stock.

	20X5	*20X4*
Gearing ratio	$\dfrac{100,000}{988,899}$	$\dfrac{100,000}{751,969}$
	= 10%	= 13%
Debt/equity ratio	$\dfrac{100,000}{868,899}$	$\dfrac{100,000}{641,969}$
	= 12%	= 16%

A company's gearing is something you often see mentioned in the financial section of the newspapers. It can have a big impact on the way a business is perceived by potential providers of finance. In the next section we find out why.

3.4 The implications of high or low gearing

The problem of a highly geared company is that it has a disproportionally large amount of liabilities and/or preference shares compared with its equity capital (or ordinary shares). Most liabilities give rise to interest payments, and all preference shares give rise to preference dividends, so that a large amount of PBIT is paid in interest and dividends before arriving at a residue available for distribution to the holders of equity.

On the other hand, in any year when a company makes a very large PBIT the providers of loan capital and preference share capital will still only get their fixed amount. The residue may be huge, and the profits remaining after loan interest and the fixed preference dividends will all belong to the ordinary shareholders.

Gearing compares two items on the balance sheet. We can also look at the impact of borrowing from the point of view of the figures in the profit and loss account.

3.5 Interest cover

The interest cover ratio shows whether a company is earning enough profits before interest and tax to pay its interest costs comfortably, or whether its interest costs are high in relation to the size of its profits, so that a fall in PBIT would then have a significant effect on profits available for ordinary shareholders.

$$\text{Interest cover} = \frac{\text{Profit before interest and tax}}{\text{Interest charges (less receipts)}}$$

An interest cover of two times or less would be low, and should really exceed three times before the company's interest costs can be considered within acceptable limits.

Note. Although preference share capital is included as prior charge capital for the gearing ratio, it is usual to exclude preference dividends from 'interest' charges. We also look at all interest payments, even interest charges on short term liabilities, and so interest cover and gearing do not quite look at the same thing.

Activity 6   **(5 minutes)**

Returning to the example of Furlong plc at the beginning of this chapter, what is the company's interest cover?

One of the worst things about interest is that it has to be paid when it is due. It is therefore highly desirable that the cash should be available at the right time, whatever profits are being earned. As you know from earlier chapters this is a matter of good working capital management.

4   LIQUIDITY AND WORKING CAPITAL RATIOS

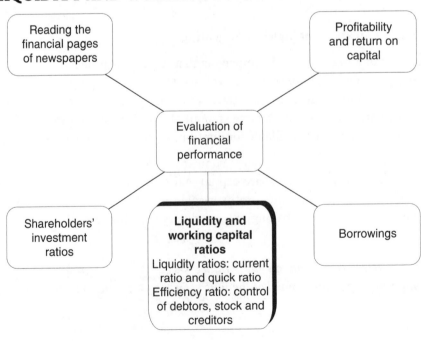

4.1 Liquidity ratios: current ratio and quick ratio

The 'standard' test of liquidity is the **current ratio**. It can be obtained from the balance sheet, and is the ratio of:

$$\frac{\text{Current assets}}{\text{Current liabilities}}$$

The idea behind this is that a company should have enough current assets that give a promise of 'cash to come' to meet its future commitments to pay off its current liabilities.

Companies are not able to convert all their current assets into cash very quickly. In particular, some manufacturing companies might hold large quantities of raw material stocks, which must be used in production to create finished goods stocks. Finished goods stocks might be warehoused for a long time, or sold on lengthy credit. In such businesses, where stock turnover is slow, most stocks are not very 'liquid' assets, because the cash cycle is so long. For these reasons, we calculate an additional liquidity ratio, known as the quick ratio or acid test ratio.

The **quick ratio**, or **acid test** ratio is:

$$\frac{\text{Current assets less stocks}}{\text{Current liabilities}}$$

This ratio should ideally be at least one for companies with a slow stock turnover. For companies with a fast stock turnover, a quick ratio can be comfortably less than one without suggesting that the company should be in cash flow trouble.

Both the current ratio and the quick ratio offer an indication of the company's liquidity position, but the absolute figures should not be interpreted too literally. It is often theorised that an acceptable current ratio is 1.5 and an acceptable quick ratio is 0.8, but these should only be used as a guide. Different businesses operate in very different ways. A supermarket, for example, has a current ratio of 0.52 and a quick ratio of 0.17. This supermarket has low debtors (people do not buy groceries on credit), low cash (good cash management), medium stocks (high stocks but quick turnover, particularly in view of perishability) and very high creditors (the supermarket buys its supplies of groceries on credit).

Compare the supermarket ratios with a manufacturing and retail company which has a current ratio of 1.44 and a quick ratio of 1.03. As this is a manufacturing and retail organisation it operates with liquidity ratios closer to the standard.

What is important is the trend of these ratios. From this, one can easily ascertain whether liquidity is improving or deteriorating. If the supermarket has traded for the last 10 years (very successfully) with current ratios of 0.52 and quick ratios of 0.17 then it should be supposed that the company can continue in business with those levels of liquidity. If in the following year the current ratio were to fall to 0.38 and the quick ratio to 0.09, then further investigation into the liquidity situation would be appropriate. It is the relative position that is far more important than the absolute figures.

Don't forget the other side of the coin either. A current ratio and a quick ratio can get bigger than they need to be. A company that has large volumes of stocks and debtors might be over-investing in working capital, and so tying up more funds in the business than it needs to. This would suggest poor management of debtors or stocks or creditors by the company.

4.2 Efficiency ratios: control of debtors, stock and creditors

A rough measure of the average length of time it takes for a company's debtors to pay what they owe is the '**debtor days**' ratio, or average debtors' payment period.

The estimated average debtors' payment period is calculated as:

$$\frac{\text{Trade debtors}}{\text{Sales}} \times 365 \text{ days}$$

The figure for sales should be taken as the turnover figure in the P & L account. The trade debtors are not the total figure for debtors in the balance sheet, which includes prepayments and non-trade debtors. The trade debtors figure will be itemised in an analysis of the debtors total, in a note to the accounts.

Sales are usually made on 'normal credit terms' of payment within 30 days. Debtor days significantly in excess of this might be representative of poor management of funds of a business. However, some companies must allow generous credit terms to win customers. Exporting companies in particular may have to carry large amounts of debtors, and so their average collection period might be well in excess of 30 days.

The trend of the collection period (debtor days) over time is probably the best guide. If debtor days are increasing year on year, this is indicative of a poorly managed credit control function (and potentially therefore a poorly managed company).

Debtor days: examples

The debtor days of Super (the supermarket) and Man (the manufacturer and retail organisation) were as follows. (*Note*. 'k' following a number denotes 'thousands'.)

	20X3		20X4	
	Trade debtors/ turnover	*Debtor days (×365)*	*Trade debtors/ turnover*	*Debtor days (×365)*
Super	£5,016k / £284,986k	= 6.4 days	£3,977k / £290,668k	= 5.0 days
Man	£458.3m / £2,059.5m	= 81.2 days	£272.4m / £1,274.2m	= 78.0 days

The differences in debtor days reflect the differences between the types of business. The supermarket has hardly any trade debtors at all, whereas the manufacturing company has far more. The debtor days are fairly constant from the previous year for both companies.

Stock turnover period

Another ratio worth calculating is the **stock turnover** period, or stock days. This is another estimated figure, obtainable from published accounts, which indicates the average number of days that items of stock are held for. As with the average debt collection period, however, it is only an approximate estimated figure, but one which should be reliable enough for comparing changes year on year.

Stock turnover is calculated as:

$$\frac{\text{Stock}}{\text{Cost of sales}} \times 365 \text{ days}$$

It is another measure of how vigorously a business is trading. A lengthening stock turnover period from one year to the next indicates one of the following.

(a) A slowdown in trading.

(b) A build-up in stock levels, perhaps suggesting that the investment in stocks is becoming excessive.

If we add together the stock days and the debtor days, this should give us an indication of how soon stock is convertible into cash. Both debtor days and stock days therefore give us a further indication of the company's liquidity.

Creditors' turnover

Creditors' turnover is ideally calculated by the formula:

$$\frac{\text{Trade creditors}}{\text{Purchases}} \times 365 \text{ days}$$

However, it is rare to find purchases disclosed in published accounts and so cost of sales serves as an approximation. The creditors' turnover ratio helps to assess a company's liquidity; an increase in creditor days is often a sign of lack of long term finance or poor management of current assets, resulting in the use of extended credit from suppliers, increased bank overdraft and so on.

Activity 7 (30 minutes)

Calculate liquidity and working capital ratios from the following accounts of Clean Group, a business which provides service support (cleaning etc) to customers worldwide.

	20X3	20X2
	£'m	£'m
Turnover	2,176.2	2,344.8
Cost of sales	(1,659.0)	(1,731.5)
Gross profit	517.2	613.3

	2003	2002
Current assets	£'m	£'m
Stocks	42.7	78.0
Debtors (note 1)	378.9	431.4
Short-term deposits and cash	205.2	145.0
	626.8	654.4
Creditors: amounts falling due within one year		
Loans and overdrafts	32.4	81.1
Corporation taxes	67.8	76.7
Dividend	11.7	17.2
Creditors (note 2)	487.2	467.2
	599.1	642.2
Net current assets	27.7	12.2

Notes

1 Trade debtors	295.2	335.5
2 Trade creditors	190.8	188.1

There are also ratios which help equity shareholders and other investors to assess the value and quality of an investment in the ordinary shares of a company. We shall look at five of these: earnings per share, dividend per share, dividend cover, P/E ratio and dividend yield.

5 SHAREHOLDERS' INVESTMENT RATIOS

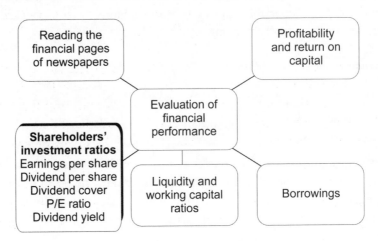

5.1 Earnings per share

It is possible to calculate the return on each ordinary share in the year. This is the earnings per share (EPS). Earnings are profits after tax, preference dividends and 'extraordinary items' (separately disclosed, large and very unusual items), which can either be paid out as a dividend to ordinary shareholders or retained in the business.

Suppose that Draught Ltd reports the following figures:

PROFIT AND LOSS ACCOUNT FOR 20X6 (EXTRACT)

	£
Profit before interest and tax	120,000
Interest	(20,000)
Profit before tax	100,000
Taxation	(40,000)
Profit after tax	60,000
Preference dividend	(1,000)
Profit available for ordinary shareholders (= earnings)	59,000
Ordinary dividend	(49,000)
Retained profits	10,000

The company has 80,000 ordinary shares and 20,000 preference shares.

Calculate earnings per share for Draught Ltd in 20X6.

SOLUTION

$$\text{EPS is } \frac{£59,000}{80,000} = 73.75 \text{ pence per share}$$

In practice there are usually further complications in calculating the EPS, but these are well beyond the scope of this book.

5.2   Dividend per share

The dividend per share in pence is self-explanatory, and clearly an item of some interest to shareholders.

5.3   Dividend cover

Dividend cover is a ratio of:

$$\frac{\text{Earnings per share}}{\text{Net dividend per (ordinary) share}}$$

It shows what proportion of profit has been paid (or proposed) as a dividend and what proportion will be retained in the business to finance future growth. A dividend cover of two times would indicate that the company had paid 50% of its profits as dividends, and retained 50% in the business to help to finance future operations. Retained profits are an important source of funds for most companies, and so the dividend cover can in some cases be quite high.

A significant change in the dividend cover from one year to the next would be worth looking at closely. For example, if a company's dividend cover were to fall sharply between one year and the next, it could be that its profits had fallen, but the directors wished to pay at least the same amount of dividends as in the previous year, so as to keep shareholder expectations satisfied.

5.4   Price to earnings ratio

The P/E ratio is the ratio of a company's current share price to the earnings per share.

A high P/E ratio indicates strong shareholder confidence in the company and its future, and a lower P/E ratio indicates lower confidence.

The P/E ratio of a company can be compared with other P/E ratios.

- Of specific companies in the same business sector
- Of other companies generally
- On average, for the business sector as a whole

5.5   Dividend yield

Dividend yield is the return a shareholder is currently expecting on the shares of a company. It is calculated as:

$$\frac{\text{Dividend on the share for the year}}{\text{Current market value of the share}} \times 100\%$$

So, if a company pays a dividend of 50p and the market price of its shares is 500p per share, the dividend yield is (50p ÷ 500p) × 100 = 10%. An investor can compare this with the return available on other investments, such as interest rates available from banks and building societies.

Shareholders look for both dividend yield and capital growth. Obviously, dividend yield is therefore an important aspect of a share's performance.

Activity 8   **(15 minutes)**

The following information is taken from the profit and loss accounts of two companies.

	Company P		Company Q	
	£m	£m	£m	£m
Profit on ordinary activities after tax		41.1		5.6
Dividends				
Preference	0.5		–	
Ordinary	20.6		5.4	
		21.1		5.4
Retained profits		20.0		0.2

In addition, we have been advised of the following.

	Company P	Company Q
Number of ordinary shares	200m	50m
Market price per share	285p	154p

Calculate the dividend yield and dividend cover of the two companies.

---

6   READING THE FINANCIAL PAGES OF NEWSPAPERS

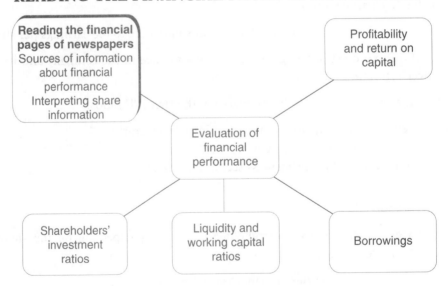

6.1   Sources of information about financial performance

All quality newspapers (such as *The Guardian, The Independent, Daily Telegraph, The Times* and, above all, the *Financial Times*) have detailed information and comment each day in their financial pages on the following.

(a) The activities in the City of London (especially the Stock Exchange).

(b) The financial results of large companies.

(c) Announcements by large companies and financial institutions of important plans, such as proposed takeovers and mergers, sales of parts of a business, expansion into new activities or geographical markets and so on.

(d) UK and overseas government policies on interest and exchange rates, industrial strategy, privatisation plans and so on.

(e) Longer term developments in the business world, such as changes in management theories or consumer tastes.

When you first try to read the financial pages, they can seem very dull and difficult to understand, especially as they are full of jargon. However, if you persevere, you will gradually find that you become familiar with the jargon and you will come to realise that the financial pages can be very helpful in developing your understanding of the financial marketplace.

There are also useful general programmes on financial matters on radio and television.

We will consolidate what you have learned so far by looking at how to interpret the share price information given in the newspapers.

6.2 Interpreting share information

Figure 6.1 Share price information from the Financial Times

The above table and notes are extracts from the *Financial Times* London Share Service.

Those shares included in the FTSE 100 index are shown in **bold** (eg Scottish & Newcastle, ICI, Boots). A ✠ in the notes column denote a FT Global 500 company – the world's 500 largest companies ranked by market capitalisation (eg Tesco, Cadbury Schweppes, Unilever).

The price shown is the **middle market price** in pence at the close of trading on the previous working day. This price is midway between the buying and selling prices at which marketmakers and brokers will deal. The difference between buying and selling prices represents the profit to the marketmakers. Just like any other business, they aim to sell their stocks (of shares) for more than they paid for them.

You will sometimes see two prices quoted, the **bid** price (the price which you would get if you sold the share to someone) and the **offer** price (the price at which you could buy the share).

If 'xd' (standing for **ex-dividend**) appears after a closing price, it means that a company is about to pay a dividend but that anyone buying the shares before the dividend payment is made will not receive the dividend. This is because companies pay dividends to all shareholders on the share register at a stated time before the payment is due. This gives them time to deal with all the administration without constantly having to change the names on the list of those to receive payment.

The column headed '+ or −' shows the changes from the last closing price in pence (or in fractions of one pound sterling for the few shares whose price is quoted in pounds rather than pence).

The columns headed 'high' and 'low' show the highest and lowest closing prices over a rolling 52-week period.

The 'Volume' column shows the number of trades made in those shares in the previous day, to the nearest 1,000 trades.

Yield stands for dividend yield. This is a measure of the return on an investment in that share.

P/E, of course, stands for P/E ratio, which is based upon the latest annual report and accounts, updated on interim figures where possible.

FOR DISCUSSION

You have £8,000 to invest in Food & Drug Retailers. Which of those shares listed above will you buy? Select no more than five different shares.

NOTES

Chapter roundup

- Ratios provide information through comparison.

    - Trends in a company's ratios from one year to the next, indicating an improving or worsening position.

    - In some cases, against a 'norm' or 'standard' for the industry or market.

    - In some cases, against the ratios of other companies, although differences between one company and another should often be expected.

- This lengthy chapter has gone into quite a lot of detail about basic ratio analysis. The ratios you should be able to calculate and/or comment on are as follows.

    - *Profitability ratios*
        - Return on capital employed
        - Net profit as a percentage of sales
        - Asset turnover ratio
        - Gross profit as a percentage of sales

    - *Liability and gearing ratios*
        - Liability ratio
        - Gearing ratio
        - Interest cover

    - *Liquidity and working capital ratios*
        - Current ratio
        - Quick ratio (acid test ratio)
        - Debtor days (average debt collection period)
        - Average stock turnover period

    - *Ordinary shareholders' investment ratios*
        - Earnings per share
        - Dividend cover
        - P/E ratio
        - Dividend yield

Quick quiz

1 What rules should be born in mind when using any method of interpretation, and why are comparisons so important?

2 What is the usual formula for ROCE?

3 ROCE can be calculated as the product of two other ratios. What are they?

4 Define the 'liabilities ratio'.

5 Give two formulae for evaluating gearing.

6 In a period when profits are fluctuating, what effect does a company's level of gearing have on the profits available for ordinary shareholders?

7 Explain 'interest cover'

8 What are the formulae for:

(a) The current ratio?
(b) The quick ratio?
(c) The debtors payment period?
(d) The stock turnover period?

9 What is earnings per share?

10 What is the formula for dividend cover?

11 What do you understand by P/E ratio?

Answers to quick quiz

1 Be aware of the industry in which the company operates, compare like with like, double-check your findings, analyse more than one accounting period's financial statements. Comparison (with previous periods, with companies in the same sector, or with companies in another sector) helps us to analyse whether the company is progressing or declining. (See section 1)

2 $\dfrac{\text{Profit on ordinary activities before interest and taxation}}{\text{Capital employed}}$ (See section 2.2)

3 Profit margin and asset turnover (See section 2.3)

4 Total liabilities as a percentage of total assets (See section 3.2)

5 Capital gearing ratio $\dfrac{\text{Prior charge capital}}{\text{Total capital}}$

Debt/equity ratio $\dfrac{\text{Prior charge capital}}{\text{Ordinary share capital plus reserves}}$

6 If profits are high, a large amount of PBIT will be available for them, but when PBIT is low there will be very little as it will be paid to the loan creditors and preference shareholders. (See section 3.4)

7 A comparison of net interest expense with profits before interest, to show whether the level of interest expense is comfortable. (See section 3.5)

8　　(a) $\dfrac{\text{Current assets}}{\text{Current liabilities}}$

　　(b) $\dfrac{\text{Current assets less stocks}}{\text{Current liabilities}}$

　　(c) $\dfrac{\text{Trade debtors}}{\text{Sales}} \times 365 \text{ days}$

　　(d) $\dfrac{\text{Stocks}}{\text{Cost of sales}} \times 365 \text{ days}$ (See section 4)

9　　$\dfrac{\text{Profits after tax, preference dividends and extraordinary items}}{\text{Number of ordinary shares}}$ (See section 5.1)

10　$\dfrac{\text{Earnings per share}}{\text{Dividend per ordinary share}}$

11　The price to earnings ratio is the ratio of the company's current ordinary share price to the earnings per share, with a high P/E showing market confidence in the share. (See section 5.4)

Answers to activities

1　　A percentage increase is calculated as follows.

$\dfrac{\text{New figures - old figure}}{\text{Old figure}}$

(a) $= \dfrac{\pounds342,130 - \pounds225,102}{\pounds225,102} = 52\%$

(b) $= \dfrac{\pounds267,930 - \pounds193,830}{\pounds193,830} = 38\%$

2　　(a) We have added back the figure for interest **payable**, as shown in Note 2 of the accounts to arrive at the profits generated from its capital (equity and loan) *including* interest receivable on surplus funds.

　　(b) It is better than a fall in the PBIT, of course, but it is difficult to say whether it is a good performance without further information. Competitors may have achieved 100% growth. Last year may have been an unusually bad one.

3　　The lower the figure you are dividing by, the higher the result will be. For example:

10/5 = 2　　　　　　10/1 = 10

If managers or companies want to look good in ROCE terms, therefore, it is in their interests not to increase capital employed by buying new assets.

4   These figures would give the following ratios.

Company A
ROCE $= \dfrac{£200,000}{£1,000,000}$ = 20%

Company B
ROCE $= \dfrac{£200,000}{£1,000,000}$ = 20%

Profit margin $= \dfrac{£200,000}{£1,000,000}$ = 20%

Profit margin $= \dfrac{£200,000}{£4,000,000}$ = 5%

Asset turnover $= \dfrac{£1,000,000}{£1,000,000}$ = 1

Asset turnover $= \dfrac{£4,000,000}{£1,000,000}$ = 4

The companies have the same ROCE, but it is arrived at in a very different fashion. Company A operates with a low asset turnover and a comparatively high profit margin whereas Company B carries out much more business, but on a lower profit margin. Company A could be operating at the luxury end of the market, whilst Company B is operating at the popular end of the market (Mercedes v Ford).

5   Your instant response may have been 'No', but a bank would be more open-minded, at least at first. What would the money be used for? If it is used to buy assets the debt ratio will still be 100%. If the assets in question consist of fantastic new machines that will generate huge profits the bank might be very interested to help. Look back at Chapter 1 for other matters that a bank would consider.

6   Interest payments should be taken gross, from the note to the accounts, and not net of interest receipts as shown in the P & L account.

	2005	*2004*
PBIT	£360,245	£247,011
Interest payable	£18,115	£21,909
	= 20 times	= 11 times

Furlong plc has more than sufficient interest cover. In view of the company's low gearing, this is not too surprising and so we finally obtain a picture of Furlong plc as a company that does not seem to have a debt problem, in spite of its high (although declining) debt ratio.

7

		2003		*2002*
Current ratio	$\dfrac{£626.8}{£599.1}$	= 1.05	$\dfrac{£654.4}{£642.2}$	= 1.02
Quick ratio	$\dfrac{£584.1}{£599.1}$	= 0.97	$\dfrac{£576.4}{£642.2}$	= 0.90
Debtors' payment period	$\dfrac{£295.2}{£2,176.2} \times 365$	= 49.5 days	$\dfrac{£335.2}{£2,344.8} \times 365$	= 52.2 days
Stock turnover period	$\dfrac{£42.7}{£1,659.0} \times 365$	= 9.4 days	$\dfrac{£78.0}{£1,731.5} \times 365$	= 16.4 days
Creditors' turnover	$\dfrac{£190.8}{£1,659.0} \times 365$	= 42.0 days	$\dfrac{£188.1}{£1,731.5} \times 365$	= 39.6 days

Clean Group is a service company and hence it would be expected to have very low stock and a very short stock turnover period. The similarity of debtors' and creditors' turnover periods means that the group is passing on most of the delay in receiving payment to its suppliers.

Clean's current ratio is a little lower than average but its quick ratio is better than average and very little less than the current ratio. This suggests that stock levels are strictly controlled, which is reinforced by the low stock turnover period. It would seem that working capital is tightly managed, to avoid the poor liquidity which could be caused by a high debtors' turnover period and comparatively high creditors.

8

	Company P £m	Company Q £m
Profit on ordinary activities after tax	41.1	5.6
Preference dividend	0.5	0.0
Earnings	40.6	5.6
Number of shares	200m	50m
EPS	20.3p	11.2p
Ordinary dividend per share	10.3p	10.8p
Dividend cover	$\dfrac{20.3}{10.3}$	$\dfrac{11.2}{10.8}$
	= 1.97 times	= 1.04 times
Dividend yield	$\dfrac{10.3}{285} \times 100\%$	$\dfrac{10.8}{154} \times 100\%$
	= 3.6%	= 7.0%

Chapter 7:
ANALYSIS OF COSTS

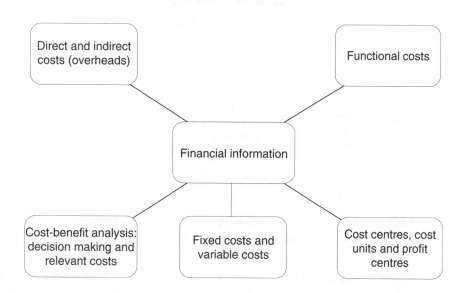

Introduction

The effective management of any resource, including finance, requires good information. Information about finance is derived from an organisation's accounting system. An accounting system records a lot more than simply who owes what to whom. It records the reasons why money was received and, more especially, the reasons why money was paid out. It does this by analysing costs in a variety of ways.

In this chapter we look at the various ways of analysing costs and at how the analyses can be used to help make decisions.

Your objectives

In this chapter you will learn about the following.

- The importance of information, and particularly financial information, to the running of a business
- How costs can be classified according to business function
- How to distinguish between direct costs and overheads
- How the responsibility for costs is divided between a number of cost centres and profit centres
- The distinction between fixed and variable costs
- What is meant by cost-benefit analysis and relevant costs
- The importance of costs in decision making

1 FINANCIAL INFORMATION

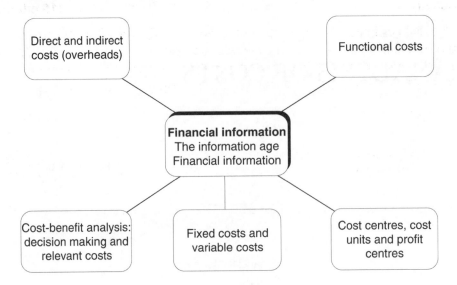

1.1 The information age

To run anything, let alone a business, we have to have information. If you look at a clock it gives you information about what the time is. If the clock rings or beeps the noise gives you the information that it is time to get up. If you turn on the radio someone will give you information about today's traffic or transport problems and the weather. When you get to work you have post and e-mails (information) to deal with or you carry out the instructions (information) your boss gives you. Modern times have quite rightly been called 'the information age'.

Definition

Information is anything that is communicated.

1.2 Financial information

Since the main objective of a business is to make a profit – to sell things for more than they cost – it follows that the most important kind of *information* used to run the business is information about money: financial information.

Aside from running the business another, more pragmatic, reason for the importance of financial information is that it is the only sort of information covering all of the activities of a business that *must*, by law, be collected. It has to be collected to satisfy the tax man. Companies have to collect it and analyse it to comply with company law, too.

By 'running the business' we mean managing resources such as people or machines or materials. In practice it may be people's *time* that a manager manages, or the type, quantity and quality of materials. But the only *reason* for managing time or quantities is because different amounts of time or quantities of material cost more or less money.

Activity 1   **(15 minutes)**

What financial information do you use in your job, if any? Who decides how you should spend your time and whether you are spending too much or too little time on an aspect of your job? What is the cost to your employer of an hour of your time? Who decides what resources you can have to help you do your job?

The most important sort of information for managing a business, then, is information about costs. To be of real value, though, this information has to be given to the person who is responsible for controlling a particular cost. We shall now look at a variety of ways in which costs can be analysed and so brought to the attention of the individuals responsible for them.

2   FUNCTIONAL COSTS

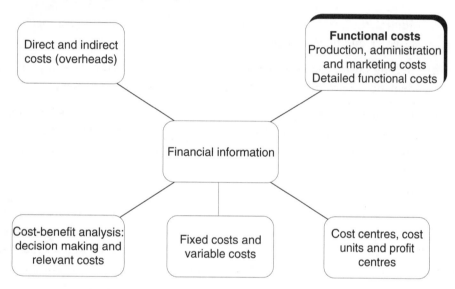

2.1   Production, administration and marketing costs

In a 'traditional' costing system for a manufacturing organisation, costs are classified as follows.

- Production or manufacturing costs
- Administration costs
- Marketing, or selling and distribution costs

Most expenses fall comfortably into one or other of these three broad classifications. Manufacturing costs are associated with the factory, selling and distribution costs with the sales, marketing, warehousing and transport departments and administration costs with general office departments (such as accounting and personnel). Classification in this way is known as classification by function. Other expenses that do not fall fully into one of these classifications might be categorised as 'general overheads' or even listed as a classification on their own (for example, research and development costs).

Activity 2 (15 minutes)

(a) Think of three specific examples of each of the above types of cost in a car manufacturer's business.

(b) Suggest what would be the equivalent of a 'production' cost in a business such as a bank that gives a service as opposed to making things.

2.2 Detailed functional costs

Functional costs include the following.

(a) **Production costs** are the costs which are incurred by the sequence of operations beginning with the supply of raw materials, and ending with the completion of the product ready for warehousing as a finished goods item.

(b) **Administration costs** are the costs of managing an organisation, that is, planning and controlling its operations, but only insofar as such administration costs are not related to the production, sales, distribution or research and development functions.

(c) **Selling costs,** sometimes known as marketing costs, are the costs of creating demand for products and securing firm orders from customers.

(d) **Distribution costs** are the costs of the sequence of operations beginning with the receipt of finished goods from the production department and making them ready for dispatch, transporting them to customers, and ending with the reconditioning for re-use of returned empty containers.

(e) **Research and development costs**
  (i) Research costs are the costs of searching for new or improved products.
  (ii) Development costs are the costs incurred between the decision to produce a new or improved product and the commencement of full, formal manufacture of the product.

(f) **Financing costs** are the costs incurred to finance the business such as loan interest.

The cost of, say, a ball-point pen includes the cost of the plastic used to make it and the ink inside it. However the pen's cost also includes things you can't touch or see, such as the cost of processing the order from WH Smith and delivering batches of pens to WH Smith's warehouse. Costs can therefore be analysed as 'direct' or 'indirect'.

3 DIRECT COSTS AND INDIRECT COSTS (OVERHEADS)

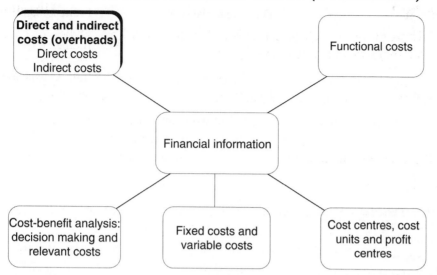

Materials, labour costs and other expenses can be classified as direct costs or as indirect costs.

Definition

> A **direct cost** is a cost that can be traced in full to the product, service, or department whose cost is being determined.

(a) Direct materials costs are the costs of materials that are known to have been used in making and selling a product (or even providing a service).

(b) Direct labour costs are the specific costs of the workforce used to make a product or provide a service. Direct labour costs are established by measuring the time taken for a job, or the time taken in 'direct production work'. Traditionally, direct labour costs have been restricted to wage-earning factory workers, but in recent years, with the development of systems for costing services ('service costing'), the costs of some salaried staff might also be treated as a direct labour cost.

(c) Other direct expenses are those expenses that have been incurred in full as a direct consequence of making a product, or providing a service, or running a department (depending on whether a product, a service or a department is being costed).

Definition

> An **indirect cost** or **overhead** is a cost that is incurred in the course of making a product, providing a service or running a department, but which cannot be traced directly and in full to the product, service or department.

Examples, respectively, might be supervisors' wages, cleaning materials and buildings insurance.

Total expenditure may therefore be analysed as follows:

Material cost	=	Direct material cost	+	Indirect material cost
+		+		+
Wages	=	Direct wages	+	Indirect wages
+		+		+
Expenses	=	Direct expenses	+	Indirect expenses
Total cost	=	Direct cost	+	Overheads

In costing a product made by a manufacturing organisation, direct costs are usually restricted to the production costs (although it is not uncommon to find a salesman's commission for selling the product as a direct selling cost). Costs are commonly built up as follows.

	£
Production costs:	
Direct materials	A
Direct wages	B
Direct expenses	C
Total direct cost	A+B+C
Production overheads	D
Full factory cost	A+B+C+D
Administration overheads	E
Selling and distribution overheads	F
Full cost of sales	A+B+C+D+E+F

You should be able to specify items of expenditure which are classifiable as direct material cost, direct labour, production overhead and so on. A list of such cost items is given here.

3.1 Direct costs

Direct material costs

All material becoming part of the product (unless used in negligible amounts and having negligible costs) is direct material, the cost of which is charged to the product as part of the prime cost. Material used in negligible amounts and/or having negligible cost can be grouped under indirect materials as part of overhead. Examples of direct material are set out below.

(a) Materials, including component parts, specially purchased for a particular job, order or process.

(b) Materials passing from one operation to another. (For example, if a product is made in two departments, when part-finished work is transferred from Department 1 to Department 2, it becomes finished work of Department 1 and a direct material cost in Department 2).

(c) Primary packing materials like cartons and boxes.

Direct labour costs

All wages paid for labour expended on work on the product itself are direct wages, the cost of which is charged to the product as part of the total direct cost. Some seemingly indirect wages (such as those paid to the foreman) which can be accurately identified with the product, may be considered a direct charge to the product and be included as direct wages.

Examples of groups of labour receiving payment as direct wages are as follows.

(a) Workers engaged in altering the condition or composition of the product (drilling holes, cutting, painting and so on)

(b) Inspectors, analysts and testers **specifically required** for such production

(c) Foremen, chargehands, shop clerks and anyone else whose wages are **specifically identified**

Direct expenses

If any expenses are incurred on a specific product other than direct material cost and direct wages those too are direct expenses, the cost of which is charged to the product as part of the total direct cost. Examples of direct expenses are as follows.

(a) The cost of special designs, drawings or layouts
(b) The hire of tools or equipment for a particular job
(c) Maintenance costs of tools, jigs, fixtures etc.

Direct expenses are also referred to as chargeable expenses.

Activity 3	(5 minutes)

A solicitor charges her clients by the hour for her services. Only hours that can be specifically identified with a particular client are regarded as chargeable.

One Monday she spends half an hour sorting through her post, half an hour on the phone to client A, an hour and a half looking through a contract for client B, two hours studying a new law on property, an hour in a meeting with her partners, and an hour and a half writing letters in reply to the day's post.

How much 'direct' or chargeable time has she spent?

3.2 Indirect costs

Production overheads

All indirect material cost, indirect wages and indirect expenses incurred in the factory from receipt of the order until its completion are included in production (or factory) overhead. Examples are as follows.

(a) **Indirect material** which cannot be traced in the finished product, such as consumable stores like lubricants or minor items of material used in negligible amounts, or amounts which it is uneconomical to allocate to a particular product, like the cost of glue in box-making.

(b) **Indirect wages,** meaning all wages not charged directly to a product, which generally include salaries and wages of non-productive personnel in the production department, such as foremen, inspectors, general labourers, maintenance staff, stores staff.

(c) **Indirect expenses** (other than material and labour) not charged directly to production. The following expenses could be included under this heading.

 LEARNING MEDIA

(i)   Rent, rates and insurance of a factory

    (ii)   Depreciation, fuel, power, repairs and maintenance of plant, machinery and factory buildings.

Production overhead is also referred to as factory overhead.

> **Activity 4**   **(5 minutes)**
>
> Why might it be 'uneconomical' to allocate the cost of glue in box-making to individual boxes?

Administration overheads

These are all indirect material costs, wages and expenses incurred in the direction, control and administration of an organisation. The following are examples.

    (a)   Depreciation of office computer equipment.

    (b)   Office salaries, including salaries of administrative directors, secretaries, accountants.

    (c)   Rent, rates, insurance, lighting, cleaning and heating of general offices, telephone, internet and postal charges, bank charges, legal charges, audit fees, depreciation and repairs of office buildings and machinery.

Definition

> **Depreciation** is a measure of how much a fixed asset wears out until it is completely useless. For example a sales rep's car might last four years before it is scrapped. If it originally cost £10,000 it would depreciate by £2,500 per year. All fixed assets except land are subject to depreciation.

Selling overheads

These are all indirect materials costs, wages and expenses incurred in promoting sales and retaining customers. Examples of selling overhead are set out below.

    (a)   Printing and stationery, such as catalogues and price lists; website maintenance costs

    (b)   Salaries and commission of salesmen, representatives and sales department staff

    (c)   Advertising and sales promotion; market research

    (d)   Rent, rates and insurance of sales offices and showrooms; bad debts and collection charges; cash discounts allowed; after-sales service

Distribution overheads

These are all indirect materials, costs, wages and expenses incurred in making the packed product ready for despatch and delivering it to the customer. Examples of distribution overhead are as follows.

(a) Cost of packing cases; materials (eg oil, spare parts) used in the upkeep of delivery vehicles; the cost of reconditioning returned packing cases, ready for re-use

(b) Wages of packers, drivers and despatch clerks

(c) Freight and insurance charges; rent, rates, insurance and depreciation of warehouses; depreciation and running expenses of delivery vehicles

You might have decided by now that you understand the distinction between direct costs and overheads, but in practice, there are many 'grey areas' where costs are not obviously direct or indirect, and a reasoned judgement has to be made in classifying them. Attempt the activity below.

Activity 5   **(15 minutes)**

A direct labour employee's wage in a particular week is made up as follows.

		£
(a)	Basic pay for normal hours worked, 36 hours at £4 per hour	144
(b)	Pay at the basic rate for overtime, 6 hours at £4 per hour	24
(c)	Overtime shift premium, with overtime paid at time-and-a-quarter 1/4 × 6 hours × £4 per hour	6
(d)	A plus payment under a group bonus (or 'incentive') scheme – bonus for the month	30
	Total gross wages in the week for 42 hours of work	204

Task

Which costs are direct? Are any indirect?

Costs consist of the costs of direct materials, direct labour, direct expenses, production overheads, administration overheads and general overheads. But how do accountants set about recording the actual expenses incurred as any one of these classifications and making individual managers responsible for them?

4 COST CENTRES, COST UNITS AND PROFIT CENTRES

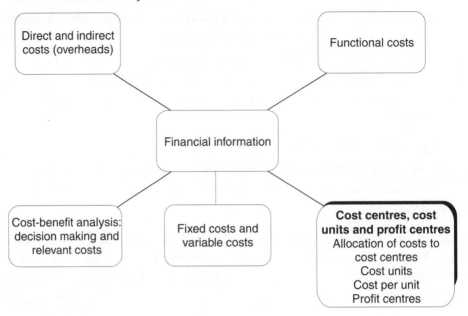

4.1 Allocation of costs to cost centres

To begin with, all costs should be recorded as a direct cost of a cost centre. Even 'overhead costs' are directly traceable to an office or an item of expense and there should be an overhead cost centre to cater for these costs.

Definition

A **cost centre** is a location, or a function, or an activity or an item of equipment. Each cost centre acts as a collecting place for certain costs before they are analysed further.

Suitable cost centres might be as follows.

(a) In a production department: the department itself, a machine within the department or group of machines, a foreman's work group, a work bench and so on.

(b) Production 'service' or 'back-up' departments, such as the stores, maintenance, production planning and control departments.

(c) Administration, sales or distribution departments, such as the personnel, accounting or purchasing departments; a sales region or salesman; or a warehouse or distribution unit.

(d) Shared costs (for example, rent, rates, electricity or gas bills) may require cost centres of their own, in order to be directly allocated. Shared cost items may be charged to separate, individual cost centres, or they may be grouped into a larger cost centre (for example, factory occupancy costs, for rents, rates, heating, lighting, building repairs, cleaning and maintenance of a particular factory).

Charging costs to a cost centre simply involves two steps.

- Identifying the cost centre for which an item of expenditure is a direct cost
- Allocating the cost to the cost centre (usually by means of a cost code)

Cost centres are always managed by someone and so they provide a basis for allocating responsibility for costs.

Once costs have been traced to cost centres, they can be further analysed in order to establish a cost per 'cost unit'. Alternatively, some items of cost may be charged directly to a cost unit, for example direct materials and direct labour costs.

4.2 Cost units

Definition

> A **cost unit** is 'a unit of product or service in relation to which costs are ascertained' (Chartered Institute of Management Accountants (CIMA), *Official Terminology*).

The unit selected must be appropriate to the business and one with which expenditure can be readily associated. For manufacturing or retail companies the cost unit is usually fairly obvious – a litre of paint for a paint manufacturer, a book for a publisher, a car for a car dealer. Care must be taken in non-manufacturing operations to ensure that the unit is a meaningful measure. For instance, in transport the cost per tonne transported may not be particularly useful. The cost per tonne carried from London to Glasgow would probably be greater than the cost per tonne from London to Dover, and it would not be easy to make comparisons for control purposes. If the cost unit was changed to a tonne-mile (the cost of transporting one tonne for one mile) then a comparison between the two journeys would be valid.

4.3 Cost per unit

Once direct costs have been measured for a cost unit, and indirect costs have been charged to a cost centre, the cost per unit can be computed.

EXAMPLE

Floggles & Co make plastic food storage boxes of various sizes in a factory made up of a moulding department and a finishing department. Each batch of 100 medium boxes uses 40kg plastic, which costs £0.60 per kg. Labour time for the moulding process for each batch is 1.5 hours, paid at a rate of £8.20 per hour. The hinges for the boxes, which cost £15 per packet of 50 pairs (one pair per box), are a patented design and royalties are payable at £0.10 per pair of hinges used in manufacture. Each batch takes 20 minutes to go through the finishing department, where labour is paid at a rate of £9.60 per hour .

Total factory indirect costs for the forthcoming period are expected to be £8,500, during which 200 batches of medium boxes are expected to be made. 60% of these are attributable to the moulding department, and 40% to the finishing department.

Task

Calculate the product cost of a batch of 100 medium boxes.

SOLUTION

Here the cost unit is a batch of 100 medium boxes. The cost of a batch can be built up as follows.

Direct costs			£
Material	plastic	*40kg × £0.60*	24.00
	hinges	*£15/50 × 100*	30.00
Labour	mouldings	*1.5 ×£8.20*	12.30
	finishing	*20/60 × £9.60*	3.20
Expenses	royalties	*100 × £0.10*	10.00
Prime cost			**79.50**
Indirect costs			
Factory	moulding	*£8,500 × 60%/200*	25.50
	finishing	*£8,500 × 40%/200*	17.00
Total production cost			**122.00**

Activity 6 (10 minutes)

It is 100 miles from A to B and 200 miles from C to D. It costs £400 for firm X to transport 10 tonnes from A to B and £720 for firm Y to transport 15 tonnes from C to D.

For each firm what is the cost per tonne and the cost per tonne-mile? Which firm would you use in future?

We have seen that a cost centre is where costs are collected. Some organisations, however, work on a profit centre basis.

4.4 Profit centres

Definition

A **profit centre** is accountable for costs and income. It may also be called a business centre, business unit or strategic business unit.

Cost centres only have costs attributed to them. Profit centres, on the other hand, also receive the income associated with those costs. For example, an organisation with two departments each making a different product will allocate the income from each product to the department where each product is made. This ensures that the organisation has some idea as to the relative profitability of each product.

Profit centre managers should normally have control over how income is raised and how costs are incurred. Not infrequently, several cost centres will comprise one profit centre.

A very important distinction in decision making is whether costs are fixed or variable. We encountered this concept briefly in Chapter 3. Here is some more detail.

5 FIXED COSTS AND VARIABLE COSTS

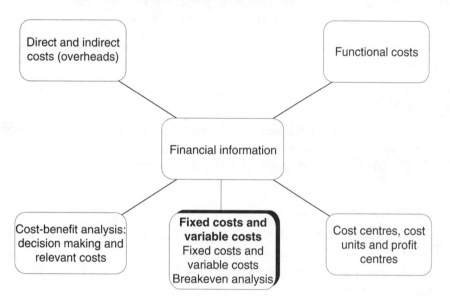

5.1 Fixed costs and variable costs

The distinction between fixed and variable costs lies in whether the amount of costs incurred will rise as the volume of activity increases, or whether the costs will remain the same, regardless of the volume of activity. Some examples are as follows.

(a) Direct material costs will rise as more units of a product are manufactured, and so they are variable costs that vary with the volume of production.

(b) Sales commission is often a fixed percentage of sales turnover, and so is a variable cost that varies with the level of sales (but not with the level of production).

(c) Telephone call charges are likely to increase if the volume of business expands, and so they are a variable overhead cost, varying with the volume of production and sales.

(d) The rental cost of business premises is a constant amount, at least within a stated time period, and so it is a fixed cost that does not vary with the level of activity conducted on the premises.

Costs can be classified as direct costs or overheads, or as fixed or variable costs. These alternative classifications are not mutually exclusive, but are complementary to each other, so that we can identify some direct costs that are fixed costs (although they are commonly variable costs) and some overhead costs that are fixed and others that are variable.

Definitions

Variable cost is that part of cost which varies with the volume of production (or level of activity).

Fixed cost is that part of cost which does not vary with the level of activity or volume of production.

Semi-variable (or semi-fixed or mixed) costs are partly variable and partly fixed.

| Activity 7 | (15 minutes) |

(a) Damien has a mobile telephone. The monthly charge is £20. Calls cost 5p per unit at all times unless more than 500 units are used in a month in which case calls cost 4p per unit. What is the annual cost if Damien uses:

(i) 250 units per month?
(ii) 600 units per month?

(b) One month Damien uses 405 units, and the next month 502. What will he find when he gets his mobile phone bill?

You have probably heard about businesses trying to 'break even' but do you really know what this means? Cost analysis is crucial to this important concept.

5.2 Breakeven analysis

The distinction between fixed costs and variable costs is very important to decision-making. This can best be illustrated by an example.

EXAMPLE

Suppose X Ltd makes a single product whose total variable costs per unit are £10. Fixed costs of the business per year are £6,000. The product can be sold for £15.

How can X Ltd decide what is the minimum number of units it will make per year?

Solution

X Ltd needs to make at least enough units to cover the £6,000 of fixed costs.

	£
Selling price per unit	15
Variable costs per unit	10
Contribution to fixed costs	5

X Ltd therefore needs to make at least £6,000/£5 = 1,200 units. At this level of production the company will break even: in other words it will not make a loss, although it will not make a profit either.

	£
Sales (1,200 × £15)	18,000
Variable costs (1,200 × £10)	(12,000)
Contribution	6,000
Fixed costs	(6,000)
Profit/loss	0

Activity 8 **(10 minutes)**

In Year 2 X Ltd is asked to pay its £6,000 of fixed costs in advance. Also, because of a slump in the market, there is no possibility of selling more than 1,000 units in Year 2. The managing director of X Ltd says, gloomily 'Well, if we're not even going to break even we may as well close down now'.

Comment on this scenario.

Definition

Contribution (or contribution to fixed costs) is the difference between an item's selling price and its variable costs. In decision making contribution is more important than 'profit', which is sales minus all costs, because some costs have to be paid no matter what decisions are taken.

6 COST-BENEFIT ANALYSIS: DECISION MAKING AND RELEVANT COSTS

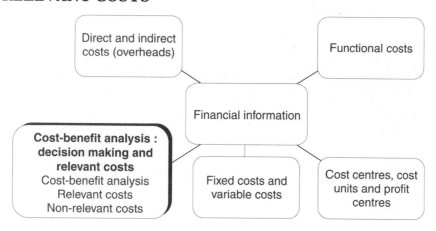

6.1 Cost-benefit analysis

Cost-benefit analysis is a very simple concept that everybody uses all the time. For example, if you were asked to work outside of normal working hours for an extra £1 an hour but this meant that your train ticket would cost an extra £2 it would only be worth doing so if you worked more than two hours.

	£
Cost	2
Benefit from, say, three hours overtime	3
Net benefit	1

This is the basis of all decision-making. If the benefits of doing something are greater than the costs of doing it the decision is to go ahead and do it. If the costs outweigh the benefits the opposite decision is made.

Though it is simple in theory, there are three major problems.

  (a) It is often very difficult to identify the costs that are relevant to a decision.

  (b) Some costs cannot be expressed in money terms. For example if you were already very tired, you could only work overtime at the 'cost' of getting more tired, but what is this cost?

  (c) Benefits can also be very hard to quantify. A benefit of working overtime might be the satisfaction of getting the job done, but what is this worth?

Unfortunately there are no definitive answers to the questions in (b) and (c). Factors that cannot be quantified in financial terms are very often the ones that most heavily influence the final decision, both in personal life and in business.

However, this does not alter the fact that financial information should be collected, analysed and used in any decision. In our example it shows us that if we do decide to work overtime, then we should work more than two hours overtime, and this is very helpful to know.

We shall concentrate on problem (a): identifying the costs that are relevant to a decision.

6.2 Relevant costs

The costs which should be used for decision making are often referred to as **relevant costs**.

Definition

A relevant cost is a future cash flow arising as a direct consequence of a decision.

(a) *Relevant costs* are **future** costs.

  (i) A decision is about the future; it cannot alter what has been done already. A cost that has been incurred in the past is totally irrelevant to any decision that is being made 'now'.

  (ii) Costs that have been incurred include not only costs that have already been paid, but also costs that are the subject of legally binding contracts, even if payments due under the contract have not yet been made. (These are known as committed costs.)

(b) Relevant costs are **cash flows**. This means that costs or charges which do not reflect additional cash spending should be ignored for the purpose of decision making. Depreciation is the main example. If you buy a car for £10,000 you might reflect depreciation by deducting £2,500 per annum from your profits for the next four years. But this £2,500 is only a cost on paper. The real cost was the £10,000 that vanished from your bank account on day 1.

(c) A relevant cost is one which **arises as a direct consequence of a decision**. Thus, only costs which will differ under some or all of the available opportunities should be considered; relevant costs are therefore sometimes referred to as *incremental costs* or *differential costs*. For example, if an employee is expected to have no other work to do during the next week, but will be paid his basic wage (of, say, £100 per week) for attending work and doing nothing, his manager might decide to give him a job which earns only £40 profit. The net gain is £40 and the £100 is irrelevant to the decision because although it is a future cash flow, it will be incurred anyway whether the employee is given work or not.

Relevant costs are therefore **future**, **incremental cash** flows. Relevant costs may also be expressed as *opportunity costs* (the benefit forgone by choosing one opportunity instead of the next best alternative). We met this concept in an earlier chapter.

6.3 Non-relevant costs

A number of terms are used to describe costs that are *irrelevant* for decision-making because they are either not future cash flows or they are costs which will be incurred anyway, regardless of the decision that is taken.

Sunk costs

A **sunk cost** is used to describe the cost of an asset which has already been acquired and which can continue to serve its present purpose, but which has no significant realisable value and no income value from any other alternative purpose.

Suppose, for example, a company purchased an item of computer equipment two years ago for £20,000. It has been depreciated down to £7,000 already, but in fact it already has no resale value because of developments in computer technology. The equipment can be used for its existing purpose for at least another year, but the company is considering whether or not to purchase more modern equipment with additional facilities and so scrap the existing equipment now.

In terms of decision making and relevant costs the existing equipment, which initially cost £20,000 but now has a value on paper of £7,000, is a sunk cost. The money has been spent and the asset has no alternative use. 'Writing off' the asset and incurring a 'paper' loss on disposal of £7,000 would be irrelevant to the decision under consideration.

Committed costs

A **committed cost** is a future cash outflow that will be incurred anyway, whatever decision is taken now about alternative opportunities. Committed costs may exist because of contracts already entered into by the organisation, which it cannot get out of.

Notional costs

A **notional cost** or **imputed cost** is a hypothetical accounting cost to reflect something for which no actual cash expense is incurred. Examples common in accounting systems include the following.

(a) Notional rent, such as that charged to the profit centres of an organisation for the use of accommodation which the organisation owns.

(b) Notional interest charges on capital, sometimes made against a profit centre or cost centre.

Fixed and variable costs

Generally you can assume the following.

- **Variable costs** will be relevant costs.
- **Fixed costs** are irrelevant to a decision.

This need not be the case, however, and you should analyse variable and fixed cost data carefully. Do not forget that 'fixed' costs may only be fixed in the short term.

Direct and indirect costs

Direct and indirect costs may be relevant or non-relevant, depending on the situation in question. Direct labour, for example, may be paid regardless of whether or not a particular product is manufactured. On the other hand, additional direct labour may be required and the cost of this would be a relevant cost.

The best way to understand relevant costs is to look at numerical examples. The example that follows includes most of the ideas we have encountered in this section. Study it carefully.

EXAMPLE: COSTS FOR DECISION MAKING

O'Reilly Ltd has been approached by a customer who would like a special job to be done for him, and who is willing to pay £22,000 for it. The job would require the following materials.

Material	Total units required	Units already in stock	Book value of units in stock £/unit	Sales value £/unit	Replacement cost £/unit
A	1,000	0	-	-	6
B	1,000	600	2	2.50	5
C	1,000	700	3	2.50	4
D	200	200	4	6.00	9

(a) Material B is used regularly by O'Reilly Ltd, and if units of B are required for this job, they would need to be replaced to meet other production demand.

(b) Materials C and D are in stock as the result of previous over-buying, and they have a restricted use. No other use could be found for material C, but the units of material D could be used in another job as substitute for 300 units of material E, which currently costs £5 per unit (of which the company has no units in stock at the moment).

(c) Book value is the cost of the stock as recorded in the company's accounting system.

(d) Sales value is the amount the stock would fetch if it had to be sold unused.

Calculate the relevant costs of material for deciding whether or not to accept the contract.

SOLUTION

(a) *Material A* is not yet owned. It would have to be bought in full at the cost of £6 per unit.

(b) *Material B* is used regularly by the company. There are existing stocks (600 units) but if these are used on the contract under review a further 600 units would have to be bought to replace them. Relevant costs are therefore 1,000 units at the replacement cost of £5 per unit.

(c) 1,000 units of *Material C* are needed and 700 are already in stock. If used for the contract, a further 300 units must be bought at £4 each. The existing stocks of 700 will not be replaced. However, if they are used for the contract, they could not be sold at £2.50 each. The realisable value of these 700 units is an opportunity cost of sales revenue forgone.

(d) The required units of *Material D* are already in stock and will not be replaced. There is an opportunity cost of using D in the contract because there are alternative opportunities either to sell the existing stocks for £6 per unit (£1,200 in total) or avoid other purchases (of *Material E*), which would cost 300 × £5 = £1,500. Since substitution for E is more beneficial, £1,500 is the opportunity cost.

(e)   Summary of relevant costs

	£
Material A (1,000 × £6)	6,000
Material B (1,000 × £5)	5,000
Material C (300 × £4) plus (700 × £2.50)	2,950
Material D	1,500
Total	15,450

(f)   The benefit to be obtained if the contract is accepted is £22,000. This is greater than the materials costs so the job should be taken on. (Note: for clarity, costs of the contract other than materials costs have been ignored.)

FOR DISCUSSION

What non-financial costs and benefits might O'Reilly Ltd also take into consideration when coming to a decision about the job?

Chapter roundup

- Financial information is essential for the management of a business. Most of it is derived from the business's accounting system and its analysis of costs.

- One way of classifying costs is according to function – production, administration, marketing and so on.

- Another classification distinguishes between direct costs and overheads. The idea of direct cost is particularly relevant to manufacturing businesses.

- Responsibility for costs is allocated by charging costs to cost centres and profit centres.

- In decision making the distinction between fixed costs and variable costs becomes very important. Contribution (to fixed costs) is the difference between selling price and variable cost.

- Cost-benefit analysis is simple in theory but difficult in practice because it is hard to identify relevant costs and because other considerations beside money have to be taken into account.

Quick quiz

1   Why is financial information important?

2   What is a production cost and a distribution cost?

3   What are the components of total direct cost?

4   Give two examples of administration overheads.

5   What is a cost centre? What would be the biggest cost centre of a mail order catalogue operation?

6   What is the difference between a cost centre and a profit centre?

7   What is the distinction between fixed costs and variable costs?

8   What is contribution?

9   Why is cost-benefit analysis difficult in practice?

10 Why are some costs irrelevant for decision making?

11 If a company accepts a contract it will have to pay a fixed rent of £500 a year for extra office space for the next five years. Is this relevant to the decision as to whether or not to accept the contract?

12 How would you categorise a telephone bill?

Answers to quick quiz

1   It allows the resources of the business to be managed; it must be collected, by law; HM Revenue and Customs requires the information. (See section 1.2)

2   Production costs are incurred in the sequence of operations from supply of raw materials to the completion of a finished goods product. Distribution costs are incurred any time between warehousing finished goods and delivery to customers. (See section 2.1)

3   Total direct costs are made up of direct material and labour costs and direct expenses. (See section 3.1)

4   Administration overheads, which are part of indirect costs, may include: depreciation of office fixtures and fittings, salaries of administrative staff and the rent and rates of offices. (See section 3.2)

5   A cost centre, which may be a location, an activity, a person or an item of equipment, is a collecting place for certain costs before they are analysed further. The biggest cost centres for a mail order catalogue would be the call centre and the warehouse. (See section 4.2)

6   A profit centre does not only collect costs, it collects income as well, and is generally expected to generate more income than costs – ie a profit. (See sections 4.2 and 4.3)

7   Fixed costs generally remain the same, whatever the level of activity, while variable costs fluctuate according to the level of activity. (See section 5.1)

8   Contribution is the amount a sold unit contributes towards covering the enterprise's fixed costs; it is the difference between the selling price and the variable cost of production. (See section 5.2)

9   In cost-benefit analysis, it can be difficult to: identify relevant costs to a decision; express some costs in money terms; quantify benefits. (See section 6.1)

10 Costs are irrelevant to decision-making when they are not future cash flows and/or the decision to be made does not affect whether the costs will be incurred or not. (See section 6.3)

11 Yes; in this case the rental expense arises directly from the decision to accept the contract.

12 It is a semi-variable cost. The rental part is a fixed cost, but the calls element will fluctuate (although not necessarily in accordance with changes in production or sales levels).

Answers to activities

1   This activity is intended to make you realise that things you do at work have financial implications, even if you personally are not aware of the precise figures involved.

2   (a) Production cost: steel, rubber, assembly line wages

Administration cost: personnel department salaries, photo-copying, office stationery

Marketing, selling, distribution: sales reps' salaries, advertising, car transporting costs.

There are, of course, lots of other possibilities.

(b) The problem is in defining exactly what the service consists of: banking, for example, is actually a collection of several different services. Supplying cash is one such service and cash machine running costs are associated with this. Keeping a record of transactions is another service and there would be associated computer and computer operator costs. The answer is a bit easier if you choose a service like a local bus service or a solicitor.

3
Direct	Hrs	Indirect	Hrs
Client A	0.5	Post	0.5
Client B	1.5	Study	2.0
Letter-writing (?)	1.5	Meeting	1.0
	3.5		3.5

Writing letters can probably be charged to individual clients, unless they were all concerned with the general administration of the practice.

4   The cost would be negligible (far less than 1p) and it would cost far more than this (in terms of time spent on record keeping and calculation) to keep track of the cost.

5   Items (a) and (b) are direct labour costs of the items produced in the 42 hours worked in week 5.

Overtime premium, item (c), is usually regarded as an overhead expense, because it is 'unfair' to charge the items produced in overtime hours with the premium. Why should an item made in overtime be more costly just because, by chance, it was made after the employee normally clocks off for the day?

Group bonus scheme payments (d) are usually overhead costs, because they cannot normally be traced directly to individual products or jobs.

In this example, the direct labour employee costs were £168 in direct costs and £36 in indirect costs, and these costs would be coded differently, to allocate them to different cost units or overhead cost centres.

6
	Firm X		*Firm Y*	
Cost per tonne	(400/10)	£40	(720/15)	£48
Cost per tonne-mile	(£40/100)	£0.40	(£48/200)	£0.24

On a cost per tonne-mile basis, Firm Y could have transported 10 tonnes from A to B for 100 × 10 × £0.24 = £240. This is cheaper than Firm X's cost so Firm Y should be used in future.

7
				£
(a)	(i)	Fixed cost (12 × £20)		240
		Variable cost (12 × 250 × £0.05)		150
				390
	(ii)	Fixed cost, as before		240
		Variable cost (12 × 600 × £0.04)		288
				528

(b)   405 × £0.05 = £20.25
      502 × £0.04 = £20.08.

Damien got 97 extra units in month 2 and paid 17p less. Note that fixed costs are not relevant to this calculation: they are the same in both cases.

8   If the company closes down now it will make a loss of £6,000. If it makes as many units as it can sell it will recover 1,000 × £5 = £5,000 as a 'contribution' to fixed costs, so the overall loss will be only £1,000. In the short term, therefore, it is worth continuing in business to minimise the loss.

In the long term (beyond Year 2) it is not worth incurring any more fixed costs unless the market picks up and there is a possibility of at least breaking even.

Chapter 8:
BUDGETS

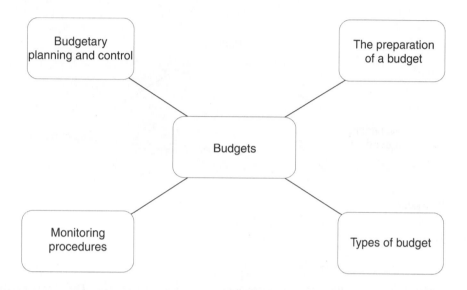

Introduction

You have heard of *the* Budget. To you it may just be an annual event when the Government makes slight changes to the amount of pay you can expect to take home. From the point of view of the Government, however, the Budget is its financial plan for the next year – how much income it expects to have (from taxes) and what it intends to spend that money on (public services and government administration).

A budget in business is a financial plan in exactly the same way. Budgets encourage forward thinking and help managers to understand how their activities must fit in with activities of other operations. Budgets also act as a yardstick against which managers can compare their actual performance.

Your objectives

In this chapter you will learn about the following.

- What a budget is and what it is for
- Methods of budget preparation
- How to prepare simple budgets
- The value of monitoring actual results against budgets
- How to prepare simple flexible budgets and calculate variances

1   BUDGETARY PLANNING AND CONTROL

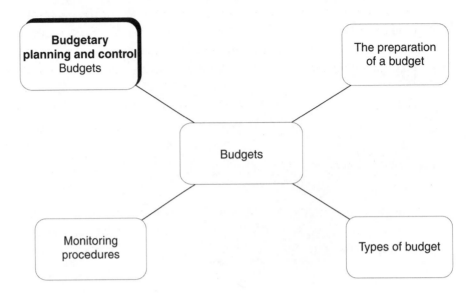

1.1   Budgets

Definition

A **budget** is basically a plan expressed in monetary terms. The plan covers income, expenditure and capital investment (buying fixed assets).

Budgets are an important source of information because they provide a system for ensuring communication, co-ordination and control within an organisation.

The objectives of a budgetary planning and control system are as follows.

(a) *To ensure the achievement of the organisation's objectives*

Objectives for the organisation as a whole, and for individual departments and operations within the organisation, are set. Quantified expressions of these objectives are then drawn up as targets to be achieved within the timescale of the budget plan.

(b) *To compel planning and decision making*

This is probably the most important feature of a budgetary planning and control system. Planning forces management to look ahead, to make decisions, to set out detailed plans for achieving the targets for each department, operation and (ideally) each manager, to anticipate problems and give the organisation purpose and direction. It thus prevents management from relying on spur of the moment or unco-ordinated planning which may be detrimental to the performance of the organisation.

(c) *To communicate ideas and plans*

A formal system is necessary to ensure that each person affected by the plans is aware of what he or she is supposed to be doing. Communication might be one-way, with managers giving orders to subordinates, or there might be a two-way dialogue and exchange of ideas.

(d) *To co-ordinate activities*

The activities of different departments or sub-units of the organisation need to be co-ordinated to ensure maximum integration of effort towards common goals. This concept of co-ordination implies, for example, that the purchasing department should base its budget on production requirements and that the production budget should in turn be based on sales expectations. Although straightforward in concept, co-ordination is remarkably difficult to achieve, and there is often conflict between departmental plans in the budget with the result that the efforts of the various departments are not fully integrated into a combined plan to achieve the company's optimum targets.

(e) *To provide a framework for responsibility*

Budgetary planning and control systems require that managers of cost and profit centres are made responsible for the achievement of budget targets for the operations under their personal control.

(f) *To establish a system of monitoring and control*

A budget is basically a yardstick against which actual performance is measured and assessed. Control over actual performance is provided by the comparisons of actual results against the budget plan. Departures from budget can then be investigated and the reasons for the departures can be divided into controllable and non-controllable factors.

(g) *To motivate employees to improve their performance*

Via a system of feedback of actual results, which lets them know how well or badly they are performing, the interest and commitment of employees can be retained. The identification of controllable reasons for departures from budget gives the managers responsible an incentive for improved future performance.

Two levels of attainment can be set.
(i)   A minimum expectations budget
(ii) A desired standards budget which provides some sort of challenge to employees

Despite the simple definition of a budget, its preparation and subsequent use provide the base for a system which should have far reaching implications for the organisation concerned.

FOR DISCUSSION

Does the organisation you work for prepare budgets? If so, do you see them and understand them? Do you see a budget for the whole organisation or just for your department? HND students should consider whether budgeting is appropriate for a college.

Budgets can be presented and used in many different ways so it is worth sharing your personal experiences with your colleagues on this course.

Having seen why organisations prepare budgets, we will now turn our attention to the mechanics of budget preparation. Even if you are not personally involved in the preparation process you may well have to work to a budget, so it is helpful to know how the figures might have been calculated. We will consider a typical budget preparation timetable in the next section. In the following section we will go on to consider the actual preparation of various budgets.

2 THE PREPARATION OF A BUDGET

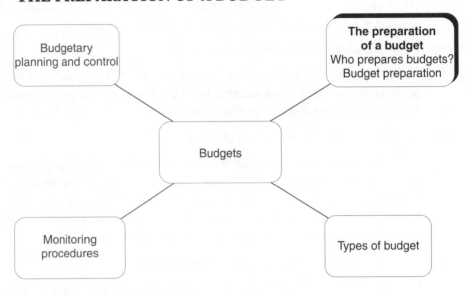

2.1 Who prepares budgets?

Managers responsible for preparing budgets should ideally be the managers whose sections are responsible for carrying out the budget, selling goods and authorising expenditure.

(a) The sales manager should draft the sales budget and selling overhead cost centre budgets.

(b) The purchasing manager should draft the material purchases budget.

(c) The production manager should draft the direct production cost budgets.

(d) Various cost centre managers should prepare the individual production, administration and distribution cost centre budgets for their own cost centre.

Definitions

The **budget period** is the time period to which the budget relates. Except for capital expenditure budgets, the budget period is commonly the accounting year (sub-divided into 12 or 13 control periods).

The co-ordination and administration of budgets is usually the responsibility of a **budget committee** (with the managing director as chairman). The budget committee is serviced by a *budget officer* who is usually an accountant. Every part of the organisation should be represented on the committee, so there should be a representative from sales, production, marketing and so on.

Let us now look at the steps involved in the preparation of a budget. The procedures will differ from organisation to organisation, but the step-by-step approach described in this chapter is indicative of the steps followed by many organisations.

2.2 Budget preparation

The annual budget is part of a longer term plan, perhaps covering five or 10 years. The longer-term plan would include a capital budget (a fixed assets purchase budget). The company may be aiming at the purchase of, say, a second factory in three years' time thus enabling the business to double its production. A key aim of the current year's budget would be to generate some of the cash needed to purchase this factory. A key feature of the budget in three years' time would be the doubling of sales when the new factory started to give results.

Less major fixed asset purchases, such as new tools, or a few new desks and chairs, are often budgeted for by means of a set annual 'allowance' for fixed assets purchase and replacement.

Step 1: *Identification of the principal budget factor*

The first task in the budgetary process is to identify the principal budget factor. This is also known as the key budget factor or limiting budget factor and it is what limits an organisation's activities.

The principal budget factor is usually sales demand: a company is usually restricted from making and selling more of its products because there would be no sales demand for the increased output at a price which would be acceptable/profitable to the company.

However the principal budget factor may alternatively be current machine capacity, distribution and selling resources, the availability of key raw materials or the availability of cash.

Once this factor is defined then the rest of the budget can be prepared. For example, if sales are the principal budget factor then the production manager can only prepare his budget after the sales budget is complete.

Step 2: *Preparation of a sales budget*

This is prepared in units of each product and also in sales value.

Step 3: *Preparation of a finished goods stock budget*

This budget decides the planned increase or decrease in finished stock levels.

Step 4: *Preparation of a production budget*

The production budget is stated in units of each product and is calculated as the sales budget in units plus or minus the budgeted change in finished goods stocks. (Goods may be produced for stock or sold out of stock and therefore planned production and sales volumes are not necessarily the same amount.)

Step 5: *Preparation of budgets of resources for production*

  (a) *Materials usage budget.* This budget is prepared for all types of materials, direct and indirect, and is stated in quantities and perhaps cost for each type of material used. It should take into account budgeted losses in production and desired levels of raw materials stocks.

  (b) *Machine utilisation budget.* This shows the operating hours required on each machine or group of machines.

  (c) *Labour budget* or *wages budget* or *personnel budget.* This budget is prepared for all grades of labour, direct and indirect. For hourly paid staff, the budget will be expressed in hours for each grade of labour and in terms of cost. It should take into account budgeted 'idle time' (when work is not possible, for example because machines have to 'warm up') and expected wage rates.

Step 6: *Preparation of overhead cost budgets*

During the preparation of the sales and production budgets, the managers of the cost centres of the organisation will prepare their draft budgets for the (department) overhead costs. There will be cost centres for each type of overhead.

  (a) *Production overheads* (for example, repairs and maintenance, stores, production control, factory supervision and so on)

  (b) *Administration overheads* (for example, budgeted costs of the accounting department, personnel department, computer department, corporate planning and so on)

  (c) *Selling and distribution overheads*, or marketing overheads (for example, budgeted costs for advertising and sales promotion, perhaps for each product group, budgeted costs of the sales force, distribution cost budgets and so on)

  (d) *Research and development department overheads*, costs incurred in product design and early market testing

Step 7: *Co-ordination and review of budgets*

Remember that it is unlikely that the above steps will be problem-free. The budgets must be reviewed in relation to one another. Such a review may indicate that some budgets are out of balance with others and need modifying so that they will be compatible with other conditions, constraints and plans. The accountant must identify such inconsistencies and bring them to the attention of the manager concerned. The revision of one budget may lead to the revision of all budgets. This process must continue until the budgeted profit and loss account, balance sheet and cash budget are acceptable.

Step 8: *Preparation of a master budget*

When all the budgets are in harmony with one another they are summarised into a master budget consisting of a budgeted profit and loss account, a balance sheet and cash budget.

Cash budgets were covered in Chapter 4. Profit and loss accounts and balance sheets were covered in Chapter 5. In the next section we consider sales budgets, production budgets and overhead budgets in a little more detail.

Activity 1   **(15 minutes)**

In pairs, see if you can define or explain the following terms without reference to the text or glossary.

(a) Raw materials
(b) Finished goods
(c) Distribution
(d) Overhead
(e) Budget
(f) Idle time
(g) Cost centre
(h) Resource

Activity 2   **(15 minutes)**

A company that manufactures and sells a range of products, with sales potential limited by market share, is considering introducing a system of budgeting.

Task

(a) List (in order of preparation) the various budgets that need to be prepared.

(b) Consider how the work can be co-ordinated in order for the budgeting process to be successful.

---

3   TYPES OF BUDGET

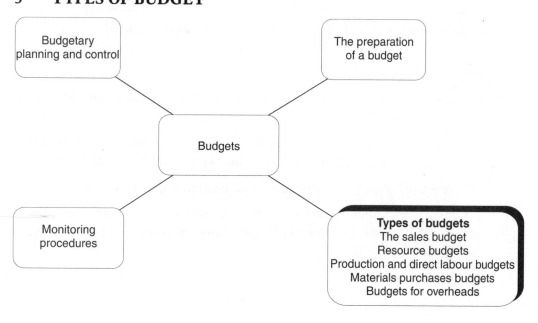

3.1 The sales budget

We have already established that, for many organisations, the principal budget factor is sales volume. The sales budget is therefore often the primary budget from which the majority of the other budgets are derived.

Before the sales budget can be prepared a sales forecast has to be made. A forecast is an estimate of what is likely to occur in the future. The forecast becomes the budget once management have accepted it as the objective or target. Sales forecasting is complex and difficult and involves the consideration of a number of factors.

(a) Past sales patterns
(b) The economic environment
(c) Results of market research
(d) Anticipated advertising during the budget period
(e) Competition
(f) Changing consumer taste
(g) New legislation
(h) Distribution and quality of sales outlets and personnel

On the basis of the sales forecast and the production capacity of the organisation, a sales budget will be prepared. This may be subdivided, possible subdivisions being by product, by sales area, by management responsibility and so on.

Here is an example.

	Units ('000)		Revenue (£'000)	
	North	*South*	*North*	*South*
Product X	2,000	3,200	1,500	2,400
Product Y	1,300	2,500	975	1,875

Activity 3 **(15 minutes)**

Interpret the sales budget shown above. What else could it show to make the information more useful?

Once the sales budget has been agreed, resource budgets can be prepared.

3.2 Resource budgets

If the principal budget factor was production capacity then the production budget would be the first to be prepared.

To assess whether production is the principal budget factor, the production capacity available must be determined. This should take into account the following factors.

(a) Available labour, including idle time, overtime and standard output rates per hour

(b) Availability of raw materials including allowances for losses during production

(c) Maximum machine hours available, including expected idle time and expected output rates per machine hour

The production budget will show the quantities and costs for each product and product group and will tie in with the sales and stock budgets. This co-ordinating process is likely to show any shortfalls or excesses in capacity at various times over the budget period. If there is likely to be a shortfall then decisions need to be made about overtime, subcontracting, machine hire, new sources of raw materials or some other way of increasing output. A significant shortfall means that production capacity is, in fact, the limiting factor.

Once the production budget has been finalised, the labour, materials and machine budgets can be drawn up. These budgets will be based on budgeted activity levels, existing stock positions and projected labour and material costs. We shall look at two examples.

3.3 Production and direct labour budgets

EXAMPLE: PRODUCTION BUDGETS

Landslide Ltd manufactures two products, A and B, and is preparing its budget for 20X7. Both products are made by the same grade of labour, grade Q. The company currently holds 800 units of A and 1,200 units of B in stock, but 250 of these units of B have just been discovered to have deteriorated in quality, and must therefore be scrapped. Budgeted sales of A are 3,000 units and of B are 4,000 units, provided that the company maintains finished goods stocks at a level equal to 3 months' sales.

Grade Q labour was originally expected to produce 1 unit of A in two hours and 1 unit of B in three hours, at an hourly rate of £5.50 per hour. In discussions with trade union negotiators, however, it has been agreed that the hourly wage rate should be raised by 50p per hour, provided that the times to produce A and B are reduced by 20%.

Task

Prepare the production budget and direct labour budget for 20X7. (You might like to cover up the solution and try this as an activity.)

SOLUTION

The expected time to produce a unit of A will now be 80% × 2 hours = 1.6 hours, and the time for a unit of B will be 2.4 hours. The hourly wage rate will be £6.

(a) *Production budget*

	Product A				Product B	
	Units	*Units*			*Units*	*Units*
Budgeted sales		3,000				4,000
Closing stocks (3/12 of 3,000)	750		(3/12 of 4,000)	1,000		
Opening stocks						
(minus stocks scrapped)	800			950		
(Decrease)/increase in stocks		(50)				50
Production		2,950				4,050

(b)   *Direct labour budget*

	Grade Q Hours	Cost £
2,950 units of Product A	4,720	28,320
4,050 units of Product B	9,720	58,320
Total	14,440	86,640

3.4   Materials purchases budgets

EXAMPLE: MATERIALS PURCHASES BUDGET

Earthquake Ltd manufactures two products, S and T, which use the same raw materials, D and E. 1 unit of S uses 3 litres of D and 4 kilograms of E. 1 unit of T uses 5 litres of D and 2 kilograms of E. A litre of D is expected to cost £3 and a kilogram of E £7.

Budgeted sales for 20X6 are 8,000 units of S and 6,000 units of T; finished goods in stock at 1 January 20X6 are 1,500 units of S and 300 units of T, and the company plans to hold stocks of 600 units of each product at 31 December 20X6.

Stocks of raw material are 6,000 litres of D and 2,800 kilograms of E at 1 January, and the company plans to hold 5,000 litres and 3,500 kilograms respectively at 31 December 20X6.

The warehouse and stores managers have suggested that a provision should be made for damages and deterioration of items held in store, as follows.

Product S :	loss of 50 units
Product T :	loss of 100 units
Material D :	loss of 500 litres
Material E :	loss of 200 kilograms

Task

Prepare a material purchases budget for 20X6. (Again, try to work through this on your own before looking at the solution below.)

SOLUTION

To calculate material purchase requirements, it is first of all necessary to calculate the budgeted production volumes and material usage requirements

(a)   *Production budget*

	Product S Units	Units	Product T Units	Units
Sales		8,000		6,000
Provision for losses		50		100
Closing stock	600		600	
Opening stock	1,500		300	
(Decrease)/increase in stock		(900)		300
Production budget		7,150		6,400

	Material D		Material E	
	Litres	Litres	Kg	Kg
Usage requirements				
To produce 7,150 units of S		21,450		28,600
To produce 6,400 units of T		32,000		12,800
Usage budget		53,450		41,400
Provision for losses		500		200
		53,950		41,600
Closing stock	5,000		3,500	
Opening stock	(6,000)		(2,800)	
(Decrease)/increase in stock		(1,000)		700
Materials purchases budget		52,950		42,300
Cost per unit		£3 per litre		£7 per kg
Cost of material purchases		£158,850		£296,100
Total purchases cost			£454,950	

Activity 4 (45 minutes)

JK Limited has recently completed its sales forecasts for the year to 31 December 20X6. It expects to sell two products J and K at prices of £135 and £145 each respectively.

Sales demand is expected to be as follows.

J   10,000 units
K   6,000 units

Both products use the same raw materials and skilled labour but in different quantities per unit.

	J	K
Material X	10 kgs	6 kgs
Material Y	4 kgs	8 kgs
Skilled labour	6 hours	4 hours

The prices expected during 20X6 for the raw materials are as follows.

Material X   £1.50 per kg
Material Y   £4.00 per kg

The skilled labour rate is expected to be £6.00 per hour.

Stocks of raw materials and finished goods on 1 January 20X6 are expected to be as follows.

Material X   400 kgs   @ £1.20 per kg
Material Y   200 kgs   @ £3.00 per kg

J   600 units   @ £70.00 each
K   800 units   @ £60.00 each

All stocks are to be reduced by 15% from their opening levels by the end of 20X6 and are valued using the FIFO method.

The company uses absorption costing, and production overhead costs are expected to be as follows.

Variable   £2.00 per skilled labour hour
Fixed   £315,900 per annum

> **Task**
>
> Prepare for the year to 31 December 20X6 the following budgets for JK Limited.
>
> (a) Production budget (in units)
> (b) Raw material purchases budget (in units and £)
> (c) Production cost budget

Finally we shall give some thought to overhead budgets. If you work for a service company, or in a service department, most of the costs connected with your work are probably overheads.

3.5 Budgets for overheads

Until fairly recently budgeting for overheads was relatively unsophisticated compared with budgeting for direct costs. Typically the figure in the budget for an overhead would simply be last year's figure plus a percentage for inflation. However, noticing a trend for overheads to form a larger and larger proportion of an organisation's total costs (mainly because of technology), academics developed a technique called Activity Based Costing (ABC).

The basic idea of ABC is simple: costs are analysed according to what causes them to be incurred. For example the costs of an accounting department are caused by things like the number of customers, the number of suppliers and the number of transactions. Once this is realised overhead budgeting can be far more scientific. For example, if sales are budgeted to increase by 5%, rather than just increasing accounting department costs by 5% it ought to be possible to predict the impact of the extra sales in terms of number of new debtors and number of new transactions. Maybe the plan is simply to sell larger quantities per existing transaction to existing customers, in which case there will be no impact on accounting costs at all.

> **Activity 5**   **(20 minutes)**
>
> Activity based costing analysis has determined that at Z Ltd it costs 14p to process a transaction and £50 per year to administer a debtors account.
>
> Z Ltd have 7,442 credit customers. The total number of transactions with customers was 447,892.
>
> Next year it is expected that 250 new credit customers will buy from Z Ltd and around 30 existing customers will be lost. Transactions are expected to be up to 470,000.
>
> What are the budgeted costs of the accounting department:
>
> (a) If last year's costs are increased by 5%?
>
> (b) If activity based costing is used to make the forecast?

The budgeting process does not stop once the budgets have been agreed. Actual results should be compared on a regular basis with the budgeted results. The frequency with which such comparisons are made depends very much on the organisation's circumstances and the sophistication of its control systems but it should occur at least monthly. Management should receive a report detailing the differences and should investigate the reasons for the differences. If the differences are within the control of management, corrective action should be taken to bring the reasons for the difference under control and to ensure that such inefficiencies do not occur in the future.

The next section describes the techniques that can be used to monitor actual performance by means of budgets.

4 MONITORING PROCEDURES

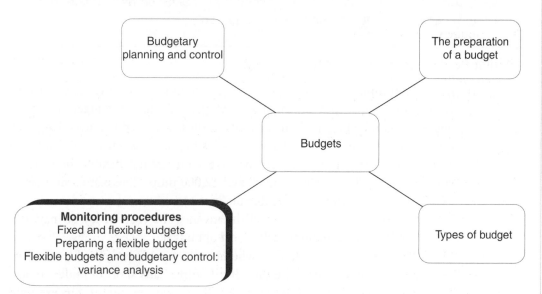

4.1 Fixed and flexible budgets

The master budget prepared before the beginning of the budget period is known as the fixed budget. By the term 'fixed', we do not mean that the budget is kept unchanged. Revisions to a fixed master budget will be made if the situation so demands.

Definitions

> The term **'fixed budget'** means the following.
>
> (a) The budget is prepared on the basis of an estimated volume of production and an estimated volume of sales, but no plans are made for the event that actual volumes of production and sales may differ from budgeted volumes.
>
> (b) When actual volumes of production and sales during a control period (month or four weeks) are achieved, a fixed budget is not adjusted (in retrospect) to the new levels of activity.
>
> A **flexible budget** recognises the existence of fixed, variable and mixed (semi-fixed, semi-variable) costs, and it is designed to change so as to relate to the actual volumes of production and sales in a period.

Flexible budgets may be used in one of two ways.

(a) **At the planning stage.** For example, suppose that a company expects to sell 10,000 units of output during the next year. A master budget (the fixed budget) would be prepared on the basis of these expected volumes. However, if the company thinks that output and sales might be as low as 8,000 units or as high as 12,000 units, it may prepare contingency flexible budgets, at volumes of, say 8,000, 9,000, 11,000 and 12,000 units. There are a number of advantages of planning with flexible budgets.

    (i) It is possible to find out well in advance the costs of lay-off pay, idle time and so on if output falls short of budget.

    (ii) Management can decide whether it would be possible to find alternative uses for spare capacity if output falls short of budget (could employees be asked to overhaul their own machines for example, instead of paying for an outside contractor?).

    (iii) An estimation of the costs of overtime, subcontracting work or extra machine hire if sales volume exceeds the fixed budget estimate can be made and it can be established whether there is a limiting factor which would prevent high volumes of output and sales being achieved.

(b) **Retrospectively.** At the end of each month (control period) or year, flexible budgets can be used to compare actual results achieved with what results should have been under the circumstances. Flexible budgets are an essential factor in budgetary control.

    (i) Management needs to be informed about how good or bad actual performance has been. To provide a measure of performance, there must be a yardstick against which actual performance can be measured.

    (ii) Every business is dynamic, and actual volumes of output cannot be expected to conform exactly to the fixed budget. Comparing actual costs directly with the fixed budget costs is meaningless.

    (iii) For useful control information, it is necessary to compare actual results at the actual level of activity achieved against the results that should have been achieved at this level of activity. These are shown by the flexible budget.

Let's look at an example of a simple flexible budget.

4.2 Preparing a flexible budget

EXAMPLE

Suppose that Lodestone Ltd expects production and sales during the next year to be 90% of the company's output capacity, that is, 9,000 units of a single product. Historical records of cost show the following details

Units of output/sales	Cost of sales
9,800	£44,400
7,700	£38,100

The company's management is not certain that the estimate of sales is correct, and has asked for flexible budgets to be prepared at output and sales levels of 8,000 and 10,000 units. The sales price per unit has been fixed at £5.

Task

Prepare appropriate budgets.

SOLUTION

If we assume that within the range 8,000 to 10,000 units of sales, all costs are fixed, variable or mixed (in other words there are no stepped costs, material discounts, overtime premiums, bonus payments etc) the fixed and flexible budgets would be based on the estimate of fixed and variable cost.

	£
Total cost of 9,800 units	44,400
Total cost of 7,700 units	38,100
Variable cost of 2,100 units	6,300

The variable cost per unit is £6,300/2,100 = £3.

	£
Total cost of 9,800 units	44,400
Variable cost of 9,800 units (9,800 × £3)	29,400
Fixed costs (all levels of output and sales)	15,000

The fixed budgets and flexible budgets might now be prepared as follows.

	Flexible budget 8,000 units £	Master budget 9,000 units £	Flexible budget 10,000 units £
Sales (× £5)	40,000	45,000	50,000
Variable costs (× £3)	(24,000)	(27,000)	(30,000)
Fixed costs	(15,000)	(15,000)	(15,000)
Profit	1,000	3,000	5,000

The above illustrates the use of flexible budgets at the planning stage. Let's now see how they can be used retrospectively for monitoring purposes.

4.3 Flexible budgets and budgetary control: variance analysis

The most important method of budgetary control is variance analysis, which in this context involves the comparison of actual results achieved during a control period (a month, or 4 weeks) with a flexible budget. The differences between actual results and expected results are called **variances** and these are used to provide a guideline for control action by individual managers.

Definition

> **Budgetary control** is the practice of establishing budgets which identify areas of responsibility for individual managers (for example production managers, purchasing managers and so on) and of regularly comparing actual results against expected results, the differences being **variances**.

Note that individual managers are held responsible for investigating differences between budgeted and actual results, and are then expected to take corrective action or amend the plan in the light of actual events.

The wrong approach to budgetary control is to compare actual results against a fixed budget. Consider the following example.

Sidewinder Limited manufactures a single product. Budgeted results and actual results for June 20X6 are shown below.

	Budget	Actual results	Variance
Production (units)	2,000	3,000	1,000
	£	£	£
Direct materials	6,000	8,500	2,500
Direct labour	4,000	4,500	500
Maintenance	1,000	1,400	400
Depreciation	2,000	2,200	200
Rent and rates	1,500	1,600	100
Other costs	3,600	5,000	1,400
Total costs	18,100	23,200	5,100

In this example, the variances are not nearly as meaningful as they could be. Costs were higher than budget because the volume of output was higher; variable costs would be expected to increase above the budgeted costs in the fixed budget. There is no information to help decide whether any action is needed for any aspect of costs or revenue. For control purposes, it is therefore necessary to know the answers to questions such as: were actual costs higher than they should have been to produce 3,000 units?

A better approach to budgetary control is as follows.

(a) Identify fixed and variable costs.
(b) Produce a flexible budget using marginal costing techniques.

In the example of Sidewinder Ltd, let us suppose that we have the following estimates of cost behaviour.

(a) Direct materials and maintenance costs are variable.

(b) Although basic wages are a fixed cost, direct labour is regarded as variable in order to measure efficiency/productivity.

(c) Rent and rates and depreciation are fixed costs.

(d) Other costs consist of fixed costs of £1,600 plus a variable cost of £1 per unit made and sold.

The budgetary control (variance) analysis should be as follows.

	Fixed budget (a)	Flexible budget (b)	Actual results (c)	Budget variance (b) – (c)
Production (units)	2,000	3,000	3,000	
	£	£	£	£
Variable costs				
Direct materials	6,000	9,000	8,500	500 (F)
Direct labour	4,000	6,000	4,500	1,500 (F)
Maintenance	1,000	1,500	1,400	100 (F)
Semi-variable costs				
Other costs	3,600	4,600	5,000	400 (A)
Fixed costs				
Depreciation	2,000	2,000	2,200	200 (A)
Rent and rates	1,500	1,500	1,600	100 (A)
Total costs	18,100	24,600	23,200	1,400 (F)

Note. (F) denotes a favourable variance (where less than expected was spent) and (A) an adverse or unfavourable variance (where more than expected was spent).

Activity 6 (15 minutes)

(a) How are the following figures in the flexible budget above calculated?

(i) Direct materials
(ii) Other costs

(b) What is depreciation and why is it the same in both the fixed and the flexible budget? Comment also on the actual depreciation figure.

We can analyse the above as follows.

(a) In producing 3,000 units the expected costs should have been, not the fixed budget costs of £18,100, but the flexible budget costs of £24,600. Instead, actual costs were £23,200 ie £1,400 less than we should have expected. The reason for the improvement is that, given output of 3,000 units, costs were lower than expected.

(b) Variable costs should have been greater than the £11,000 in the fixed budget because the company produced 3,000 units instead of 2,000 units. Costs should have increased by ½ (6,000 + 4,000 + 1,000) = £5,500, which was budgeted as the variable cost of 1,000 units. This is the difference between the fixed and flexible budgets. Semi-variable costs should have risen by £1,000 for the increased production. (We do not take fixed costs into account since they remain unchanged as activity levels change.)

(c) A full variance analysis statement would be as follows.

	£	£
Fixed budget costs		18,100
Budgeted difference due to increased production		
level (£5,500 + £1,000)		6,500
Flexible budget costs		24,600
Variances		
Direct materials cost	500 (F)	
Direct labour cost	1,500 (F)	
Maintenance cost	100 (F)	
Other costs	400 (A)	
Depreciation	200 (A)	
Rent and rates	100 (A)	
		1,400 (F)
Actual costs		23,200

Such a statement could be prepared by the accountant and then circulated to senior management and/or operational management in a periodically-prepared budgetary control report. Operational management may then be asked to investigate the reasons for large variances so that they can decide whether any corrective action is necessary.

Figure 8.1 shows a variety of common variances that can be calculated and suggests possible reasons why they might have occurred.

Brief summary of the possible causes of variances

Variance	Favourable	Adverse
Material price	Unforeseen discounts received. Greater care taken in purchasing. Change in material standard	Price increase. Careless purchasing. Change in material standard
Material usage	Material used of higher quality than standard/less wastage. More efficient use made of material. Errors in allocating material to jobs	Defective material. Excessive waste. Theft. Stricter quality control. Errors in allocating material to jobs
Labour rate	Use of apprentices or other workers at a rate of pay lower than standard	Wage rate increase. Excessive overtime, with overtime premium charged to (direct) labour costs
Idle time		Machine breakdown. Non-availability of material. Illness or injury to worker
Labour efficiency	Output produced more quickly than expected, that is actual output in excess of standard output set for same number of hours because of worker motivation, better quality of equipment or materials. Errors in allocating time to jobs	Lost time in excess of standard allowed. Output lower than standard set because of deliberate restriction, lack of training, or substantial materials used. Errors in allocating time to jobs

Brief summary of the possible causes of variances

Variance	Favourable	Adverse
Fixed overhead price	Savings in costs incurred	Increase in cost of services used
	More economical use of services	Excessive use of services
		Change in type of service used

Figure 8.1 Common causes of variance

One way of monitoring performance, then, is to compare actual results with what was originally planned. Another way is to compare actual results with results achieved in the past and with results achieved by other businesses.

Activity 7 (10 minutes)

One month an unfavourable variance of £10,000 arises because a company uses hundreds of kilograms more materials than was expected.

Who is responsible for this variance?

NOTES

Chapter roundup

- The objectives of a budgetary planning and control system are as follows.

  - To ensure the achievement of the organisation's objectives
  - To compel planning
  - To communicate ideas and plans
  - To co-ordinate activities
  - To provide a framework for responsibility accounting
  - To establish a system of control
  - To motivate employees to improve their performance

- A budget is a quantified plan of action for a forthcoming accounting period.

- Managers responsible for preparing budgets should ideally be the managers responsible for carrying out the budget.

- The budget committee is the co-ordinating body in the preparation and administration of budgets.

- The principal budget factor should be identified at the beginning of the budgetary process, and the budget for this is prepared before all the others.

- Once prepared, the resource budgets must be reviewed to ensure they are consistent with one another.

- The budgeting process does not end for the current period once the budget period has begun: budgeting should be seen as a continuous and dynamic process.

- The master budget consists of a budgeted profit and loss account, balance sheet and cash budget.

- Budgets can be used as a yardstick against which actual results can be compared. If done regularly this is an effective way of monitoring the success of the business. Ideally, flexible budgets should be used.

Quick quiz

1   What are the objectives of a system of budgetary planning and control?

2   What is meant by the term principal budget factor?

3   What are the steps in the preparation of a budget?

4   What factors need to be considered when forecasting sales?

5   When might production capacity be the principal budget factor?

6   What is the basic idea of ABC?

7   What do you understand by 'flexible budgets'?

8   What is a variance?

9   Why might there be an adverse material usage variance?

Answers to quick quiz

1   To facilitate achievement of the organisation's objectives; to compel systematic planning and decision-making; to communicate ideas and plans; to co-ordinate activities; to allocate responsibility; to facilitate a system of monitoring and control; to motivate employees. (See section 1.1)

2   The principal budget factor is the factor that most significantly limits the organisation's activities. Usually it is sales (there is usually only a limited market, or a limited share of a market, that an enterprise can hope to achieve) but it may also be finance, or availability of raw materials, or people of the right quality. (See section 2.2)

3   *Step   Action*

      1   Identify principal budget factor
      2   Prepare sales budget
      3   Prepare finished goods stock budget
      4   Prepare production budget
      5   Prepare production resources budget
      6   Prepare overhead cost budgets
      7   Combine, co-ordinate and review budgets
      8   Complete master budget (See section 2.2)

4   Past sales patterns; results of market research; planned marketing activity; competition; distribution channels; economic environment; changing customer tastes; new legislation. (See section 3.1)

5   When demand exceeds the factory's current ability to manufacture, for reasons such as shortage of raw materials, skilled labour or machine capacity.

6   Costs are analysed by what causes them to be incurred rather than simply by where they occurred (in a cost centre, for instance). (See section 3.5)

7   A flexible budget, in recognising the existence of fixed, variable and semi-fixed costs, changes so as to relate to actual volumes in the period. (See section 4.1)

8   The difference between expected and actual results. (See section 4.3)

9   There may have been: defective materials; excessive waste; theft; stricter quality control (a rise in standards); errors in allocating material to jobs in the cost accounting department. (See section 4.3)

Answers to activities

1   (a)   Raw materials are things like steel and rubber that a business does work on to make finished products.

    (b)   Finished goods are manufactured items that are ready to sell.

    (c)   Distribution is the function of a business that sees to it that the finished stock is in a place where the customer can buy it, or is delivered directly to the customer's premises.

    (d)   An overhead is a cost which is incurred in the course of making a product, delivering a service, or running a department, but which cannot be traced directly to the product, service or department.

    (e)   A budget is a plan expressed in money.

(f) Idle time is time when workers are at work and being paid but are unable to get on with their job, perhaps because they are waiting for other workers to finish their job or because a machine breaks down.

(g) A cost centre is a location, a function, an activity or an item of equipment.

(h) A resource is something that is used in the operations of a business – people, materials, machines, time, space (land and buildings), finance and information.

2 (a) The sequence of budget preparation will be roughly as follows.

(i) Sales budget. (The market share limits demand and so sales are the principal budget factor. All other activities will depend upon this forecast.)

(ii) Finished goods stock budget (in units)

(iii) Production budget (in units)

(iv) Production resources budgets (materials, machine hours, labour)

(v) Overhead budgets for production, administration, selling and distribution, research and development and so on

Other budgets required will be the capital expenditure budget, the working capital budget (debtors and creditors) and, very importantly, the cash budget.

(b) Procedures for preparing budgets can be contained in a budget manual which shows which budgets must be prepared when and by whom, what each functional budget should contain and detailed directions on how to prepare budgets including, for example, expected price increases, rates of interest, rates of depreciation and so on.

The formulation of budgets can be co-ordinated by a budget committee comprising the senior executives of the departments responsible for carrying out the budgets: sales, production, purchasing, personnel and so on.

The budgeting process may also be assisted by the use of a spreadsheet/computer budgeting package.

3 The budget shows that 2 million units of product X will be sold in the north and 1.3 million of product Y, while 3.2 million units of product X will be sold in the south and 2.5 million of product Y. It also shows the income that will be received in each case.

The budget could helpfully show totals as follows.

| | Units ('000) | | | Revenue (£'000) | | |
	North	South	Total	North	South	Total
Product X	2,000	3,200	5,200	1,500	2,400	3,900
Product Y	1,300	2,500	3,800	975	1,875	2,850
	3,300	5,700	9,000	2,475	4,275	6,750

It would also be useful to show the selling price per unit. (In fact it is 75p for both products in both regions.)

4 (a) *Production budget*

	J Units	K Units
Opening stock	(600)	(800)
Closing stock (85%)	510	680
Sales	10,000	6,000
	9,910	5,880

(b) *Raw materials purchases budget*

	X kg	Y kg
Opening stock	(400)	(200)
Production (per (a))		
J (10 kg/4 kg)	99,100	39,640
K (4 kg/8 kg)	35,280	47,040
	133,980	86,480
Closing stock	340	170
	134,320	86,650
Cost per kg	£1.50	£4.00
Purchase cost	£201,480	£346,600

(c) *Production cost budget*

	£
Materials	
Opening stock (400 kg × £1.20) + (200 kg × £3)	1,080
Purchases £(201,480 + 346,600)	548,080
	549,160
Closing stock (340 kg × £1.50) + (170 kg × £4)	(1,190)
	547,970
Skilled labour (W1)	497,880
Variable overhead (W2)	165,960
Fixed overhead	315,900
	1,527,710

Workings

1 Labour cost budget

	J	K
Units produced per (a)	9,910	5,880
Hours per unit	6	4
Total hours	59,460	23,520

(59,460 + 23,520) = 82,980 hours × £6 = £497,880

2 Variable overheads

82,980 hours (W1) × £2 = £165,960

5 (a)

	£
Credit customers' costs (7,442 × £50)	372,100
Transaction costs (447,892 × £0.14)	62,705
	434,805
Increase by 5%	£456,545

(b)

	£
Credit customers' costs ((7,442 + 250 − 30) × £50)	383,100
Transaction costs (470,000 × £0.14)	65,800
	448,900

6   This activity is to encourage you to study and work through the figures for yourself.

(a) (i)   Direct materials are a variable cost. If 3,000 units are produced instead of 2,000 the cost may be expected to be:

£6,000 × 3,000/2,000 = £9,000

(ii) Other costs are part variable and part fixed. The fixed part should not be expected to change.

	£
Fixed cost	1,600
Variable cost (3,000 × £1)	3,000
	4,600

(b)   Depreciation is a measure of how much a fixed asset has worn out during a period. It is stated in the information given to be a fixed cost. The actual results suggest that it may not be, or that new information has come to light that means that the original estimate was 'wrong' (though depreciation is only ever an estimate).

7   The variance might have been caused by the department that uses the materials if they did so wastefully. Alternatively the purchasing department may have bought poor quality materials to try to save money, meaning that more materials were wasted. This is an example of how the price of something might affect its usage – the so-called interdependence of variances. Another possibility is that the original estimate was wrong in the first place – whoever prepared the budget would then be responsible.

(*Note*. If you answered along the lines that the extra kilograms might have been used because the production department made more units than expected you are wrong. Remember that the budget should be flexed to allow for this before any variances are calculated.)

Chapter 9:

PRICING DECISIONS

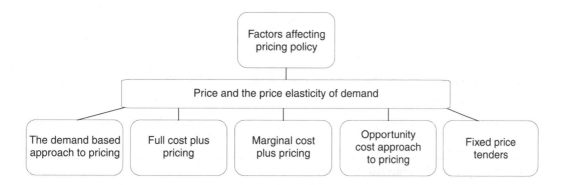

Introduction

Price can go by many names: fares, tuition fees, rent, assessments and so on. All profit organisations and many non-profit-making organisations face the task of setting a price for their products or services.

In the past, setting a price was the single most important decision made by the sales department, but in modern marketing philosophy, price, whilst important, is not necessarily the predominant factor. Modern businesses seek to interpret and satisfy customer wants and needs by modifying existing products or introducing new products to the range. This contrasts with earlier production-oriented times when the typical reaction was to cut prices in order to sell more of an organisation's product.

Nevertheless, proper pricing of an organisation's products or services is essential to its profitability and hence its survival, and price can be used to differentiate a product and an organisation from competitors.

As you go through this chapter, consider how it relates to everything you have learned about so far. The results of the company you have looked at may have been affected by pricing decisions.

Your objectives

In this chapter you will learn about the following.

- The factors which may influence an organisation's pricing policy
- The importance of the price elasticity of demand to an organisation setting or changing prices
- The demand-based approach to setting prices
- Approaches to pricing using absorption costing, marginal costing and opportunity costing
- The procedure for preparing cost estimates for fixed price quotations and tenders
- The procedure for monitoring costs against fixed prices

1 FACTORS AFFECTING PRICING POLICY

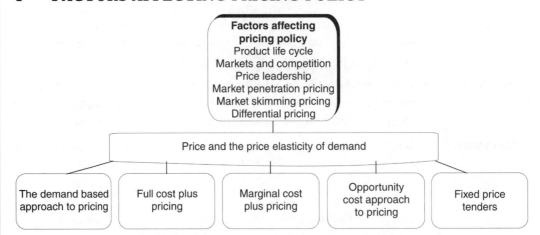

In practice, there are many more influences on pricing policy than the cost of a product or service.

Influence	Explanation/example
Price sensitivity	Sensitivity to price levels will vary amongst purchasers. **Those that can pass on the cost of purchases will be the least sensitive** and will therefore respond more to other elements of perceived value. For example, the business traveller will probably be more concerned about the level of service and quality of food in looking for a hotel than price, since his or her employer will be paying the bill. In contrast, a family on holiday are likely to be very price sensitive when choosing an overnight stay.
Price perception	Price perception is **the way customers react to prices**. For example, customers may react to a price increase by buying more. This could be because they expect further price increases to follow (they are 'stocking up').
Quality	This is an aspect of price perception. In the absence of other information, customers tend to **judge quality by price**. Thus a price change may send signals to customers concerning the quality of the product. A price rise may indicate improvements in quality, a price reduction may signal reduced quality, for example through the use of inferior components.
Intermediaries	If an organisation distributes products or services to the market through independent intermediaries, the **objectives of these intermediaries complicate the pricing decision**. Such intermediaries are likely to deal with a range of suppliers and their aims concern their own profits rather than those of suppliers.
Competitors	In setting prices, an organisation sends out signals to rivals. *Competitors are likely to react to these signals in some way.* In some industries (such as petrol retailing) *pricing moves in unison*; in others, price changes by one supplier may initiate a *price war*, with each supplier undercutting the others. Competition is discussed in more detail below.

Influence	Explanation/example
Suppliers	If an organisation's suppliers *notice a price rise* for the organisation's products, they *may seek a rise* in the price for their supplies to the organisation on the grounds that it is now able to pay a higher price.
Inflation	In periods of inflation the organisation may need to change prices to reflect increases in the prices of supplies, labour, rent and so on. Such changes may be needed to keep relative (real) prices unchanged.
Uniqueness	When a *new product* is introduced for the first time there are no existing reference points such as customer or competitor behaviour; *pricing decisions are most difficult to make* in such circumstances. It may be possible to seek alternative reference points, such as the price in another market where the new product has already been launched, or the price set by a competitor.
Incomes	In times of *rising incomes*, *price* may become *less important than product quality* or convenience of access (distribution). When income levels are *falling* and/or unemployment levels rising, *price* will become much *more important*.
Product range	Products are often interrelated, being complements to each other or substitutes for one another. *Pricing* is then likely *to focus* on the profit from the *whole range* rather than the profit on each single product. Take, for example, the use of *loss leaders:* a very low price for one product is intended to make consumers buy additional products in the range which carry higher profit margins. A good example is selling razors at very low prices whilst selling the blades for them at a higher profit margin; similarly the price of inkjet printer cartridges can be very high relative to the price of the printer itself.
Ethics	Ethical considerations may be a further factor, for example whether or not to exploit short-term shortages through higher prices.
Substitute products	These are products which could be transformed for the same use. For example if the price of train travel rises it comes under competition from cheaper coach travel and more expensive air travel.

1.1 Product life cycle

A typical product has a life cycle of four stages.

(a) **Introduction**. The product is introduced to the market. Heavy **capital expenditure** will be incurred on product development and perhaps also on the purchase of new fixed assets and building up stocks for sale.

On its introduction to the market, the product will begin to earn some revenue, but initially demand is likely to be small. Potential customers will be unaware of the product or service, and the organisation may have to spend further on **advertising** to bring the product or service to the attention of the market.

(b) **Growth**. The product gains a bigger market as demand builds up. Sales revenues increase and the product begins to make a profit. The initial costs of the **investment** in the new product are gradually **recovered**.

(c) **Maturity**. Eventually, the growth in demand for the product will slow down and it will enter a period of relative maturity. It will continue to be profitable. The product may be **modified or improved, as a means of sustaining its demand**.

(d) **Saturation and decline**. Except for some 'essential' items (eg milk, or bread), the market will at some stage have bought enough of the product and it will therefore reach 'saturation point'. Demand will start to fall. For a while, the product will still be profitable in spite of declining sales, but eventually it will become a **loss-maker** and this is the time when the organisation should decide to stop selling the product or service, and so the product's life cycle should reach its end.

It is useful to relate the above life cycle and pricing factors to real life examples. As you continue through the chapter try to think of firms and products which are good examples of the theories described.

1.2 Markets and competition

The price that an organisation can charge for its products will be determined to a greater or lesser degree by the type of market in which it operates.

Definitions

> **Perfect competition**: many buyers and many sellers all dealing in an identical product. No single producer or user has any market power and both must accept the prevailing market price.
>
> **Monopoly**: one seller who dominates many buyers. The monopolist can use his market power to set a profit-maximising price.
>
> **Oligopoly**: relatively few competitive companies dominate the market. Whilst each large firm has the ability to influence market prices, the unpredictable reaction from the other giants makes the final industry price indeterminate.

In **established industries** dominated by a few major firms, it is generally accepted that a price initiative by one firm will be countered by a price reaction by competitors. In these circumstances, **prices tend to be fairly stable**, unless pushed upwards by inflation or strong growth in demand.

If a **rival cuts its prices** in the expectation of increasing its market share, a **firm has several options**.

(a) It will **maintain its existing prices** if the expectation is that only a small market share would be lost, so that it is more profitable to keep prices at their existing level. Eventually, the rival firm may drop out of the market or be forced to raise its prices.

(b) It may maintain its prices but respond with a **non-price counter-attack**. This is a more positive response, because the firm will be securing or justifying its current prices with a product change, advertising, or better back-up services.

(c) It may **reduce its prices**. This should protect the firm's market share so that the main beneficiary from the price reduction will be the consumer.

(d) It may **raise its prices** and respond with a **non-price counter-attack**. The extra revenue from the higher prices might be used to finance an advertising campaign or product design changes. A price increase would be based on a campaign to emphasise the quality difference between the firm's own product and the rival's product.

EXAMPLE

When leading supermarkets began expanding into superstores, price wars forced other retailers to make pricing decisions. With the advent of US-led hypermarkets these decisions will again be on the agenda not only for firms such as Tesco, Asda and Sainsbury, but also for smaller retailers.

1.3 Price leadership

It is not unusual to find that large corporations emerge as price leaders. The price leader indicates to the other firms in the market what the price will be, and competitors then set their prices with reference to the leader's price.

A price leader will have the dominant influence over price levels for a class of products and may actually lead without other firms moving its prices at all. For example, if other firms tried to raise prices and the leader did not follow, the upward move in prices would be halted.

The price leader generally has a large, if not necessarily the largest, market share. The greater the number of firms in an industry, the weaker will be the role of a price leader.

1.4 Market penetration pricing

Market penetration pricing is a policy of **low prices** when the product is **first launched** in order to obtain sufficient penetration into the market. A penetration pricing policy may be appropriate in the following circumstances.

(a) If the firm wishes to **discourage new entrants** into the market.

(b) If the firm wishes to **shorten the initial period of the product's life cycle** in order to enter the growth and maturity stages as quickly as possible.

(c) If there are significant **economies of scale** to be achieved from a high volume of output, so that quick penetration into the market is desirable in order to gain unit cost reductions.

(d) If **demand is likely to increase as prices fall.**

Penetration prices are prices which aim to secure a substantial share in a substantial total market. A firm might therefore **deliberately build excess production capacity** and set its prices very low. As demand builds up the spare capacity will be used up gradually and unit costs will fall; the firm might even reduce prices further as unit costs fall. In this way, early losses will enable the firm to dominate the market and have the lowest costs.

1.5 Market skimming pricing

In contrast, market skimming involves charging high prices when a product is first launched and spending heavily on advertising and sales promotion to obtain sales. As the product moves into the later stages of its life cycle (growth, maturity and decline) progressively lower prices will be charged. The profitable 'cream' is thus skimmed off in stages until sales can only be sustained at lower prices.

The aim of market skimming is to gain high unit profits early in the product's life. High unit prices make it more likely that competitors will enter the market than if lower prices were to be charged. Such a policy may be appropriate in the following circumstances.

(a) Where the **product is new and different,** so that customers are prepared to pay high prices so as to be one up on other people who do not own it.

(b) Where the strength of **demand** and the sensitivity of demand to price are **unknown**. It is better from the point of view of marketing to start by charging high prices and then reduce them if the demand for the product turns out to be price elastic than to start by charging low prices and then attempt to raise them substantially if demand appears to be insensitive to higher prices.

(c) Where the firm can identify **different market segments** for the product, each prepared to pay progressively lower prices, so that it may be possible to continue to sell at higher prices to some market segments when lower prices are charged in others. This is discussed further below.

(d) Where products may have a **short life cycle,** and so need to recover their development costs and make a profit relatively quickly.

EXAMPLE

Sony used price skimming with their original Playstation, Playstation 2 and Playstation 3.

Initially the price is high because it is a new product. The pricing of games follows the same pattern. The price falls over time attracting more consumers.

1.6 Differential pricing

In certain circumstances the **same product** can be sold at **different prices** to **different customers**. There are a number of bases on which such prices can be set.

Basis	Example
By **market segment**	A cross-channel ferry company would market its services at different prices in England, Belgium and France, for example. Services such as cinemas and hairdressers are often available at lower prices to old age pensioners and/or juveniles.
By **product version**	Many car models have 'add on' extras which enable one brand to appeal to a wider cross-section of customers. The final price need not reflect the cost price of the add on extras directly: usually the top of the range model would carry a price much in excess of the cost of provision of the extras, as a prestige appeal.
By **place**	Theatre seats are usually sold according to their location so that patrons pay different prices for the same performance according to the seat type they occupy.
By **time**	This is perhaps the most popular type of price discrimination. Rail operating companies, for example, are successful price discriminators, charging more to rush hour rail commuters whose demand remains the same whatever the price charged at certain times of the day.

Activity 1   **(5 minutes)**

Can you think of any more examples of products or services which are sold to different customers at different prices on the basis of time?

2   PRICE AND THE PRICE ELASTICITY OF DEMAND

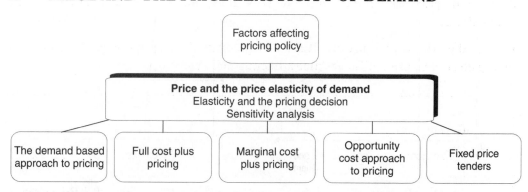

Economists argue that the higher the price of a good, the lower will be the quantity demanded. We have already seen that in practice it is by no means as straightforward as this (some goods are bought **because** they are expensive, for example Aston Martin cars), but you know from your personal experience as a consumer that the theory is essentially true. An important concept in this context is price elasticity of demand (PED).

Definition

> The **price elasticity of demand** measures the extent of change in demand for a good following a change to its price.

Price elasticity of demand (η) is measured as:

$$\frac{\text{\% change in sales demand}}{\text{\% change in sales price}}$$

Demand is said to be **elastic** when a **small change in the price** produces a **large change in the quantity demanded**. The PED is then greater than 1. *Example:* A product such as a Ford Focus car, would be expected to have relatively high demand elasticity.

Demand is said to be **inelastic** when a **small change in the price** produces only a **small change in the quantity demanded**. The PED is then less than 1. *Example:* Mains electricity for domestic use, a 'necessity' that cannot easily be replaced by alternative energy sources, and so demand will be relatively inelastic.

Strictly speaking, demand is elastic (PED > 1) when a cut in price results in a bigger **percentage** expansion in demand. Thus, in Figure 9.1 (a), a cut in price from £12 to £6 (50% reduction) leads to an expansion in demand from 100 to 300 (200% expansion).

$$\text{PED} = \frac{200\%}{50\%} = 4.0$$

Total revenue *rises* from $100 \times £12 = £1,200$ to $300 \times £6 = £1,800$

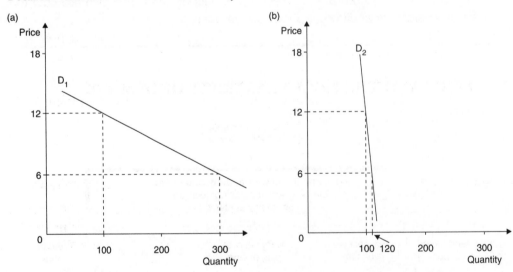

Figure 9.1 Price elasticity

Demand is inelastic (PED < 1) when a cut in price results in a smaller percentage expansion in demand. Thus, in Figure 9.1(b), a cut in price from £12 to £6 (50% reduction) leads to an expansion in demand from 100 to 120 units (20% expansion).

$$\text{PED} = \frac{20\%}{50\%} = 0.4$$

and total revenue **falls** from $100 \times £12 = £1,200$ to $120 \times £6 = £720$.

(PED will be negative for all 'normal' demand curves. Hence it is usual to omit the use of + and – signs.)

Price elasticity can, of course, apply also to price rises. What has been stated so far merely operates in reverse. Therefore, if price is increased and revenue falls, demand is elastic. The following table summarises the situation.

Price	Revenue	Demand
Decrease	Rises	Elastic
Increase	Falls	Elastic
Decrease	Falls	Inelastic
Increase	Rises	Inelastic

2.1 Elasticity and the pricing decision

An awareness of the concept of elasticity can assist management with pricing decisions.

(a) In circumstances of **inelastic demand, prices should be increased** because revenues will increase and total costs will reduce (because quantities sold will reduce).

(b) In circumstances of **elastic demand**, increases in prices will bring decreases in revenue and decreases in price will bring increases in revenue. Management therefore have to **decide whether the increase/decrease in costs will be less than/greater than the increases/decreases in revenue.**

(c) In situations of **very elastic demand**, overpricing can lead to a massive drop in quantity sold and hence a massive drop in profits, whereas underpricing can lead to costly stock outs and, again, a significant drop in profits. **Elasticity must therefore be reduced by creating a customer preference which is unrelated to price** (through advertising and promotional activities).

(d) In situations of **very inelastic demand**, customers are not sensitive to price. **Quality, service, product mix and location are therefore more important** to a firm's pricing strategy.

Activity 2 **(15 minutes)**

The price of a good is £1.20 per unit and annual demand is 800,000 units. Market research indicates that an increase in price of 10 pence per unit will result in a fall in annual demand of 75,000 units. What is the price elasticity of demand?

2.2 Sensitivity analysis

Sensitivity analysis, in its broadest form is the determination of the effects on planned outcome of changes made to input values.

In the context of pricing, this may be the analysis of changes in expected sales revenue arising from changes in selling price. This is very closely linked to price elasticity of demand.

NOTES

EXAMPLE

A product is currently being sold at £25 per unit, at which there is a demand of 120,000 units per annum. It is thought that a £1 increase in price will lead to a 10,000 fall in demand.

How sensitive is sales revenue to price changes?

Currently, total revenue is 120,000 × £25 = £3,000,000.

If the price is increased by £1, demand will fall to 110,000 units and total revenue will be 110,000 × £26 = £2,860,000.

This represents a fall in revenue of £140,000. As a percentage of the original revenue this is £140,000/£3,000,000 × 100 = 4.67%

So a £1 increase in price leads to a 4.67% fall in revenue. This is a measure of sensitivity of revenue to price changes.

From our previous discussion on price elasticity, you should be able to see that in this situation, demand must be elastic, as a price increase has lead to a fall in revenue. You should also appreciate that the sensitivity will change as you move along the demand curve, as the price elasticity changes.

For example, if we make a further increase in price of £1, to £27, demand will fall by a further 10,000 units, to 100,000. Revenue will be £2,700,000, a further fall of £(2,860,000 − 2,700,000) = £160,000. This represents a further fall of 5.6%.

So as the price increases, the revenue will become more and more sensitive to £1 price rises.

3 THE DEMAND BASED APPROACH TO PRICING

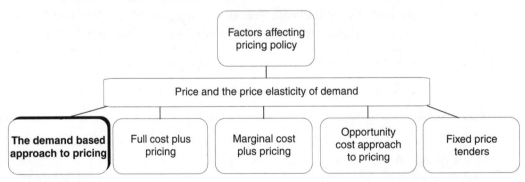

A difficulty with a demand-based approach to pricing is to find a balance between theory and practice.

(a) **Price theory** or **demand** theory is based on the idea that a connection can be made between price, quantity demanded and sold, and total revenue. Demand varies with price, and so if an estimate can be made of demand at different price levels, it should **be possible to derive either a profit-maximising price** or a revenue-maximising price.

The theory of demand cannot be applied in practice, however, unless realistic estimates of demand at different price levels can be made.

(b) In practice, businesses might not make estimates of demand at different price levels, but they might still make pricing decisions on the basis of demand conditions and competition in the market.

Some larger organisations go to considerable effort to estimate the demand for their products or services at differing price levels by producing estimated demand curves. A knowledge of demand curves can be very useful.

For example, a large transport authority might be considering an increase in fares. The effect on total revenues and profit of the increase in fares could be estimated from a knowledge of the demand for transport services at different price levels. If an increase in the price per ticket caused a large fall in demand, because demand was price elastic, total revenues and profits would fall whereas a fares increase when demand is price inelastic would boost total revenue, and since a transport authority's costs are largely fixed, this would probably boost total profits too.

Many businesses enjoy something akin to a monopoly position, even in a competitive market. This is because they develop a unique marketing mix, for example a unique combination of price and quality, or a monopoly in a localised area. The significance of a monopoly situation is as follows.

(a) The business does not have to 'follow the market' on price, in other words it is not a 'price-taker', but has more choice and flexibility in the prices it sets. **At higher prices**, demand for its products or services will be less. **At lower prices**, demand for its products or services will be higher.

(b) There will be a selling price at which the business can maximise its profits.

Activity 3 **(20 minutes)**

Gnu Ltd sells a product which has a variable cost of £8 per unit. The sales demand at the current sales price of £14 is 3,000 units. It has been estimated by the marketing department that the sales volume would fall by 100 units for each addition of 25 pence to the sales price. Establish whether the current price of £14 is the optimal price which maximises contribution.

Hint: consider the contribution earned at prices above and below £14.

4 FULL COST PLUS PRICING

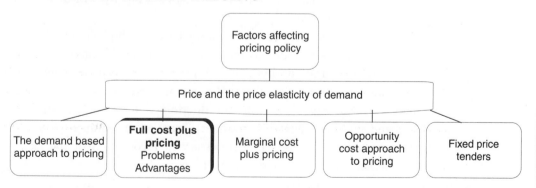

A traditional approach to pricing products is full cost plus pricing, whereby the sales price is determined by **calculating the full cost of the product and adding a percentage**

mark-up for profit. The term **target pricing** is sometimes used, which means setting a price so as to achieve a target profit or return on capital employed.

In full cost plus pricing, the full cost may be a fully absorbed **production** cost only, or it may include some absorbed administration, selling and distribution overhead. The full cost might also include some opportunity costs as well, such as the opportunity cost of a production resource that is in short supply, so that **'full cost' need not be the cost as it might be established in the accounts**.

A business might have an idea of the percentage profit margin it would like to earn and so might decide on an average profit mark-up as a general guideline for pricing decisions. This would be particularly useful for businesses that carry out a large amount of **contract work** or **jobbing work**, for which individual job or contract prices must be quoted regularly to prospective customers. The **percentage profit mark-up** does not have to be fixed, but can be **varied to suit** demand conditions in the market.

The full cost plus approach to pricing is commonly used in practice, but varying the size of the profit mark-up gives the pricing decisions much-needed flexibility so as to adapt to demand conditions.

4.1   Problems with full cost plus pricing

There are serious problems with relying on a full cost approach as a basis for pricing decisions.

(a) Perhaps the most significant problem with cost plus pricing is that it fails to recognise that since demand may be determined by price, **there will be a profit-maximising combination of price and demand**. A cost plus based approach to pricing will be most unlikely to arrive at the profit-maximising price.

(b) Prices must be adjusted to market and demand conditions: the decision cannot simply be made on a cost basis only.

(c) Output volume, a key factor in the fixed overhead absorption rate, must be budgeted. **A full cost plus pricing decision cannot be made without a knowledge of demand and demand cannot be estimated without a knowledge of price**: a vicious circle.

    (i) One solution is to estimate likely demand (from past experience in the case of established products) and calculate an absorption rate on this assumed volume of output. Provided that actual volume equals or exceeds the estimated volume of sales, the company will achieve (or exceed) its target profit.

    (ii) Another solution is to set a price on the basis of a budgeted production volume and allow stocks to build up for a time if demand is below production volume at this price. A price review can be made when demand conditions are known better, and either of the following decisions could be taken. A **price reduction** could be made to stimulate demand if this seems appropriate. Production volumes could be reduced and **prices raised** if necessary in recognition of the lack of demand at the original budgeted volumes.

(d) Further objections to full cost plus pricing as the basis for pricing decisions can be listed as follows.

(i)   It **fails to allow for competition**. A company may need to match the prices of rival firms when these take a price-cutting initiative.

(ii) A full cost plus basis for a pricing decision is a means of ensuring that, in the long run, a company succeeds in covering all its fixed costs and making a profit out of revenue earned. However, in the short term it is **inflexible**. A firm may tender a cost plus price that results in a contract going elsewhere, although a lower price would have been sufficient to cover incremental costs and opportunity costs. In the **short term**, rapidly-changing environmental factors might dictate the need for lower (or higher) prices than long-term considerations would indicate.

(iii) Full cost plus prices tend to ignore opportunity costs.

(iv) Where more than one product is sold by a company, the price decided by a cost plus formula depends on the method of apportioning fixed costs between the products.

EXAMPLE: FULL COST PLUS PRICING WITH MORE THAN ONE PRODUCT

Botham Ltd is attempting to decide sales prices for two products, Richies and Eddies. The products are both made by the same workforce and in the same department. 30,000 direct labour hours are budgeted for the year.

The budgeted fixed costs are £30,000 and it is expected that the department will operate at full capacity. Variable costs per unit are as follows.

		Richies £		Eddies £
Materials		4		4
Labour	(2 hours)	6	(3 hours)	9
Expenses	(1 machine hour)	2	(1 machine hour)	2
		12		15

Expected demand is 7,500 Richies and 5,000 Eddies. You are required to calculate the unit prices which give a profit of 20% on full cost if overheads are absorbed:

(a) On a direct labour hour basis

(b) On a machine hour basis

SOLUTION

(a) *A direct labour hour basis*

$$\frac{\text{Budgeted fixed costs}}{\text{Budgeted labour hours}} = \frac{£30,000}{(15,000 + 15,000)} = £1$$

Absorption rate: £1 per direct labour hour

	Richies £	Eddies £
Variable costs	12.00	15.00
Overhead absorbed	2.00	3.00
	14.00	18.00
Profit (20%)	2.80	3.60
Price	16.80	21.60

The total budgeted profit would be £(21,000 + 18,000) = £39,000.

(b) *A machine hour basis*

$$\frac{\text{Budgeted fixed costs}}{\text{Budgeted machine hours}} = \frac{£30,000}{(7,500 + 5,000)} = \frac{£30,000}{12,500} = £2.40$$

Absorption rate : £2.40 per machine hour

	Richies £	Eddies £
Variable costs	12.00	15.00
Overhead absorbed	2.40	2.40
Full cost	14.40	17.40
Profit (20%)	2.88	3.48
Price	17.28	20.88

The total budgeted profit would be £(21,600 + 17,400) = £39,000.

(c) The different bases for charging overheads result in different prices for both Richies (difference of 48p per unit) and Eddies (difference of 72p per unit).

It is unlikely that the expected sales demand for the products would be the same at both sales prices. It is questionable whether one (or either) product might achieve expected sales demand at the higher price. In other words, although the budgeted profit is £39,000 whichever overhead absorption method is used, this assumes that budgeted sales would be achieved regardless of the unit price of each product. This is an unrealistic basis on which to make a decision.

4.2 Advantages of full cost plus pricing

The advantages of full cost plus pricing are as follows.

(a) Since the size of the profit margin can be varied at management's discretion, a decision based on a price in excess of full cost should ensure that **a company working at normal capacity will cover all its fixed costs and make a profit.** Companies may benefit from cost plus pricing in the following circumstances.

(i)   When they carry out large contracts which must make a sufficient profit margin to cover a fair share of fixed costs

(ii) If they must justify their prices to potential customers (for example, for government contracts)

(iii) If they find it difficult to estimate expected demand at different sales prices

(b) It is a **simple, quick and cheap** method of pricing which can be delegated to junior managers. This may be particularly important with jobbing work where many prices must be decided and quoted each day.

Activity 4	**(5 minutes)**

A product's full cost is £4.75 and it is sold at full cost plus 70%. A competitor has just launched a similar product selling for £7.99. How will this affect the first product's mark up?

5 MARGINAL COST PLUS PRICING

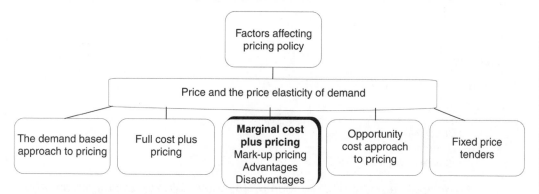

5.1 Mark-up pricing

Instead of pricing products or services by adding a profit margin on to full cost, a business might add a profit margin on to marginal cost (either the marginal cost of production or else the marginal cost of sales). This is sometimes called **mark-up pricing**.

For example, if a company budgets to make 10,000 units of a product for which the variable cost of production is £3 a unit and the fixed production cost £60,000 a year, it might decide to fix a price by adding, say, $33^1/_3$% to full production cost to give a price of £9 × $1^1/_3$ = £12 a unit. Alternatively, it might decide to add a profit margin of, say, 250% on to the variable production cost, to give a price of £3 × 350% = £10.50.

5.2 Advantages

The **advantages** of a marginal cost plus approach to pricing are as follows.

(a) It is a **simple and easy** method to use.

(b) The **mark-up can be varied** and so, provided that a rigid mark-up is not used, mark-up pricing can be adjusted to reflect demand conditions.

(c) It draws management attention to contribution and the effects of higher or lower sales volumes on profit.

(d) Mark-up pricing is **convenient where there is a readily identifiable basic variable cost. Retail industries** are the most obvious example, and it is quite common for the prices of goods in shops to be fixed by adding a mark-up (20% or $33^1/_3$%, say) to the purchase cost. A retailer might buy in items of pottery, for example at £3 each, add a mark-up of one third and resell the items at £4.

5.3 Disadvantages

There are, of course, **drawbacks** to marginal cost plus pricing.

(a) Although the size of the mark-up can be varied in accordance with demand conditions, it **does not ensure that sufficient attention is paid to competitors' prices and profit maximisation**.

(b) It ignores fixed overheads in the pricing decision, but the price must be high enough to ensure that a profit is made after covering fixed costs. Pricing decisions **cannot ignore fixed costs altogether**.

Activity 5	**(10 minutes)**

A product has the following costs.

	£
Direct materials	5
Direct labour	3
Variable overhead	7

Fixed overheads are £10,000 per month. Budgeted sales for the month are 400 units. What profit mark-up needs to be added to marginal cost to break even?

6 OPPORTUNITY COST APPROACH TO PRICING

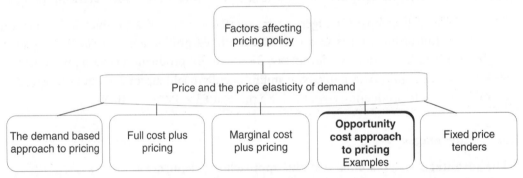

The opportunity cost approach to pricing can be used to set a full cost plus price or marginal cost plus price which includes the opportunity costs of the resources consumed in making and selling the item.

EXAMPLE: FULL COST-PLUS PRICING AND OPPORTUNITY COSTS

Pun Ltd has begun to produce a new product, Product Dit, for which the following cost estimates have been made.

	£
Direct materials	27
Direct labour: 4 hrs at £5 per hour	20
Variable production overheads: machining, ½ hr at £6 per hour	3
	50

Production fixed overheads are budgeted at £300,000 per month and because of the shortage of available machining capacity, the company will be restricted to 10,000 hours of machine time per month. The absorption rate will be a direct labour rate, however, and budgeted direct labour hours are 25,000 per month.

It is estimated that the company could obtain a minimum contribution of £10 per machine hour on producing items other than product Dit. The company wishes to make a profit of 20% on full production cost from product Dit.

You are required to calculate the full cost plus price.

SOLUTION

Let us begin by calculating a price based on *not* including opportunity costs.

	£
Direct materials	27.00
Direct labour (4 hours)	20.00
Variable production overheads	3.00
Fixed production overheads	
(at $\dfrac{£300,000}{25,000}$ = £12 per direct labour hour)	48.00
Full production cost	98.00
Profit mark-up (20%)	19.60
Selling price per unit of product Dit	117.60

The price if we include machine time opportunity costs is as follows.

	£
Full production cost as above	98.00
Opportunity cost of machine time:	
contribution forgone (½ hr × £10)	5.00
Adjusted full cost	103.00
Profit mark-up (20%)	20.60
Selling price per unit of product Dit	123.60

The inclusion of opportunity costs therefore raises the price by £6.

Activity 6 **(15 minutes)**

Reeves Ltd and its rival Mortimer Ltd both produce individually packaged biscuits and cakes which are sold through confectionery retailers and newsagents' shops throughout the country. It is estimated that Reeves currently has a 50% share of this market, while Mortimer has approximately a 40% share. Discuss the options which are open to Reeves if Mortimer cuts the prices of its products.

Managing Financial Resources and Decisions

7 FIXED PRICE TENDERS

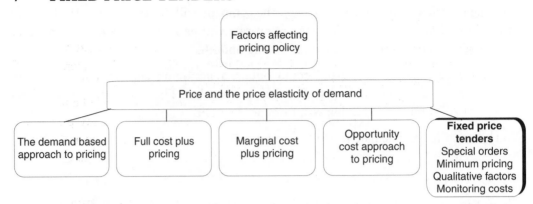

7.1 Special orders

A special order is a **one-off revenue earning opportunity**. These may arise in the following situations.

(a) When a business has a regular source of income but also has some **spare capacity** allowing it to take on extra work if demanded. For example a brewery might have a capacity of 500,000 barrels per month but only be producing and selling 300,000 barrels per month. It could therefore consider special orders to use up some of its spare capacity.

(b) When a business has no regular source of income and **relies exclusively on its ability to respond to demand**. A building firm is a typical example as are many types of sub-contractors. In the service sector consultants often work on this basis.

In the case of (a), a firm would normally attempt to cover its longer-term running costs in its prices for its regular product. Pricing for special orders need therefore take no account of unavoidable fixed costs. This is clearly not the case for a firm in (b)'s position, where special orders are the only source of income for the foreseeable future.

Questions featuring pricing for special orders typically present a scenario in which a firm has to decide whether to submit a fixed price tender for a contract. The basic approach in both situations is to determine the price at which the firm would break even if it undertook the work, that is, the minimum price that it could afford to charge.

7.2 Minimum pricing

A minimum price is the price that would have to be charged so that the **following costs are just covered**.

(a) The **incremental costs** of producing and selling the item

(b) The **opportunity costs** of the resources consumed in making and selling the item

A minimum price would leave the business no better or worse off in financial terms than if it did not sell the item.

220

Two essential points about a minimum price are as follows.

    (a)   It is **based on relevant costs**.

    (b)   It is **unlikely that a minimum price would actually be charged** because if it were, it would not provide the business with any incremental profit. However, the minimum price for a job shows the following.

        (i)   An absolute minimum below which the price should not be set

        (ii)   The incremental profit that would be obtained from any price that is actually charged in excess of the minimum (For example, if the minimum price is £20,000 and the actual price charged is £24,000, the incremental profit on the sale would be £4,000.)

If there are no scarce resources and a company has spare capacity, the minimum price of a job is the incremental cost of carrying it out. Any price in excess of this minimum would provide an incremental contribution towards profit.

If there are scarce resources, minimum prices must include an allowance for the opportunity cost of using the scarce resources on the job (instead of using the resources on the next most profitable product).

EXAMPLE: OPPORTUNITY COSTS AND MINIMUM PRICE

Gladiator Ltd has just completed production of an item of special equipment for a customer, only to be notified that this customer has now gone into liquidation. After much effort, the sales manager has been able to interest a potential buyer who might buy the machine if certain conversion work could first be carried out.

    (a)   The sales price of the machine to the original buyer had been fixed at £138,600 and had included an estimated normal profit mark-up of 10% on total costs. The costs incurred in the manufacture of the machine were as follows.

	£
Direct materials	49,000
Direct labour	36,000
Variable overhead	9,000
Fixed production overhead	24,000
Fixed sales and distribution overhead	8,000
	126,000

    (b)   If the machine is converted, the production manager estimates that the cost of the extra work required would be as follows.

Direct materials (at cost) £9,600
Direct labour
Department X: 6 workers for 4 weeks at £210 per worker per week
Department Y: 2 workers for 4 weeks at £160 per worker per week

    (c)   Variable overhead would be 20% of direct labour cost, and fixed production overhead would be absorbed as follows.

Department X: 83.33% of direct labour cost

Department Y: 25% of direct labour cost

(d)　Additional information is available as follows.

　　(i)　In the original machine, there are three types of material.

　　　　(1)　Type A could be sold for scrap for £8,000.

　　　　(2)　Type B could be sold for scrap for £2,400 but it would take 120 hours of casual labour paid at £4.50 per hour to put it into a condition in which it would be suitable for sale.

　　　　(3)　Type C would need to be scrapped, at a cost to Gladiator Ltd of £1,100.

　　(ii)　The direct materials required for the conversion are already in stock. If not needed for the conversion they would be used in the production of another machine in place of materials that would otherwise need to be purchased, and that would currently cost £8,800.

　　(iii)　The conversion work would be carried out in two departments, X and Y. Department X is currently extremely busy and working at full capacity; it is estimated that its contribution to fixed overhead and profits is £2.50 per £1 of labour.

　　　　Department Y, on the other hand, is short of work but for organisational reasons its labour force, which at the moment has a workload of only 40% of its standard capacity, cannot be reduced below its current level of eight employees, all of whom are paid a wage of £160 per week.

　　(iv)　The designs and specifications of the original machine could be sold to an overseas customer for £4,500 if the machine is scrapped.

　　(v)　If conversion work is undertaken, a temporary supervisor would need to be employed for four weeks at a total cost of £1,500. It is normal company practice to charge supervision costs to fixed overhead.

　　(vi)　The original customer has already paid a non-returnable deposit to Gladiator Ltd of 12.5% of the selling price.

Task

Calculate the minimum price that Gladiator Ltd should quote for the converted machine. Explain clearly how you have reached this figure.

SOLUTION

The minimum price is the price which reflects the opportunity costs of the work. These are established as follows.

(a)　Past costs are not relevant, and the £126,000 of cost incurred should be excluded from the minimum price calculation. It is necessary, however, to consider the alternative use of the direct materials which would be forgone if the conversion work is carried out.

	£
Type A	
Revenue from sales as scrap (note (i))	8,000
Type B	
Revenue from sales as scrap,	
minus the additional cash costs necessary to	
prepare it for sale (£2,400 – (120 × £4.50)) (note (i))	1,860
Type C	
Cost of disposal if the machine is not converted	
(a negative opportunity cost) (note (ii))	(1,100)
Total opportunity cost of materials types A, B and C	8,760

By agreeing to the conversion of the machine, Gladiator Ltd would therefore lose a net revenue of £8,760 from the alternative use of these materials.

Notes

(i) Scrap sales would be lost if the conversion work goes ahead.

(ii) These costs would be incurred unless the work goes ahead.

(b) The cost of additional direct materials for conversion is £9,600, but this is an historical cost. The relevant cost of these materials is the £8,800 which would be spent on new purchases if the conversion is carried out. If the conversion work goes ahead, the materials in stock would be unavailable for production of the other machine mentioned in item (d)(ii) of the question and so the extra purchases of £8,800 would then be needed.

(c) Direct labour in departments X and Y is a fixed cost and the labour force will be paid regardless of the work they do or do not do. The cost of labour for conversion in department Y is not a relevant cost because the work could be done without any extra cost to the company.

In department X, however, acceptance of the conversion work would oblige the company to divert production from other profitable jobs. The minimum contribution required from using department X labour must be sufficient to cover the cost of the labour and variable overheads and then make an additional £2.50 in contribution per direct labour hour.

Department X: costs for direct labour hours spent on conversion

6 workers × 4 weeks × £210 =	£5,040
Variable overhead cost £5,040 × 20% =	£1,008
Contribution forgone by diverting labour from other work £2.50 per £1 of labour cost = £5,040 × 250% =	£12,600

(d) Variable overheads in department Y are relevant costs because they will only be incurred if production work is carried out. (It is assumed that if the workforce is idle, no variable overheads would be incurred.)

Department Y 20% of (2 workers × 4 weeks × £160) = £256

(e) If the machine is converted, the company cannot sell the designs and specifications to the overseas company. £4,500 is a relevant (opportunity) cost of accepting the conversion order.

(f) Fixed overheads, being mainly unchanged regardless of what the company decides to do, should be ignored because they are not relevant (incremental) costs. The additional cost of supervision should, however, be included as a relevant cost of the order because the £1,500 will not be spent unless the conversion work is done.

(g) The non-refundable deposit received should be ignored and should not be deducted in the calculation of the minimum price. Just as costs incurred in the past are not relevant to a current decision about what to do in the future, revenues collected in the past are also irrelevant.

Estimate of minimum price for the converted machine:

	£	£
Opportunity cost of using the direct materials types A, B and C		8,760
Opportunity cost of additional materials for conversion		8,800
Opportunity cost of work in department X		
Labour	5,040	
Variable overhead	1,008	
Contribution forgone	12,600	
		18,648
Opportunity cost: sale of designs and specifications		4,500
Incremental costs:		
Variable production overheads in department Y		256
Fixed production overheads (additional supervision)		1,500
Minimum price		42,464

Activity 7 (15 minutes)

Brown Ltd has recently shut down its London factory which used to make cushions, although all the stocks of raw materials and machinery are still there awaiting disposal. A former customer has just asked whether he could be supplied with one last delivery of 500 cushions. You ascertain the following facts.

(a) There is sufficient covering material in stock. This originally cost £400 but has a disposal value of £190.

(b) There is sufficient stuffing in stock. This originally cost £350. It was to have been shipped to the Bristol factory at a cost of £80. The Bristol factory would currently expect to pay £500 for this quantity.

(c) Labour costs would be £450.

(d) A supervisor could be spared from the Bristol factory for the week needed to produce the cushions. His normal wage is £160 and his rail fare and hotel bill in London would amount to £135.

(e) Before the factory was closed, fixed overheads were absorbed at 200% of direct labour cost.

Task

Calculate the minimum price that could be quoted.

Activity 8 (10 minutes)

Dyer Ltd has decided to price its jobs as follows.

(a) It calculates the minimum price for the job using relevant costs.
(b) It adds £5,000 to cover fixed costs.
(c) It adds a 10% profit margin to the total cost.

A customer who has work to be performed in May says he will award the contract to Dyer Ltd if its bid is reduced by £5,000. Assess whether the contract should be accepted.

In setting the price, management must decide **how much profit** it would consider reasonable on the job. A simple cost-plus approach can be used (for example, add 10% to the minimum price) but the company management should **consider the effect that the additional jobs will have** on the activities engaged in by the company and whether these activities will create additional unforeseen costs.

Sometimes an organisation may depart from its typical price-setting routine and 'low-ball' bid jobs. The rationale behind **low-ball bids** is to obtain the job so as to have the opportunity to introduce products or services to a particular market segment. During the recession of the early 1990s, there were many reports of accountancy firms 'low balling' – submitting tenders for audit and other work at very low prices. As well as the shortage of work resulting from the recession, one of the reasons behind this was probably often the desire to gain a competitive edge. By gaining new clients with low priced audit work, the firms hoped to 'cross-sell' other more lucrative services, such as consultancy, to the same clients.

'Low ball' pricing may provide work for a period of time, but cannot be continued in the long term. To remain in business, an organisation must set selling prices which cover total variable costs and an appropriate amount of fixed costs, and provide a reasonable profit margin.

7.3 Qualitative factors

When setting prices, management must consider qualitative as well as quantitative issues.

(a) Will setting a low bid price cause the customer (or others) to feel that a **precedent** has been established for future prices?

(b) Will the contribution margin on a bid set low enough to acquire the job, **earn a sufficient amount to justify the additional burdens** placed on management or employees by the activity?

(c) How, if at all, will fixed price tenders **affect the organisation's normal sales?**

(d) If the job is taking place during a period of low business activity (off-season or during a recession), is management willing to take the business at a **lower contribution or profit margin simply to keep a valued workforce employed?**

7.4 Monitoring costs against fixed prices

Once the tender has been submitted and accepted, management must ensure that actual costs do not exceed the estimated costs, since for every cost overrun, profit is eroded.

NOTES

Actual costs must therefore monitored in detail on a regular basis. **Variances** between actual and estimated costs must be **investigated**. If the estimates are found to be incorrect then profit forecasts must be revised; if actual costs are too high they must be brought under control and back in line with estimates.

The last point takes us back to budgeting (Chapter 8). As you can see from this chapter, the pricing decision is complex. The context of the decision must be considered along with a number of other factors.

Chapter roundup

- In practice in the modern world there are many more influences on pricing policy than the cost of a product or service.

- A typical product has a life cycle of four stages

- Competition affects pricing policy. A price leader indicates to the other firms in the market what the price will be.

- Market penetration pricing and market skimming pricing are pricing policies for new products.

- Differential pricing involves selling the same product at different prices to different customers.

- The price of elasticity of demand measures the extent of change in demand for a good following a change in price. Demand can be elastic or inelastic.

- The demand-based approach to pricing involves determining a profit-maximising price.

- Using full cost plus pricing, the sales price is determined by calculating the full cost of the product and adding a percentage mark-up for profit. The approach is unlikely to arrive at a profit-maximising price.

- Marginal cost plus pricing (mark-up pricing) involves adding a profit margin to the marginal cost of production or the marginal cost of sales.

- The opportunity cost approach to pricing involves including the opportunity costs of resources consumed in making and selling the item in the cost of the product and then adding a profit margin.

- Fixed price tenders involve an analysis of relevant costs. A margin is often added to the minimum price.

Quick quiz

1   Name ten influences (apart from cost) on pricing policy.

2   What are the four stages of the product life cycle?

3   What price is first charged for a product under a policy of market penetration pricing?

4   What are the four bases on which the same product can be sold at different prices to different customers?

5   Demand is elastic when a small price change produces a large change in quantity demanded. True or false?

6   What form of pricing is useful for businesses that carry out a large amount of jobbing or contract work?

7   Describe two drawbacks to marginal cost plus pricing?

8   What costs does a minimum price cover?

9   What qualitative issues should management consider when submitting a fixed price quotation.

Answers to quick quiz

1   Price sensitivity, price perception, quality, intermediaries, competitors, suppliers, uniqueness, incomes, product range, ethics, substitute products

2   Introduction, growth, maturity, decline

3   A low price

4   By maker segment, by product version, by place, by time

5   True

6   Full cost plus pricing

7   Although the size of the mark-up can be varied in accordance with demand conditions, it does not ensure that sufficient attention is paid to demand conditions, competitors' prices and profit maximisation.

   It ignores fixed overheads in the pricing decision, but the price must be high enough to ensure that a profit is made after covering fixed costs. Pricing decisions cannot ignore fixed costs altogether.

8   • The incremental costs of producing and selling the item

   • The opportunity costs of the resources consumed in making and selling the item

9   Will setting a low bid price cause the customer (or others) to feel that a precedent has been established for future prices?

   Will the contribution margin on a bid set low enough to acquire the job, earn a sufficient amount to justify the additional burdens placed on management or employees by the activity?

   How, if at all, will fixed price tenders affect the organisation's normal sales?

If the job is taking place during a period of low business activity (off-season or during a recession), is management willing to take the business at a lower contribution or profit margin simply to keep a valued workforce employed?

Answers to activities

1 Off-peak travel bargains, hotel prices, telephone and electricity charges are examples.

2 Annual demand at £1.20 per unit is 800,000 units.

Annual demand at £1.30 per unit is 725,000 units.

$$\text{\% change in demand} \quad = \quad \frac{75,000}{800,000} \times 100\% = 9.375\%$$

$$\text{\% change in price} \quad = \quad \frac{10p}{120p} \times 100\% = 8.333\%$$

$$\text{Price elasticity of demand} \quad = \quad \frac{-9.375}{8.333} = -1.125$$

Ignoring the minus sign, price elasticity is 1.125.

The demand for this good, at a price of £1.20 per unit, would be referred to as *elastic* because the price elasticity of demand is greater than 1.

3

Sales price	Unit contribution	Sales volume	Total contribution
£	£	Units	£
13.00	5.00	3,400	17,000
13.25	5.25	3,300	17,325
13.50	5.50	3,200	17,600
13.75	5.75	3,100	17,825
14.00	6.00	3,000	18,000
14.25	6.25	2,900	18,125
14.50	6.50	2,800	18,200
14.75	6.75	2,700	*18,225
15.00	7.00	2,600	18,200

* Contribution would be maximised at a price of £14.75, and sales of 2,700 units.

The current price is not optimal.

4 Price needs to be reduced to £7.99

$$\text{Mark-up therefore needs to be} \left(\frac{7.99 - 4.75}{4.75} \right) \times 100\% = 68\%$$

The mark-up therefore needs to be reduced by 2%.

5 To breakeven, total contribution = fixed costs

Let selling price = p

Unit contribution = p – 15

Total monthly contribution $\qquad$ = 400 (p – 15)

At breakeven point, $\quad$ 400(p – 15) $\quad$ = 10,000

$\qquad\qquad\qquad\qquad$ p – 15 $\quad$ = 25

$\qquad\qquad\qquad\qquad\qquad$ p $\quad$ = 40

Profit mark-up = $\dfrac{40-15}{15} \times 100\% = 166^2/_3\%$

6   If a rival cuts its prices in the expectation of increasing its market share, a firm has several options.

   (a) Reeves could *maintain its existing prices* if the expectation is that only a small market share would be lost, so that it is more profitable to keep prices at their existing level. Eventually Mortimer may drop out of the market or be forced to raise its prices.

   (b) Reeves may *maintain its prices but respond with non-price measures.* This is a more positive response, because the firm will be securing or justifying its current prices with a product change or advertising.

   (c) It may *reduce its prices.* This should protect the firm's market share so that the main beneficiary from the price reduction will be the consumer.

   (d) It may *raise its prices and respond with non-price measures.* The extra revenue from the higher prices might be used to finance an advertising campaign or packaging design changes. A price increase would be based on a campaign to emphasise the quality difference between the firm's own product and the rival's product.

7   The minimum price is estimated from the relevant costs of producing the cushions.

	£
Covering material (the opportunity cost of this material is its scrap value of £190	
The original cost is irrelevant because it is a historical cost, not a future cash flow)	190
Stuffing (the opportunity cost of the stuffing is the savings forgone by not sending it to Bristol, net of the transport costs of getting it to Bristol: £(500 – 80))	420
Labour: incremental cost	450
Supervisor's expenses: incremental expense item	135
Minimum price	1,195

The supervisor's basic wage and the overheads are irrelevant to the decision because these are costs that would be incurred anyway, even if the cushions were not produced.

8   Yes or no.

Yes, if there is no other work available, because Dyer will at least earn a contribution towards fixed costs of 10% of the minimum cost.

No, if by accepting this reduced price it would send a signal to other prospective customers that they too could negotiate such a large reduction.

LEARNING MEDIA

Chapter 10:

INVESTMENT AND PROJECT APPRAISAL

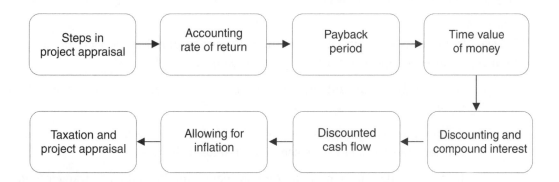

Introduction

In this chapter, we look at how potential investments and projects are assessed. The management of an organisation will have a number of investment decisions to make as time moves on. These decisions vary from which carpet to purchase for the boardroom, through which production machine should be purchased to manufacture widgets, to whether to invest in a new business venture.

A number of considerations must be made before an investment is agreed and implemented. These are covered in this chapter.

Your objectives

In this chapter you will learn about the following.

- The methods of project appraisal: accounting rate of return, payback and discounted cash flow

- The concepts of time preference, the opportunity cost of finance and the cost of capital

- Relevant cash flows

- Net present value and internal rate of return methods

- The implications of taxation and inflation in discounted cash flow

Managing Financial Resources and Decisions

1 STEPS IN PROJECT APPRAISAL

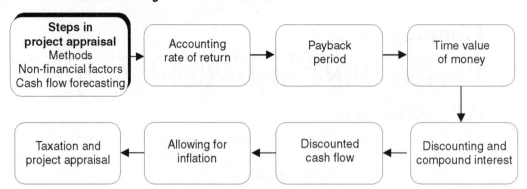

We have already discussed capital expenditure. Proper appraisal of projects involving capital expenditure is important for the following reasons.

(a) A relatively significant amount of the resources of the business will be involved.

(b) A capital investment decision may be difficult to reverse, and on any reversal considerable costs may have been incurred for little benefit.

(c) Investment decisions need to be considered in the light of strategic and tactical decisions of the company. The decision made should be consistent with the company's long-term objective, which will usually be the maximisation of the wealth of shareholders

(d) Future benefits need detailed evaluation since they are often difficult to predict. Consequently, there may be a high degree of risk and uncertainty.

The **decision making and control cycle** in appraisal or evaluation of a capital project has the following key stages.

(a) **Initial investigation of the proposal.** Is it feasible, technically and commercially? What are its main risks? Does it match the firm's long-term strategic objectives?

(b) **Detailed evaluation.** Once the feasibility of the project has been established, a detailed investigation will examine expected cash flows arising from the project, using methods such as those we will identify and use below. The effects of **risk** may be analysed by evaluating the effects on the cash flows of different 'What if...?' outcomes occurring: this is called **sensitivity analysis**. Sources of necessary **finance** will need to be considered. If there are not enough funds to undertake all proposals, they should be ranked in order of priority.

(c) **Authorisation.** For capital projects that are significant relative to the size of the company, authorisation rules will require that the decision to go ahead is made by senior management or by the board of directors. Those making the decision must be satisfied that an appropriately detailed evaluation has been carried out, that the proposal meets the necessary criteria to contribute to profitability, and that it is consistent with the overall strategy of the enterprise.

(d) **Implementation.** Once the decision has been made that the project will be undertaken, responsibility for the project should be assigned to a *project manager* or other responsible person. The required resources will need to be made available to this manager, who should be given specific targets to achieve.

(e) **Project monitoring**. After the start of the project, progress should be monitored and senior management should be informed on the progress of the project regularly. The project can be monitored more effectively if the costs and benefits originally expected are reassessed in the light of unforeseen events happening in the course of the project.

(f) **Post-completion audit**. At the end of the project, a post-completion audit should be carried out in order to make use of what can be learned from the experience in the planning of future projects.

Audit of project performance can bring the following advantages.

(a) **Better future investment decisions**. The audit can identify where mistakes have been made, so that similar mistakes can be avoided in the future. It may also identify areas of success which might be replicated in future projects.

(b) **Better current investment decisions**. Awareness that an audit will be carried out at a later date may encourage managers involved to be more realistic and not unduly optimistic in their judgements. The data used in current appraisals may be improved as a result.

(c) **Contribution to performance evaluation**. A project audit can provide feedback to project managers and to senior management which is of use in the process of management control and performance assessment.

1.1 Methods of project appraisal

There are three principal methods of evaluating whether a capital project is of value to an enterprise.

(a) **The accounting rate of return (or return on investment)**. This method calculates the profits that will be earned by a project and expresses this as a percentage of the capital invested in the project. The higher the rate of return, the higher a project is ranked. This method is based on **accounting results** rather than cash flows.

(b) **The payback period.** This method of investment appraisal calculates the length of time a project will take to recoup the initial investment, in other words how long a project will take to pay for itself. The method is based on **cash flows**.

(c) **Discounted cash flow (DCF)**, which may be sub-divided into two approaches.

   (i) The **net present value (NPV) method** considers all relevant cash flows associated with a project over the whole of its life and adjusts those occurring in future years to their *'present value'* by discounting at a rate called the *'cost of capital'*. The NPV method should be used where possible, since it is consistent with the objective of maximising shareholder wealth.

   (ii) The **internal rate of return (IRR) method** involves comparing the rate of return expected from the project calculated on a discounted cash flow basis with the rate used as the cost of capital. Projects with an IRR higher than the cost of capital are worth undertaking.

1.2 Non-financial factors

A decision maker should always bear in mind *non-financial factors* that affect a decision, and you may be asked to identify these in a question. Such 'non-financial' factors may have indirect financial implications, for example at a later stage.

Possible non-financial factors

(a) **Legal issues.** Possible legal actions should be considered.

(b) **Ethical issues.** Unethical actions by a company could be damaging if not illegal.

(c) **Changes to regulations.** Many governments have regulations designed to promote competition, for example.

(d) **Political issues.** A future change of government in the country concerned could affect plans.

(e) **Quality implications.** Poorer quality materials or equipment may be cheaper but may lead to problems later on, for example problems relating to breakdowns and warranty claims by customers.

(f) **Personnel issues.** Personnel may be affected significantly by decisions, and the impact on personal relations, motivation and working culture may need to be considered.

(g) **Coherence.** The project may affect existing branding. A cheap version of a product may bring the perceived quality of existing products down in the consumers eyes.

EXAMPLE

Richard Branson's Virgin is associated with innovative products. It has broken into many different markets, including

- Cola
- Trains
- Mortgages
- Mobiles
- Wine

Investing in a new product should not be a problem for Virgin. Compare this with the prospect of a 'budget Jaguar'! If Jaguar were to sell an economy car model for, say, £15,000, how would this affect their current products?

Non-financial considerations and the general context is an important aspect of decision making. Compare this with the evaluation of financial performance in Chapter 6. Again we need to look at the wider picture. This is a key skill.

1.3 Cash flow forecasting

Before looking at each of these methods in turn it is worth emphasising one problem common to all of them, that of estimating future cash flows. *Cash flow forecasting* is never easy, but in capital budgeting the problems are particularly acute. This is because the period under consideration may not be merely a year or two, but five, ten, perhaps twenty years. It is therefore important that decision makers should consider that variations in the estimates might affect their decision.

2 ACCOUNTING RATE OF RETURN

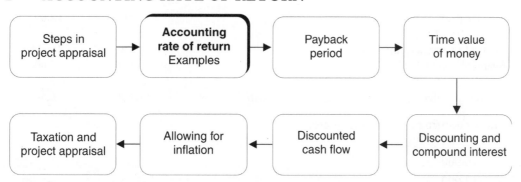

A capital investment project may be assessed by calculating the **return on investment (ROI)** or **accounting rate of return (ARR)** and comparing it with a pre-determined target level. A formula for ARR which is common in practice is:

$$ARR = \frac{\text{Estimated average profits}}{\text{Estimated average investment}} \times 100\%$$

Other formulae you may come across use total profits for the numerator, or initial investment for the denominator. Various combinations are possible, but the important thing is to be consistent once a method has been selected.

EXAMPLE: EVALUATING A PROJECT USING ARR

Queen Limited is contemplating the purchase of a new machine and has two alternatives.

	Machine A	Machine B
Cost	£10,000	£10,000
Estimated scrap value	£2,000	£3,000
Estimated life	4 years	4 years
Estimated future cash flows		
Year 1	£5,000	£2,000
2	£5,000	£3,000
3	£3,000	£5,000
4	£1,000	£5,000

The only difference between annual cash flows and annual profits is depreciation.

Based on the ARR method, which of the two machines would be purchased?

SOLUTION

Since ARR is based on accounting results rather than cash flows we must adjust the cashflows for depreciation. We can think of the value of the investment as the amount of money tied up in it. The average of this value is the average of the initial investment and the residual value.

	A	B
	£	£
Total cash flows	14,000	15,000
Total depreciation	8,000	7,000
Total profits after depreciation	6,000	8,000
Average profits (4 years)	£1,500	£2,000
Value of investment initially	10,000	10,000
Eventual residual value	2,000	3,000
	12,000	13,000
∴ Average value of investment (÷ 2)	6,000	6,500

The accounting rates of return are:

$$X = \frac{£1,500}{£6,000} = 25\%$$

$$Y = \frac{£2,000}{£6,500} = 31\%$$

Machine B would therefore be chosen. (Example end)

In the example above, note how as much weight was attached to cash inflows at year four as to those at year one, whereas the management of Queen Limited would favour high cash inflows in the early years. Early cash flows are less risky and they improve liquidity. For this reason, they might choose machine A despite its lower ARR. One of the disadvantages of the ARR method is that it does not take account of the timing of cash inflows and outflows.

Advantages of ARR	Disadvantages of ARR
A widely understood measure of accounting profitability.	Based on accounting profits rather than cash flow, giving too much emphasis to costs as conventionally defined which are not relevant to project performance.
Readily available from accounting data.	
	Fails to take account of the timing of cash inflows and outflows.

3   THE PAYBACK PERIOD

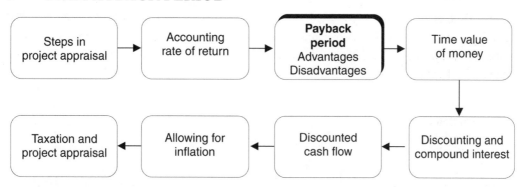

The **payback period** method is one which gives greater weight to cash flows generated in earlier years. The payback period is the length of time required before the total cash inflows received from the project is equal to the original cash outlay. In other words, it is the length of time the investment takes to pay itself back.

In the previous example, machine A pays for itself within two years and machine B in three years. Using the payback method of investment appraisal, machine A is preferable to machine B.

The payback method has obvious disadvantages. Consider the case of two machines for which the following information is available.

		Machine P	Machine Q
		£	£
Cost		10,000	10,000
Cash inflows year	1	1,000	5,000
	2	2,000	5,000
	3	6,000	1,000
	4	7,000	500
	5	8,000	500
		24,000	12,000

Machine Q pays back at the end of Year 2 and machine P not until early in Year 4. Using the payback method machine Q is to be preferred, but this ignores the fact that the total profitability of P (£24,000) is double that of Q.

Advantages of payback method	Disadvantages of payback method
It is widely used in practice, even if often only as a supplement to more sophisticated methods. Its use will tend to minimise the effects of risk and help liquidity, because greater weight is given to earlier cash flows which can probably be predicted more accurately than distant cash flows.	Total profitability is ignored. It ignores any cash flows that occur after the project has paid for itself. A project that takes time to get off the ground but earns substantial profits once established might be rejected if the payback method is used.

A more scientific method of investment appraisal is the use of discounted cash flow (DCF) techniques. Before DCF can be understood it is necessary to know something about the time value of money.

4 THE TIME VALUE OF MONEY

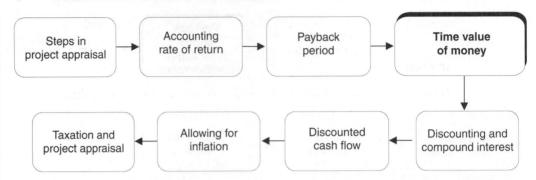

Money is spent to earn a profit. For example, if an item of machinery costs £6,000 and would earn profits (ignoring depreciation) of £2,000 per year for three years, it would not be worth buying because its total profit (£6,000) would only just cover its cost.

Clearly then, items of capital expenditure must earn profits or make savings to justify their costs, but we would also say that the size of profits or return must be sufficiently large to justify the investment. In the example given in the previous paragraph, if the machinery costing £6,000 made total profits of £6,300 over three years, the return on the investment would be £300, or an average of £100 per year. This would be a very low return, because it would be much more profitable to invest the £6,000 somewhere else (for example, on deposit at a bank).

We must recognise that if a capital investment is to be worthwhile, it must earn at least a minimum profit or return so that the size of the return will compensate the investor (the business) for the **length** of time which the investor must wait before the profits are made. (For example, if a company could invest £6,000 now to earn revenue of £6,300 in one week's time, a profit of £300 in seven days would be a very good return. If it takes three years to earn the revenue, however, the return would be very low.)

When capital expenditure projects are evaluated, it is therefore appropriate to decide whether the investment will make enough profits to allow for the **time value** of capital tied up. The time value of money reflects people's **time preference** for £100 now over £100 at some time in the future. DCF is an evaluation technique which takes into account the time value of money.

5 DISCOUNTING AND COMPOUND INTEREST

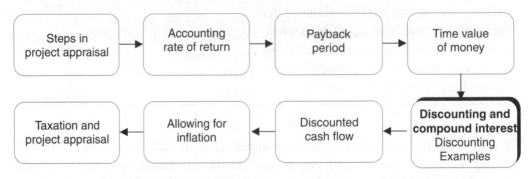

If we were to invest £1,000 now in a bank account which pays interest of 10% per annum, with interest calculated once each year at the end of the year, we would expect the following returns.

(a) After one year, the investment would rise in value to:

£1,000 plus 10% = £1,000 (1 + 10%) = £1,000 × (1.10) = £1,100

Interest for the year would be £100. We can say that the rate of **simple interest** is 10%.

(b) If we keep all our money in the bank account, after two years the investment would now be worth:

£1,100 × 1.10 = £1,210.

Interest in year two would be £(1,210 − 1,100) = £110.

Another way of writing this would be to show how the original investment has earned interest over two years as follows.

£1,000 × (1.10) × (1.10) = £1,000 × $(1.10)^2$ = £1,210

(c) Similarly, if we keep the money invested for a further year, the investment would grow to £1,000 × (1.10) × (1.10) × (1.10) = £1,000 × $(1.10)^3$ = £1,331 at the end of the third year. Interest in year three would be £(1,331 − 1,210) = £121.

This example shows how **compound interest** works. The amount of interest earned each year gets larger because we earn interest on both the original capital and also on the interest now earned in earlier years.

A formula which can be used to show the value of an investment after several years which earns compound interest is:

$S = P(1 + r)^n$

where

S = future value of the investment after n years
P = the amount invested now
r = the rate of interest, as a proportion. For example, 10% = 0.10, 25% = 0.25, 8% = 0.08
n = the number of years of the investment

EXAMPLE

Suppose that we invest £2,000 now at 10%. What would the investment be worth after the following number of years?

(a) Five years
(b) Six years

The future value of £1 after n years at 10% interest is given in the following table.

n	$(1 + r)^n$ with $r = 0.10$
1	1.100
2	1.210
3	1.331
4	1.464
5	1.611
6	1.772
7	1.949

The solution is as follows.

SOLUTION

(a) After five years:

$S = £2,000 \ (1.611) = £3,222$

(b) After six years:

$S = £2,000 \ (1.772) = £3,544$

The principles of compound interest are used in discounted cash flow, except that discounting is compounding in reverse.

5.1 Discounting

With **discounting**, we look at the size of an investment after a certain number of years, and calculate how much we would need to invest now to build up the investment to that size, given a certain rate of interest. This may seem complicated at first, and an example might help to make the point clear. With discounting, we can calculate how much we would need to invest now at an interest rate, of say, 6% to build up the investment to (say) £5,000 after four years.

The compound interest formula shows how we calculate a future sum S from a known current investment P, so that if $S = P \ (1 + r)^n$, then:

$$P = \frac{S}{(1+r)^n} = S \times \frac{1}{(1+r)^n}$$

This is the basic formula for discounting, which is sometimes written as: $P = S(1 + r)^{-n}$

$[\ (1 + r)^{-n}$ and $\dfrac{1}{(1+r)^n}$ mean exactly the same thing.]

EXAMPLE

To build up an investment to £5,000 after four years at 6% interest, we would need to invest now:

$$P = £5,000 \times \frac{1}{(1 + 0.06)^4}$$

$$= £5,000 \times 0.792 = £3,960$$

5.2 Further examples of discounting

If you have never done any discounting before, the basic principle and mathematical techniques might take some time to get used to. The following examples might help to make them clearer.

(a) A business person wants to have £13,310 in three years' time, and has decided to put some money aside now which will earn interest of 10% per annum. How much money must he put aside in order to build up the investment to £13,310 as required?

Solution $\quad P \quad = £13,310 \times \dfrac{1}{(1.10)^3} = £10,000$

Proof. After one year the investment would be worth £10,000 × 1.10 = £11,000; after two years it would be £11,000 × 1.10 = £12,100; and after three years it would be £12,100 × 1.10 = £13,310.

(b) Another businessman has two sons who are just 18 years and 17 years old. He wishes to give them £10,000 each on their 20th birthdays and he wants to know how much he must invest now at 8% interest to pay this amount.

The following table is relevant, giving values r = 8% or 0.08. Note that you can read the figures in the 'present value' column from the Present Value Table in the Appendix to this Course Book: look down the 8% column.

Year n	Future value of £1 $(1 + r)^n$	Present value of £1 $(1 + r)^{-n}$
1	1.080	0.926
2	1.166	0.857
3	1.260	0.794
4	1.360	0.735

The investment must provide £10,000 after two years for the elder son and £10,000 after three years for the younger son.

	After n years n =	Discount factor 8%		Amount provided £	Present value £
Elder son	2	0.857	×	10,000	8,570
Younger son	3	0.794	×	10,000	7,940
Total investment required					16,510

Proof. After two years the investment of £16,510 will be worth £16,510 × 1.166 = £19,251. After paying £10,000 to the elder son, £9,251 will be left after two years. This will earn interest of 8% in year three, to be worth £9,251 × 1.08 = £9,991 at the end of the year. This is almost enough to pay £10,000 to the younger son. The difference (£9) is caused by rounding errors in the table of discount (present value) factors and compound (future value) factors.

(c) A company is wondering whether to invest £15,000 in a project which will pay £20,000 after two years. It will not invest unless the return from the investment is at least 10% per annum. Is the investment worthwhile? The present value of £1 in two years time at 10% interest is 0.826.

SOLUTION

The return of £20,000 after two years is equivalent to an investment now at 10% of £20,000 × 0.826 = £16,520.

In other words, in order to obtain £20,000 after two years, the company would have to invest £16,520 now at an interest rate of 10%. The project offers the same payment at a cost of only £15,000, so that it must provide a return in excess of 10% and it is therefore worthwhile.

	£
Present value of future profits at 10%	16,520
Cost of investment	15,000
The investment in the project offers the same return, but at a cost lower by	1,520

6   DISCOUNTED CASH FLOW

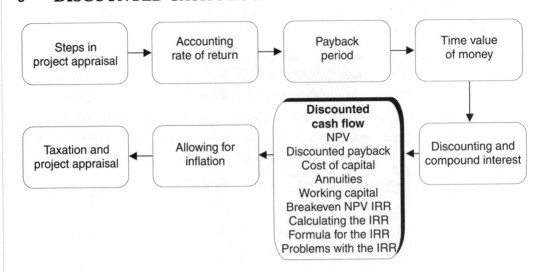

Definition

> **Discounted cash flow** is a technique of evaluating capital investment projects, using discounting arithmetic to determine whether or not they will provide a satisfactory return.

A typical investment project involves a payment of capital for fixed assets at the start of the project and then there will be profits coming in from the investment over a number of years.

The word 'profits' however, is not really appropriate in DCF, for two main reasons.

(a) The cost of a fixed asset is charged against profits each year as depreciation in the normal financial accounts. In DCF, however, depreciation must be ignored because the full cost of the asset is treated as a capital investment at the start of the project. It would therefore be wrong to charge depreciation against profits as well because this would be 'double-counting' the cost.

(b) The return on an investment only occurs when the investor receives payments in cash. There is a difference between accounting profits and cash receipts less cash payments and in DCF it is the *cash flows* which are considered more relevant. For example, suppose that a company makes profits of £5,000 before depreciation during one year, but in that time increases its debtors by £1,000. The cash received in the year would not be £5,000, but only £4,000. In DCF, the return for the year would be taken as the cash flow of £4,000, not the profit of £5,000.

In addition it should be noted that DCF methods use relevant cash flows only, as studied in Chapter 7.

As we noted earlier, DCF can be used in either of two ways: the **net present value method,** or the **internal rate of return** (sometimes called DCF yield, DCF rate of return) method. We will now look at each method in turn.

6.1 The net present value (NPV) method of DCF

The **net present value (NPV) method** of evaluation is as follows.

(a) Determine the present value of costs. In other words, decide how much capital must be set aside to pay for the project. Let this be £C.

(b) Calculate the present value of relevant future cash benefits from the project. To do this we take the cash benefit in each year and discount it to a present value. This shows how much we would have to invest now to earn the future benefits, if our rate of return were equal to the cost of capital. ('Cost of capital' is explained below.) By adding up the present value of benefits for each future year, we obtain the total present value of benefits from the project. Let this be £B.

(c) Compare the present value of costs £C with the present value of benefits £B. The net present value is the difference between them: £(B – C).

(d) If the NPV is positive, the present value of benefits exceeds the present value of costs. This in turn means that the project will earn a return in excess of the cost of capital. Therefore, the project should be accepted.

(e) If the NPV is negative, this means that it would cost us more to invest in the project to obtain the future cash receipts than it would cost us to invest somewhere else, at a rate of interest equal to the cost of capital, to obtain an equal amount of future receipts. The project would earn a return lower than the cost of capital and would not be worth investing in.

EXAMPLE: THE NPV METHOD

A company is wondering whether to invest £18,000 in a project which would make extra profits (before depreciation is deducted) of £10,000 in the first year, £8,000 in the second year and £6,000 in the third year. Its cost of capital is 10% (in other words, it would require a return of at least 10% on its investment). You are required to evaluate the project.

SOLUTION

In DCF we make several assumptions. One such assumption is that discounted cash flows (payments or receipts) occur on the last day of each year. For example, although profits are £10,000 during the course of Year 1, we assume that the £10,000 is not received until the last day of Year 1. Similarly, the profits of £8,000 and £6,000 in Years 2 and 3 are assumed to occur on the last day of Years 2 and 3 respectively. The cash payment of £18,000 occurs 'now' at the start of Year 1. To be consistent, we say that this payment occurs on the last day of the current year which is often referred to as year 0.

The NPV is now calculated with discounting arithmetic. Note that the Present Value Table in the Appendix to this Course Book gives us the following values.

Year	Present value of £1	
n	$(1 + r)^{-n}$	where r = 0.10
1	0.909	
2	0.826	
3	0.751	

NOTES

Year	Cash flow	Present value factor	Present value
	£	10%	£
0	(18,000)	1.000	(18,000)
1	10,000	0.909	9,090
2	8,000	0.826	6,608
3	6,000	0.751	4,506
		NPV	2,204

The NPV is positive, which means that the project will earn more than 10%. (£20,204 would have to be invested now at 10% to earn the future cash flows; since the project will earn these returns at a cost of only £18,000 it must earn a return in excess of 10%.)

Activity 1   **(15 minutes)**

A project would involve a capital outlay of £24,000. Profits (before depreciation) each year would be £5,000 for six years. The cost of capital is 12%. Is the project worthwhile?

(Use the Present Value Table in the Appendix.)

If the NPV method is followed, expected **shareholder wealth** will be maximised. If the NPV of a project is positive, shareholders will be better off if the project is accepted. *Problems* with the NPV method are as follows.

(a) Some managers are unfamiliar with the concept of NPV.

(b) It can be difficult to identify an appropriate discount rate.

(c) For simplicity, cash flows are sometimes all assumed to occur at year ends: this assumption may be unrealistic.

6.2 Discounted payback method

We have seen how discounting cash flows is a way of reflecting the time value of money in investment appraisal. The further into the future a cash flow is expected to be, the more uncertain it tends to be, and the returns or interest paid to the suppliers of capital (ie to investors) in part reflects this uncertainty. The **discounted payback technique** is an adaptation of the payback technique, which we looked at earlier, taking some account of the time value of money. To calculate the discounted payback period, we establish the time at which the net present value of an investment becomes positive.

FOR DISCUSSION: DISCOUNTED PAYBACK PERIOD

We can calculate the discounted payback period for the example above. Having produced a net present value analysis as in the solution above, we calculate the discounted payback period as follows.

Year	Present value	Cumulative PV
	£	£
0	(18,000)	(18,000)
1	9,090	(8,910)
2	6,608	(2,302)
3	4,506	2,204
	2,204	

SOLUTION

If we assume now that cash flows in Year 3 are even, instead of occurring on the last day of the year, the discounted payback period can be estimated as follows.

Discounted payback period = 2 yrs + 2,302/4,506 yrs

= 2.51 yrs, say 2 ½ years

This compares with a non-discounted payback period of two years for the same project, since the initial outlay of £18,000 is recouped in money terms by Year 2. The discounted payback period of 2½ years suggests that if the project must be terminated within that period, it will not have added value to the company.

Like the basic payback method, the discounted payback method fails to take account of positive cash flows occurring after the end of the payback period.

6.3 The cost of capital

We have mentioned that the appropriate discount rate to use in investment appraisal is the company's **cost of capital**. In practice, this is a difficult figure to determine. It is often suggested that the discount rate which a company should use as its cost of capital is one that reflects the return expected by its investors in shares and loan stock. Investors will expect to receive a return at least as high as that which they could receive from alternative investments with the same level of risk, and this level of return can be termed the **opportunity cost of finance**.

Shareholders expect dividends and capital gains; loan stock investors expect interest payments. A company must make enough profits from its own operations (and this includes capital expenditure projects) to pay dividends and interest. The average return is the weighted average of the return required by shareholders and loan stock investors. The cost of capital is therefore the **weighted average cost** of all the sources of capital which a company uses.

6.4 Annuities

In DCF the term 'annuities' refers to an annual cash payment which is the same amount every year for a number of years, or else an annual receipt of cash which is the same amount every year for a number of years.

In Activity 1 above, the profits are an annuity of £5,000 per annum for six years. The present value of profits (£20,560 as shown in the answer at the end of the chapter) is the present value of an annuity of £5,000 per annum for six years at a discount rate of 12%.

NOTES

When there is an annuity to be discounted, there is a shortcut method of calculation. You may already have seen what it is. Instead of multiplying the cash flow each year by the present value factor for that year, and then adding up all the present values (as shown in the solution above), we can multiply the annuity by the sum of the present value factors.

Thus we could have multiplied £5,000 by the sum of (0.893 + 0.797 + 0.712 + 0.636 + 0.567 + 0.507) = 4.112. We then have £5,000 × 4.112 = £20,560.

This quick calculation is made even quicker by the use of 'annuity' tables. These show the sum of the present value factors each year from year one to year n.

The Annuity Table in the Appendix to this Course Book shows the following.

Years N	Present value of £1 received per year $\dfrac{[1-(1+r)^{-n}]}{r}$	Notes
1	0.893	PV factor for year 1 only
2	1.690	(0.893 + 0.797)
3	2.402	(add 0.712)
4	3.038	(add 0.636)
5	3.605	(add 0.567)
6	4.112	(add 0.507)

EXAMPLE

A project would involve a capital outlay of £50,000. Profits (before depreciation) would be £12,000 per year. The cost of capital is 10%. Would the project be worthwhile if it lasts the following numbers of years?

(a)   Five years
(b)   Seven years

SOLUTION

We can find the discount factors from the Annuity Table in the Appendix.

(a)   *If the project lasts five years*

Years	Cash flow £	Discount factor 10%	Present value £
0	(50,000)	1.000	(50,000)
1 – 5	12,000 pa	3.791	45,492
		NPV	(4,508)

(b)   *If the project lasts seven years*

Years	Cash flow £	Discount factor 10%	Present value £
0	(50,000)	1.000	(50,000)
1 – 7	12,000 pa	4.868	58,416
		NPV	8,416

The project is not worthwhile if it last only five years, but it would be worthwhile if it lasted for seven years. The decision to accept or to reject the project must depend on management's view about its duration.

Activity 2 **(20 minutes)**

(a) A project would cost £39,500. It would earn £10,000 per year for the first three years and then £8,000 per year for the next three years. The cost of capital is 10%. Is the project worth undertaking?

(b) Another project would cost £75,820. If its life is expected to be five years and the cost of capital is 10%, what are the minimum annual savings required to make the project worthwhile?

Use the Annuity Table in the Appendix to derive your answers.

6.5 Working capital

You might be given a problem in which you are told that in addition to capital expenditure on plant and machinery, a project would require some investment in **working capital** (ie stocks and debtors). To understand how this situation would be treated in DCF, it is necessary to remember the following.

(a) An increase in working capital leads to a reduction in expected total cash receipts and a decrease in working capital leads to an increase in cash receipts.

(b) If a project needs working capital, the amount of capital required should be treated as an **outflow** (payment of cash), usually at the start of the project life (ie year 0).

(c) Once the project ends, the working capital will no longer be needed and can be reduced to zero. This will cause an additional inflow of cash, usually in the last year of the project.

EXAMPLE: WORKING CAPITAL

A project would involve the purchase of some plant for £25,000 and an investment in working capital of £6,000. It would earn £10,000 per year for four years. The cost of capital is 9%. Is the project worthwhile?

SOLUTION

Year		*Cash flow* £	*Discount factor* 9%	*Present value* £
0	Plant	(25,000)	1.000	(25,000)
0	Working capital increase	(6,000)	1.000	(6,000)
1-4	Income	10,000pa	3.240	32,400
4	Working capital decrease	6,000	0.708	4,248
			NPV	5,648

The NPV is positive and the project is worthwhile. Note that the net cost of the working capital invested makes a difference of £(6,000 – 4,248) = £1,752 to the NPV.

NOTES

6.6 Calculating a 'breakeven' NPV

You might be asked to calculate how much income would need to be generated for the NPV of a project to be zero. This is referred to as **breakeven NPV**.

EXAMPLE: BREAKEVEN NPV

For the project in the example above, calculate how much the annual income from the project could reduce before the NPV would reach a 'breakeven' zero level.

SOLUTION

For every £1 reduction in the annual income of £10,000, the NPV will fall by £1 × 3.240 = £3.240.

'Breakeven' fall in income = £5,648 ÷ 3.240 = £1,743

Annual income of £10,000 − £1,743 = £8,257 will result in a 'breakeven' NPV of zero.

6.7 Internal rate of return (IRR)

The *internal rate of return method* of DCF involves two steps.

(a) Calculating the rate of return which is expected from a project
(b) Comparing the rate of return with the cost of capital

If a project earns a higher rate of return than the cost of capital, it will be worth undertaking (and its NPV would be positive). If it earns a lower rate of return, it is not worthwhile (and its NPV would be negative). If a project earns a return which is exactly equal to the cost of capital, its NPV will be 0 and it will only just be worthwhile.

6.8 Calculating the internal rate of return

You may find the method of calculating the rate of return to be rather unsatisfactory because it involves some guesswork and approximation. An example will help to illustrate the technique.

Suppose that a project would cost £20,000 and the annual net cash inflows are expected to be as follows. What is the internal rate of return of the project?

Year	Cash flow £
1	8,000
2	10,000
3	6,000
4	4,000

The IRR is a rate of interest at which the NPV is 0 and the discounted (present) values of benefits add up to £20,000. We need to find out what interest rate or cost of capital would give an NPV of 0. The way we do this is to guess what it might be, and calculate the NPV at this cost of capital. It is most unlikely that the NPV will turn out to be 0, but we are hoping that it will be nearly 0.

We repeat this exercise until we find two rates of return.

(a) One at which the NPV is a small positive value. The actual IRR will be higher than this rate of return.

(b) One at which the NPV is a small negative value. The actual IRR will be lower than this rate of return.

The actual IRR will then be found (approximately) by using the two rates in (a) and (b).

In our example, we might begin by trying discount rates of 10%, 15% and 20%.

Year	Cash flow	Discount factor at 10%	Present value at 10%	Discount factor at 15%	Present value at 15%	Discount factor at 20%	Present value at 20%
	£		£		£		£
0	(20,000)	1.000	(20,000)	1.000	(20,000)	1.000	(20,000)
1	8,000	0.909	7,272	0.870	6,960	0.833	6,664
2	10,000	0.826	8,260	0.756	7,560	0.694	6,940
3	6,000	0.751	4,506	0.658	3,948	0.579	3,474
4	4,000	0.683	2,732	0.572	2,288	0.482	1,928
Net present value			2,770		756		(994)

The IRR is more than 15% but less than 20%. We could try to be more accurate by trying a discount rate of 16%, 17%, 18% or 19%, but in this solution we will use the values for 15% and 20% to estimate the IRR.

To estimate the IRR, we now assume that the NPV falls steadily and at a constant rate between £756 at 15% and £(994) at 20%. This represents a fall of £(756 + 994) = £1,750 in NPV between 15% and 20%. This is an average fall of:

$$\frac{£1,750}{(20-15)\%} = £350 \text{ in NPV for each 1\% increase in the discount rate.}$$

Since the IRR is where the NPV is 0, it must be $\dfrac{£756}{£350} \times 1\%$ above 15%, ie about 2.2% above 15% = 17.2%.

6.9 A formula for the IRR

A formula for making this calculation (which is known as **interpolation**) is as follows.

$$IRR = A + \left[\frac{a}{a+b} \times (B - A) \right]$$

where A is the discount rate which provides the positive NPV
        a is the amount of the positive NPV
        B is the discount rate which provides the negative NPV
        b is the amount of the negative NPV but the minus sign is ignored

In our example, using this formula, the IRR would be calculated as follows.

$$15\% + \left[\frac{756}{756 + 994} \times (20 - 15) \right]\%$$

$$= \quad 15\% + [\, 0.432 \times 5 \,]\%$$
$$= \quad 15\% + 2.16\%$$

$$= \quad 17.16\%, \text{ say } 17.2\%$$

6.10 Problems with the IRR method

(a) Some managers are unfamiliar with the IRR method.

(b) It may give conflicting recommendations with mutually exclusive projects, because the result is given in relative terms (percentages), and not in absolute terms (£s) as with NPV.

(c) Projects with unconventional cash flows can produce negative or multiple IRRs.

(d) IRR may be confused with ARR or return on capital employed (ROCE), since all give answers in percentage terms.

7 ALLOWING FOR INFLATION

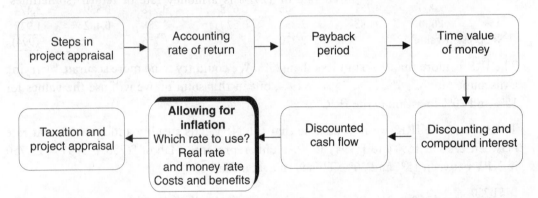

We now consider the effect of **inflation** on the appraisal of capital investment proposals. As we saw earlier, inflation refers to a sustained increase in the level of prices over a period of time. As the inflation rate increases so will the minimum return required by an investor. For example, you might be happy with a return of 5% in an inflation-free world, but if inflation was running at 15% you would expect a considerably greater yield.

You won't be expected to carry out detailed calculations of a net present value involving inflation – but looking at some examples involving calculations will help you understand the points involved.

EXAMPLE: INFLATION (1)

A company is considering investing in a project with the following cash flows.

Time	Actual cash flows
	£
0	(15,000)
1	9,000
2	8,000
3	7,000

The company requires a minimum return of 12½% under the present and anticipated conditions. Inflation is currently running at 4% a year, and this rate of inflation is expected to continue indefinitely. Should the company go ahead with the project?

Let us first look at the company's required rate of return. Suppose that it invested £1,000 for one year on 1 January, then on 31 December it would require a minimum return of £125. With the initial investment of £1,000, the total value of the investment by 31 December must therefore increase to £1,125. During the course of the year the purchasing value of the pound would fall due to inflation. We can restate the amount received on 31 December in terms of the purchasing power of the pound at 1 January as follows.

Amount received on 31 December in terms of the value of the pound at 1 January

$$= \frac{£1,125}{(1.04)^1} = £1,082$$

In terms of the value of the pound at 1 January, the company would make a profit of £82 which represents a rate of return of 8.2% in 'today's money' terms. This is known as the **real rate of return**. The required rate of 12½% is a money rate of return (sometimes called a nominal rate of return). The money rate measures the return in terms of the pound which is, of course, falling in value. The real rate measures the return in constant price level terms.

The two rates of return and the inflation rate are linked by the equation:

(1 + money rate) = (1 + real rate) × (1 + inflation rate)

where all the rates are expressed as proportions.

In our example:

(1 + 0.125) = (1 + 0.082) × (1 + 0.04) = 1.125

7.1 Which rate is used in discounting?

We must decide which rate to use for discounting, the real rate or the money rate. The rule is as follows. If the cash flows are expressed in terms of the actual number of pounds that will be received or paid on the various future dates, we use the **money rate** for discounting. If the cash flows are expressed in terms of the value of the pound at time 0 (that is, in constant price level terms), we use the **real rate**.

The cash flows given in the above example are expressed in terms of the actual number of pounds that will be received or paid at the relevant dates. We should, therefore, discount them using the money rate of return.

Time	Cash flow	Discount factor		PV
	£	12½%		£
0	(15,000)	1.000		(15,000)
1	9,000	0.889		8,001
2	8,000	0.790	(W1)	6,320
3	7,000	0.702		4,914
				4,235

The project has a positive net present value of £4,235.

Working

The discount factors for 12½% have been worked out from the basic formula, eg for

time 2 $\frac{1}{(1.125)^2} = 0.790$

The future cash flows can be re-expressed in terms of the value of the pound at time 0 as follows, given inflation at 4% a year.

Time	Actual cash flow £	Cash flow at time 0 price level		£
0	(15,000)			(15,000)
1	9,000	$9,000 \times \dfrac{1}{1.04}$	=	8,654
2	8,000	$8,000 \times \dfrac{1}{(1.04)^2}$	=	7,396
3	7,000	$7,000 \times \dfrac{1}{(1.04)^3}$	=	6,223

The cash flows expressed in terms of the value of the pound at time 0 can now be discounted using the real rate of 8.2%.

Time	Cash flow £	Discount factor 8.2%	PV £
0	(15,000)	1.00	(15,000)
1	8,654	$\dfrac{1}{1.082}$	7,998
2	7,396	$\dfrac{1}{(1.082)^2}$	6,317
3	6,223	$\dfrac{1}{(1.082)^3}$	4,913
		NPV	4,228

The NPV is the same as before (and the present value of the cash flow in each year is the same as before) apart from rounding differences with a net total of £7.

7.2 The real rate of interest and the money rate of interest

In practice the **nominal or money rate** of interest or return is the **market rate** of interest or market rate of return. This is evident from the way rates of interest tend to rise whenever inflation rises. The real rate of return is not consciously used by investors, whose investment decisions are based on money rates of interest and the future money values of dividends and capital growth.

The money rate of interest is used when the money rate is below the rate of inflation, as it has been in the UK when the rate of inflation rises. When this occurs, the effective real rate of interest is negative so invested wealth will decline in purchasing power. Even so, an investor might prefer to invest some of his money, for the following reasons.

(a) There is a limit to the amount of money needed for immediate spending. It is better to invest any surplus funds even at the negative rate to earn some interest than to hold cash which earns nothing.

(b) There may not be higher return alternatives at a satisfactory level of risk.

7.3 Costs and benefits which inflate at different rates

Not all costs and benefits will rise in line with the general level of inflation. In such cases, we can apply the money rate to inflated values to determine a project's NPV.

EXAMPLE: INFLATION (2)

Rice Ltd is considering a project which would cost £5,000 now. The annual benefits, for four years, would be a fixed income of £2,500 a year, plus other savings of £500 a year in Year 1, rising by 5% each year because of inflation. Running costs will be £1,000 in the first year, but would increase at 10% each year because of inflating labour costs. The general rate of inflation is expected to be 7½% and the company's required money rate of return is 16%.

You are required to evaluate whether the project is worthwhile. Ignore taxation.

SOLUTION

The cash flows at inflated values are as follows.

Year	Fixed income	Other savings	Running costs	Net cash flow
	£	£	£	£
1	2,500	500	1,000	2,000
2	2,500	525	1,100	1,925
3	2,500	551	1,210	1,841
4	2,500	579	1,331	1,748

The NPV of the project is as follows.

Year	Cash flow	Discount factor	PV
	£	16%	£
0	(5,000)	1.000	(5,000)
1	2,000	0.862	1,724
2	1,925	0.743	1,430
3	1,841	0.641	1,180
4	1,748	0.552	965
			+ 299

The NPV is positive and the project would seem to be worthwhile.

---

8 TAXATION AND PROJECT APPRAISAL

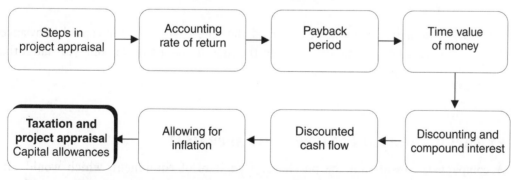

The effect of *taxation* on capital budgeting is theoretically quite simple. Organisations must pay tax, and the effect of undertaking a project will be to increase or decrease tax payments each year. These incremental tax cash flows should be included in the cash flows of the project for discounting to arrive at the project's NPV.

When taxation is ignored in the DCF calculations, the discount rate will reflect the pre-tax rate of return required on capital investments. When taxation is included in the cash flows, a post-tax required rate of return should be used.

8.1 Capital allowances

Capital allowances are used to reduce taxable profits, and the consequent reduction in a tax payment should be treated as a cash saving arising from the acceptance of a project. In the UK, writing down allowances are generally allowed on the cost of *plant and machinery* at the rate of 25% on a *reducing balance basis*. Thus if a company purchases plant costing £80,000, the subsequent writing down allowances would be as follows.

Year		Capital allowance £	Reducing balance £
1	(25% of cost)	20,000	60,000
2	(25% of RB)	15,000	45,000
3	(25% of RB)	11,250	33,750
4	(25% of RB)	8,438	25,312

When the plant is eventually sold, the difference between the sale price and the reducing balance amount at the time of sale will be treated as:

(a) A taxable profit if the sale price exceeds the reducing balance, and

(b) A tax allowable loss if the reducing balance exceeds the sale price.

Questions often assume that this loss will be available immediately, though in practice the balance less the sale price continues to be written off at 25% a year as part of a pool balance unless the asset has been de-pooled.

The cash saving on the capital allowances (or the cash payment for the charge) is calculated by multiplying the allowance (or charge) by the corporation tax rate.

There are two possible assumptions about the time when capital allowances start to be claimed.

(a) It can be assumed that the first claim for capital allowances occurs at the start of the project (at Year 0) and so the first tax saving occurs one year later (at Year 1).

(b) Alternatively it can be assumed that the first claim for capital allowances occurs later in the first year, so the first tax saving occurs one year later, that is, Year 2.

EXAMPLE: TAXATION AND PROJECT APPRAISAL

A company is considering the purchase of an item of equipment, which would earn profits before tax of £25,000 a year. Depreciation charges would be £20,000 a year for six years. Capital allowances would be £30,000 a year for the first four years. Corporation tax is at 30%.

What would be the annual net cash inflows of the project:

(a) For the first four years

(b) For the fifth and sixth years,

assuming that tax payments occur in the same year as the profits giving rise to them, and there is no balancing charge or allowance when the machine is scrapped at the end of the sixth year?

SOLUTION

(a)

	Years 1-4	Years 5-6
	£	£
Profit before tax	25,000	25,000
Add back depreciation	20,000	20,000
Net cash inflow before tax	45,000	45,000
Less capital allowance	30,000	0
	15,000	45,000
Tax at 30%	4,500	13,500

Years 1–4 Net cash inflow after tax = £45,000 – £4,500 = £40,500

(b)   Years 5–6 Net cash inflow after tax = £45,000 – £13,500 = £31,500

Activity 3   (5 minutes)

A company is considering the purchase of a machine for £150,000. It would be sold after four years for an estimated realisable value of £50,000. By this time capital allowances of £120,000 would have been claimed. The rate of corporation tax is 30%. What are the tax implications of the sale of the machine at the end of four years?

BPP
LEARNING MEDIA

Chapter roundup

- A long-term view of benefits and costs must be taken when reviewing a capital expenditure project.

- The accounting rate of return method, sometimes called the return on investment method, calculates the estimated average profits as a percentage of the estimated average investment.

- The payback period is the time taken for the initial investment to be recovered in the cash inflows from the project. The payback method is particularly relevant if there are liquidity problems, or if distant forecasts are very uncertain.

- Discounted cash flow techniques take account of the time value of money – the fact that £1 received now is worth more because it could be invested to become a greater sum at the end of a year, and even more after the end of two years, and so on. As with payback, discounted cash flow techniques use cash figures before depreciation in the calculations.

- The discounted payback method applies discounting to arrive at a payback period after which the NPV becomes positive.

- Annuities are an annual cash payment or receipt which is the same amount every year for a number of years.

- The net present value method calculates the present value of all cash flows, and sums them to give the net present value. If this is positive, then the project is acceptable.

- The internal rate of return technique uses a trial and error method to discover the discount rate which produces the NPV of zero. This discount rate will be the return forecast for the project.

- Inflation is a feature of all economies, and it needs to be accommodated in financial planning. Taxation implications must also sometimes be considered.

Quick quiz

1   What is the formula usually used for calculating the accounting rate of return?

2   What is the payback period?

3   Why should depreciation be excluded from DCF calculations?

4   What is the yardstick for acceptance of projects when using the net present value method?

5   What is the discounted payback period?

6   What is the cost of capital?

7   What are the two steps involved in calculating the internal rate of return?

8   What is the relationship between the money rate of return, the real rate of return and the rate of inflation?

Answers to quick quiz

1   $ARR = \dfrac{\text{Estimated average profits}}{\text{Estimated average investment}} \times 100\%$

2   The length of time required before the total of the cash inflows received from the project is equal to the original cash outlay.

3   Depreciation does not reflect additional cash spent, and so is not a relevant cost.

4   Accept the project if the net present value is positive.

5   The time after which the net present value of an investment becomes positive.

6   The weighted average cost of all sources of capital for an enterprise, used as the discount rate in investment appraisal.

7   Firstly, calculate the rate of return expected; secondly, compare the rate of return with the cost of capital.

8   (1 + money rate) = (1 + real rate) × (1 + inflation rate)

Answers to activities

1

Years	Cash flow £	Present value factor	Present value £	£
0	(24,000)	1.000		(24,000)
1	5,000	0.893	4,465	
2	5,000	0.797	3,985	
3	5,000	0.712	3,560	
4	5,000	0.636	3,180	
5	5,000	0.567	2,835	
6	5,000	0.507	2,535	
				20,560
		NPV		(3,440)

The NPV is negative and so the project is not worthwhile.

2   (a)
Present value of £1 per annum, years 1-6	4.355
Less present value of £1 per annum, years 1-3	2.487
Gives present value of £1 per annum, years 4-6	1.868

Year	Cash flow £	Discount factor 10%	Present value £
0	(39,500)	1.000	(39,500)
1 – 3	10,000 pa	2.487	24,870
4 – 6	8,000 pa	1.868	14,944
		NPV	314

The NPV is positive, but only just (£314). The project therefore promises a return a little above 10%. If we are confident that the estimates of cost and benefits for the next six years are accurate, the project is worth undertaking. However, if there is some suspicion that earnings may be a little less than the figures shown, it might be prudent to reject it.

(b) The project will just be worthwhile if the NPV is 0. For the NPV to be 0 the present value of benefits must equal the present value of costs, £75,820.

PV of benefits = annual savings × present value of £1 per year for 5 years (at 10%)

£75,820 = annual savings × 3.791

Annual savings $= \dfrac{£75,820}{3.791} = £20,000$

This example shows that annuity tables can be used to calculate an annual cash flow from a given investment.

3　There will be a balancing charge on the sale of the machine of £(50,000 – (150,000 – 120,000)) = £20,000. This will give rise to a tax payment of 30% × £20,000 = £6,000.

BPP
LEARNING MEDIA

PRESENT VALUE TABLES

PRESENT VALUE TABLE

Present value of $1 = (1+r)^{-n}$ where r = discount rate, n = number of periods until payment

This table shows the present value of £1 per annum, receivable or payable at the end of *n* years.

Periods (n)	Discount rates (r)									
	1%	2%	3%	4%	5%	6%	7%	8%	9%	10%
1	0.990	0.980	0.971	0.962	0.952	0.943	0.935	0.926	0.917	0.909
2	0.980	0.961	0.943	0.925	0.907	0.890	0.873	0.857	0.842	0.826
3	0.971	0.942	0.915	0.889	0.864	0.840	0.816	0.794	0.772	0.751
4	0.961	0.924	0.888	0.855	0.823	0.792	0.763	0.735	0.708	0.683
5	0.951	0.906	0.863	0.822	0.784	0.747	0.713	0.681	0.650	0.621
6	0.942	0.888	0.837	0.790	0.746	0.705	0.666	0.630	0.596	0.564
7	0.933	0.871	0.813	0.760	0.711	0.665	0.623	0.583	0.547	0.513
8	0.923	0.853	0.789	0.731	0.677	0.627	0.582	0.540	0.502	0.467
9	0.914	0.837	0.766	0.703	0.645	0.592	0.544	0.500	0.460	0.424
10	0.905	0.820	0.744	0.676	0.614	0.558	0.508	0.463	0.422	0.386
11	0.896	0.804	0.722	0.650	0.585	0.527	0.475	0.429	0.388	0.350
12	0.887	0.788	0.701	0.625	0.557	0.497	0.444	0.397	0.356	0.319
13	0.879	0.773	0.681	0.601	0.530	0.469	0.415	0.368	0.326	0.290
14	0.870	0.758	0.661	0.577	0.505	0.442	0.388	0.340	0.299	0.263
15	0.861	0.743	0.642	0.555	0.481	0.417	0.362	0.315	0.275	0.239

	11%	12%	13%	14%	15%	16%	17%	18%	19%	20%
1	0.901	0.893	0.885	0.877	0.870	0.862	0.855	0.847	0.840	0.833
2	0.812	0.797	0.783	0.769	0.756	0.743	0.731	0.718	0.706	0.694
3	0.731	0.712	0.693	0.675	0.658	0.641	0.624	0.609	0.593	0.579
4	0.659	0.636	0.613	0.592	0.572	0.552	0.534	0.516	0.499	0.482
5	0.593	0.567	0.543	0.519	0.497	0.476	0.456	0.437	0.419	0.402
6	0.535	0.507	0.480	0.456	0.432	0.410	0.390	0.370	0.352	0.335
7	0.482	0.452	0.425	0.400	0.376	0.354	0.333	0.314	0.296	0.279
8	0.434	0.404	0.376	0.351	0.327	0.305	0.285	0.266	0.249	0.233
9	0.391	0.361	0.333	0.308	0.284	0.263	0.243	0.225	0.209	0.194
10	0.352	0.322	0.295	0.270	0.247	0.227	0.208	0.191	0.176	0.162
11	0.317	0.287	0.261	0.237	0.215	0.195	0.178	0.162	0.148	0.135
12	0.286	0.257	0.231	0.208	0.187	0.168	0.152	0.137	0.124	0.112
13	0.258	0.229	0.204	0.182	0.163	0.145	0.130	0.116	0.104	0.093
14	0.232	0.205	0.181	0.160	0.141	0.125	0.111	0.099	0.088	0.078
15	0.209	0.183	0.160	0.140	0.123	0.108	0.095	0.084	0.074	0.065

ANNUITY TABLE

Present value of an annuity of 1 ie $\dfrac{1-(1+r)^{-n}}{r}$

where r = discount rate

 n = number of periods

Periods					Discount rates (r)					
(n)	1%	2%	3%	4%	5%	6%	7%	8%	9%	10%
1	0.990	0.980	0.971	0.962	0.952	0.943	0.935	0.926	0.917	0.909
2	1.970	1.942	1.913	1.886	1.859	1.833	1.808	1.783	1.759	1.736
3	2.941	2.884	2.829	2.775	2.723	2.673	2.624	2.577	2.531	2.487
4	3.902	3.808	3.717	3.630	3.546	3.465	3.387	3.312	3.240	3.170
5	4.853	4.713	4.580	4.452	4.329	4.212	4.100	3.993	3.890	3.791
6	5.795	5.601	5.417	5.242	5.076	4.917	4.767	4.623	4.486	4.355
7	6.728	6.472	6.230	6.002	5.786	5.582	5.389	5.206	5.033	4.868
8	7.652	7.325	7.020	6.733	6.463	6.210	5.971	5.747	5.535	5.335
9	8.566	8.162	7.786	7.435	7.108	6.802	6.515	6.247	5.995	5.759
10	9.471	8.983	8.530	8.111	7.722	7.360	7.024	6.710	6.418	6.145
11	10.37	9.787	9.253	8.760	8.306	7.887	7.499	7.139	6.805	6.495
12	11.26	10.58	9.954	9.385	8.863	8.384	7.943	7.536	7.161	6.814
13	12.13	11.35	10.63	9.986	9.394	8.853	8.358	7.904	7.487	7.103
14	13.00	12.11	11.30	10.56	9.899	9.295	8.745	8.244	7.786	7.367
15	13.87	12.85	11.94	11.12	10.38	9.712	9.108	8.559	8.061	7.606

	11%	12%	13%	14%	15%	16%	17%	18%	19%	20%
1	0.901	0.893	0.885	0.877	0.870	0.862	0.855	0.847	0.840	0.833
2	1.713	1.690	1.668	1.647	1.626	1.605	1.585	1.566	1.547	1.528
3	2.444	2.402	2.361	2.322	2.283	2.246	2.210	2.174	2.140	2.106
4	3.102	3.037	2.974	2.914	2.855	2.798	2.743	2.690	2.639	2.589
5	3.696	3.605	3.517	3.433	3.352	3.274	3.199	3.127	3.058	2.991
6	4.231	4.111	3.998	3.889	3.784	3.685	3.589	3.498	3.410	3.326
7	4.712	4.564	4.423	4.288	4.160	4.039	3.922	3.812	3.706	3.605
8	5.146	4.968	4.799	4.639	4.487	4.344	4.207	4.078	3.954	3.837
9	5.537	5.328	5.132	4.946	4.772	4.607	4.451	4.303	4.163	4.031
10	5.889	5.650	5.426	5.216	5.019	4.833	4.659	4.494	4.339	4.192
11	6.207	5.938	5.687	5.453	5.234	5.029	4.836	4.656	4.486	4.327
12	6.492	6.194	5.918	5.660	5.421	5.197	4.988	4.793	4.611	4.439
13	6.750	6.424	6.122	5.842	5.583	5.342	5.118	4.910	4.715	4.533
14	6.982	6.628	6.302	6.002	5.724	5.468	5.229	5.008	4.802	4.611
15	7.191	6.811	6.462	6.142	5.847	5.575	5.324	5.092	4.876	4.675

APPENDIX

Edexcel Guidelines for the HND/HNC Qualification in Business

This book is designed to be of value to anyone who is studying Managing Financial Resources and Decisions, whether as a subject in its own right or as a module forming part of any business-related degree or diploma.

However, it provides complete coverage of the topics listed in the Edexcel guidelines for Core Unit 2. We include the Edexcel Guidelines here for your reference, mapped to the topics covered in this book.

EDEXCEL GUIDELINES FOR CORE UNIT 2: MANAGING FINANCIAL RESOURCES AND DECISIONS

Description of the Unit

This Unit is designed to give learners a broad understanding of the ways in which finance is managed within a business organisation. Learners will learn how to evaluate the different sources of finance, compare the ways in which these are used and will learn how to use financial information to make decisions. Included will be consideration of decisions relating to pricing and investment, as well as budgeting. Finally, they will learn techniques for the evaluation of financial performance.

Summary of learning outcomes

To achieve this unit a learner must:

1   Explore the **sources of finance** available to a business

2   Analyse the implications of **finance as a resource** within a business

3   Make **financial decisions** based on financial information

4   Analyse and evaluate the **financial performance** of a business

Content

Covered in chapter(s)

1 Sources of finance

Range of sources: sources for different businesses, long-term such as share capital, retained earnings, loans, third-party investment, short/medium-term such as hire purchase and leasing, working capital, stock control, cash management, debtor factoring.

1, 2, 3, 4

Implications of choices: legal, financial and dilution of control implications, bankruptcy.

2

Choosing a source: advantages and disadvantages of different sources, suitability for purpose eg matching of term of finance to term of project.

1, 2

2 Finance as a resource

Finance costs: tangible costs eg interest, dividends; opportunity costs eg loss of alternative projects when using retained earnings; tax effects.

3

Financial planning: the need to identify shortages and surpluses eg cash budgeting; implications of failure to finance adequately, overtrading.

3, 4

Decision making: information needs of different decision makers.

7, 8

Accounting for finance: how different types of finance and their costs appear in the financial statements of a business, the interaction of assets and liabilities on the balance sheet.

5

3 Financial decisions

Budgeting decisions: analysis and monitoring of cash and other budgets.

4, 8

Costing and pricing decisions: calculation of unit costs, use within pricing decisions, sensitivity analysis.

7, 8, 9

Investment appraisal: payback period, accounting rate of return, discounted cashflow techniques ie net present value, internal rate of return.

10

Nature of long-term decisions: nature of investment, importance of true value of money, cash flow, assumptions in capital investment decisions, advantages and disadvantages of each method.

10

4 Financial performance

Terminology: introduction to debit, credit, books of prime entry, accounts and ledgers, trial balance, final accounts

5

Financial statements: basic form, structure and purpose of main financial statements ie balance sheet, profit and loss account, cashflow statement, notes, preparation not required; distinctions between different types of business ie limited company, partnership, sole trader.

1, 5

Interpretation: use of key accounting ratios for profitability, liquidity, efficiency, and investment, comparison both external ie other companies, industry standards and internal ie previous periods, budgets.

6

Outcomes and assessment criteria

Outcomes	Assessment criteria **To achieve each outcome a student must demonstrate the ability to:**
1 Explore the **sources of finance** available to a business	• identify the sources of finance available to a business • assess the implications of the different sources • select appropriate sources of finance for a business project
2 Analyse the implications of **finance as a resource** within a business	• assess and compare the costs of different sources of finance • explain the importance of financial planning • describe the information needs of different decision makers • describe the impact of finance on the financial statements
3 Make **financial decisions** based on financial information	• analyse budgets and make appropriate decisions • calculate unit costs and make pricing decisions using relevant information • assess the viability of a project using investment appraisal techniques
4 Analyse and evaluate the **financial performance** of a business	• explain the purpose of the main financial statements • describe the differences between the formats of financial statements for different types of business • analyse financial statements using appropriate ratios and comparisons, both internal and external

Delivery

Understanding will be developed via exposure to a variety of case studies. It will also be useful to look at a number of sets of financial statements. The form and structure of these statements must be understood, although learners are not required to actually prepare the statements. That said, simple examples which *do* require accounts to be prepared may aid understanding of the formats.

Assessment

Assessment may be by way of case study or project, based on specific business organisations. The organisations can be simulated, but learners may benefit from the analysis of a variety of real organisations. Assessment of the decision making outcome is likely to require a simulated case study.

Links

This unit links with other units within the specification: Unit 6: *Business Decision Making, Unit 9: Management Accounting, Unit 10: Financial Reporting, Unit 11: Financial Systems and Auditing* and *Unit 12: Taxation.*

This unit also covers some of the underpinning knowledge and understanding for the following units of the NVQ in Accounting at level 4: *Contributing to the management of cost and enhancement of value, Contributing to the planning and allocation of resources.*

The unit covers financial topics essential for learners wishing to make a career in this field and wishing to gain membership of a professional accounting body.

Resources

Suggested reading

Text books

Sufficient library resources should be available to enable learners to achieve this unit. Texts that are particularly relevant are:

- Cox, D and Fardon, M – *Management of Finance* (Osborne Books, 2003), ISBN 1872962238

- Dyson, J R – *Accounting for Non-Accounting Learners* (Pitman, 2003), ISBN 0273646834

Journals/Newspapers

The financial and mainstream press can provide useful background reading, and can also be a useful source of case studies and financial information. Copies of published financial reports are available from companies themselves, or via the *Financial Times* (a free online ordering service is available).

Videos

A number of videos are available covering the financial aspects of business.

Websites

The professional accounting bodies all have websites with lots of useful information and links. The *Financial Times* website includes a free service providing copies of financial reports. Biz/ed provides a wealth of useful resources aimed at learners and teachers.

- www.aat.co.uk/   The Association of Accounting Technicians
- www.ft.com   The Financial Times
- www.accountingtechnician.co.uk/   Accounting Technician magazine
- www.bized.ac.uk   Biz/ed

GLOSSARY

Asset Something *owned* by a business, for example a factory or a van.

Associated company A company in which a holding company has a very large interest, although it does not control it.

Bad debt A debt that is never repaid.

Balance sheet A statement of the assets, liabilities and capital of a business at a given moment in time. The balance sheet can also be called the Statement of Financial Position.

Bonds Very large fixed interest loans. The term is often used interchangeably with debentures. *Commercial paper* is just another term for this sort of loan.

Books of prime entry or **day books** refer to a set of 'books' in which transactions are initially recorded in the accounting system; it is in these 'books' that information is recorded from the source documents at the start of the accounting process. Each of the books record only a particular type of transaction eg credit sales, credit purchases etc.

Budget A plan expressed in monetary terms.

Budget committee Responsible for the co-ordination and administration of budgets (with the managing director as chairman). Every part of the organisation should be represented on the committee, so there should be a representative from sales, production, marketing and so on.

Budget period The time period to which the budget relates. Except for capital expenditure budgets, the budget period is commonly the accounting year (sub-divided into 12 or 13 control periods).

Budgetary control The practice of establishing budgets which identify areas of responsibility for individual managers (for example production managers, purchasing managers and so on) and of regularly comparing actual results against expected results.

Capital Capital is used with a number of slightly different meanings.

(a) *Capital* is the *money* with which a business starts up - your life savings, for example, or a large redundancy payment might be used to set up a business.

(b) *Capital* is the also the name given to the assets that are used in a business. If you use your redundancy money to buy a pub and all its contents then the building, the furniture, the beer stocks and so on are all your capital.

(c) Sometimes *capital* is the name given to money invested, for example £10,000 savings in a building society or £10,000 worth of ICI shares.

Contribution (or contribution to fixed costs) The difference between an item's selling price and its variable costs. In decision making contribution is more important than 'profit', which is sales minus *all* costs, because some costs have to be paid no matter what decisions are taken.

Cost centre A location, a function, an activity or an item of equipment. Each cost centre acts as a collecting place for certain costs before they are analysed further.

Cost unit 'A unit of product or service in relation to which costs are ascertained' (Chartered Institute of Management Accountants, *Official Terminology*).

Current assets Cash, stocks and debtors.

Current liabilities Amounts that must be paid out within one year.

Debentures Amounts loaned to a company. Debentures are usually secured: ie lenders have the right to seize assets if the loan is not repaid.

Depreciation A measure of how much a fixed asset wears out until it is completely useless.

Direct cost One that can be traced in full to the product, service or department whose cost is being determined.

Director (of a company) A person who takes part in making decisions and managing a company's affairs. Private companies must have at least one director and public companies must have at least two. Directors have to be re-elected by the shareholders at regular intervals.

Discounted cash flow A technique of evaluating capital investment projects, using discounting arithmetic to determine whether or not they will provide a satisfactory return.

Effectiveness When resources are used to achieve the desired ends.

Efficiency When resources input to a process produce the optimum (maximum) amount of outputs.

Environment The organisation's surroundings, not just the 'green' environment. For example an organisation's technological environment is all the developments that are taking place in the world in technology. Similarly there is a legal environment, an economic environment and so on.

Equity The ordinary shares of a company.

Eurobonds Bonds that are bought and sold on an international basis (not necessarily in Euros).

Fixed assets Things, like buildings and machines, that a business intends to keep and use for a long period.

Fixed budget The budget is prepared on the basis of an estimated volume of production and an estimated volume of sales, but no plans are made for the event that actual volumes of production and sales may differ from budgeted volumes.

Fixed cost That part of cost which does not vary with the level of activity or volume of production.

Fixed overheads Overheads which do not change no matter how much is produced.

Flexible budget Recognises the existence of fixed, variable and mixed (semi-fixed, semi-variable) costs, and it is designed to change so as to relate to the actual volumes of production and sales in a period.

Goodwill The amount paid to buy a business in excess of the value of its assets.

Holding company A company which controls another, its subsidiary, by holding the majority of its shares. The term parent company is sometimes used instead.

Income statement Term used under international terminology for the profit and loss account.

Indirect cost A cost that is incurred in the making of a product or providing a service, but which cannot be traced directly and in full to that product or service.

Information is anything that is communicated.

Intangible fixed asset A fixed asset that does not have a physical existence. It cannot be 'touched'. A good example is a trade mark. 'Coca-Cola' is a trade mark. It is an asset because it helps the Coca-Cola company to make profits -

people buy things with the trade mark Cola-Cola in preference to other types of cola.

Lead time The time between starting something and finishing it. Thus supply lead time is the time between placing an order for an item and actually receiving it. Production lead time is the time between starting to make something and completing it.

Liability A debt *owed* by a business, for example an overdraft at the bank.

Liquid assets Assets that are easily converted into cash. For example Sainsbury's can easily convert packets of washing powder (stock) into cash by selling them. Cash itself is included when measuring the liquidity of a business.

Minority interest The shares held in a subsidiary by people other than the holding company. For example a holding company may own 95% of the shares and another person or company may own the other 5%.

Monopoly One seller who dominates many buyers. The monopolist can use his market power to set a profit-maximising price.

Nominal or **general ledger** A file, hard or soft copy, which contains all the separate accounts of a business. In other words, a general ledger is an accounting record which summarises the financial affairs of a business.

Non-current assets Term used by international GAAP for fixed assets (that is, assets with a life of over (usually) one year).

Objectives Things that an organisation is trying to achieve, for example increase sales by 10% or increase market share by 20%.

Oligopoly Relatively few competitive companies dominate the market. Whilst each large firm has the ability to influence market prices, the unpredictable reaction from the other giants makes the final industry price indeterminate.

Opportunity cost The value of the alternative action which you go without because you do the first action.

Overheads Expenses on things not used directly in the production of the finished item, for example factory rental or the cost of lighting a factory.

Payables IAS term for creditors.

Perfect competition Many buyers and many sellers all dealing in an identical product. Neither producer nor user has any market power and both must accept the prevailing market price.

Price elasticity of demand Measures the extent of change in demand for a good following a change to its price.

Private company A company that is prohibited from offering its shares to the general public.

Profit and loss account A record of income generated and expenditure incurred over a given period. The profit and loss account can also be the Statement of Financial Performance or under International terminology, the income statement.

Profit centre A location, or a function accountable for costs and income. It may also be called a *business centre, business unit* or *strategic business unit*.

Public company (plc) A company that can invite the general public to subscribe for shares.

Published accounts Accounts are not published in the sense that you can go and buy a copy in a bookshop or a newsagents. 'Published' means that they are available for consultation by the general public. You have to pay a small fee to a government body called Companies House to see them. All companies have to publish their accounts in this way.

Raw materials Things that are processed to make the finished product. For example steel is a raw material used to make cars.

Receivables IAS term for debtors.

Resource A means of doing something. A business's resources are sometimes referred to as the four Ms - manpower, machinery, materials and money.

Revenue Under international terminology, turnover (sales) is listed under the term 'revenue'.

Securities This term is commonly used to mean any sort of investment that can be bought and sold in the financial markets. (Some would object to this definition, but this is how you will find the word used in financial writing.)

Semi-variable costs Costs which are partly variable and partly fixed.

Share premium The amount paid for a new share in excess of the share's 'nominal value'. For example when the water industry was privatised shares had a nominal value of £1 but buyers had to pay a total of £2.40 to acquire them (spread over about a year and a half). The extra £1.40 is the share premium.

Subsidiary A company under the control of another company, its holding company or 'parent'.

Trade creditors People you owe money to because you have bought things from them that go into making your product or service. (Other creditors include employees, HMRC, the landlord for rent and so on.)

Trade debtors People who owe you money because they have bought products or services from your business. (Non-trade debtors ('other debtors') are people who owe you money for other reasons: for example, you may have earned 70 days' interest on a bank deposit but not yet have received the money because it is only paid every three months.)

Turnover Another word for sales.

Variable cost That part of cost which varies with the volume of production (or level of activity).

Variable overheads Overheads which change depending on how much is produced – for example, if the factory is running for longer it will need to be lit for longer.

What if? analysis A way of looking at a problem by considering what would happen in different circumstances (or 'scenarios'). For example, what if sales demand is 10,000 units, or 20,000 units? What are the different implications for staffing the production department?

INDEX

BPP LEARNING MEDIA

Review Form – Business Essentials – Managing Financial Resources and Decisions (9/07)

BPP Learning Media always appreciates feedback from the students who use our books. We would be very grateful if you would take the time to complete this feedback form, and return it to the address below.

Name: _____   Address: _____

_____

_____

How have you used this Course Book?
(Tick one box only)

☐ Home study (book only)

☐ On a course: college _____

☐ Other _____

Why did you decide to purchase this Course book? *(Tick one box only)*

☐ Have used BPP Learning Media Texts in the past

☐ Recommendation by friend/colleague

☐ Recommendation by a lecturer at college

☐ Saw advertising

☐ Other _____

During the past six months do you recall seeing/receiving any of the following?
(Tick as many boxes as are relevant)

☐ Our advertisement

☐ Our brochure with a letter through the post

Your ratings, comments and suggestions would be appreciated on the following areas

	Very useful	Useful	Not useful
Introductory pages	☐	☐	☐
Topic coverage	☐	☐	☐
Summary diagrams	☐	☐	☐
Chapter roundups	☐	☐	☐
Quick quizzes	☐	☐	☐
Activities	☐	☐	☐
Discussion points	☐	☐	☐

	Excellent	Good	Adequate	Poor
Overall opinion of this Course book	☐	☐	☐	☐

Do you intend to continue using BPP Learning Media Business Essentials Course books?   ☐ Yes   ☐ No

Please note any further comments and suggestions/errors on the reverse of this page.

Please return this form to: Pippa Riley, BPP Learning Media Ltd, FREEPOST, London, W12 8BR

Review Form (continued)

Please note any further comments and suggestions/errors below